```
809                           161255
The

    Theories of literary genre.
```

**Learning Resources Center
Nazareth College of Rochester, N. Y.**

THEORIES OF LITERARY GENRE

YEARBOOK OF
COMPARATIVE CRITICISM

VOLUME VIII

Theories
of
Literary Genre

Edited by

Joseph P. Strelka

THE PENNSYLVANIA STATE
UNIVERSITY PRESS
University Park and London

Library of Congress Cataloging in Publication Data
Main entry under title:

Theories of literary genre.

  (Yearbook of comparative criticism; v. 8)
  Includes index.
  1. Literary form. I. Strelka, Joseph, 1927–
II. Series.
PN45.5.T5   809   76-41807
ISBN 0-271-01243-9

Copyright © 1978 The Pennsylvania State University
All rights reserved
Printed in the United States of America

CONTENTS

PREFACE   vii
Joseph P. Strelka

BASIC THEORETICAL PROBLEMS

DICHOTOMY OF ARTISTIC GENRES   3
Henri Bonnet

LITERATURE AND THE IMAGINATION:
A THEORY OF GENRES   17
Albert William Levi

TOWARD A DEFINITION OF LITERARY GENRES   41
Adrian Marino

MORE THAN KIN AND LESS THAN KIND:
THE LIMITS OF GENRE THEORY   57
John Reichert

LITERARY GENRES:
SOME IDIOSYNCRATIC CONCEPTS   80
Ernest L. Stahl

SPECIAL ASPECTS OF GENRE THEORY

SEMANTIC MODES AND LITERARY GENRES   94
Robert Champigny

THE AESTHETIC FUNCTION OF DETAIL AND
SILHOUETTE IN LITERARY GENRES   112
Horst S. Daemmrich

GENERATIVE CLASSIFICATIONS IN MEDIEVAL
LITERATURE   123
Johannes A. Huisman

THE GENRES OF ORAL NARRATIVE   150
Bruce A. Rosenberg

STRUCTURE AND RECEPTION   166
Rolf Tarot

CONTEMPORARY GENRE CRITICISM

ORDER WITHOUT BORDERS:
RECENT GENRE THEORY IN THE
ENGLISH-SPEAKING COUNTRIES   192
Paul Hernadi

OBSERVATIONS ON THE DEFINITION,
EVOLUTION, AND SEPARATION OF GENRES IN
THE STUDY OF FRENCH LITERATURE   209
Herman P. Salomon

A MORPHOLOGICAL GENRE THEORY:
AN ANSWER TO A PLURALISM OF FORMS   229
Klaus Weissenberger

STRUCTURAL AND SEMIOTIC GENRE THEORY   254
Thomas G. Winner

LIST OF CONTRIBUTORS   269

INDEX OF NAMES   275

PREFACE

Theory of genres is not only one of the oldest, but also one of the most genuinely literary principles of order in literary studies. There seems, however, to be little agreement on how to use the concept of genre to create such order. The individual genres themselves undergo constant change and evolution. Genre criticism itself, furthermore, is also, for both intrinsic and extrinsic reasons, dynamic rather than static. The dynamic nature of the genres with all its complex critical implications has recently been pointed out in a sophisticated study by Gerhard Kaiser.[1] In spite of the dynamic nature of genre-criticism and the implied differences and even contradictions of viewpoints, the situation seems not entirely hopeless. Some viewpoints, for example, the strict nominalistic stand of Croce and his followers, who see no validity whatever in genre-criticism, are so extreme that they will never gain general recognition. Genre-criticism, after all, while it has often led to such abuses as a classical authoritarianism, has nevertheless been widely recognized as filling a legitimate and urgent need.

The concept of genre itself has been repeatedly questioned by recent criticism. There is a surprising degree of agreement among critics from Karl Viëtor and Austin Warren to Tzvetan Todorov that we should limit the concept to specific historical kinds rather than include the basic categories of epic, drama, and lyric.[2] Other theoreticians, for example, the great Swiss critic Emil Staiger, have tried to make the traditional concept of these categories more flexible by taking a phenomenological approach. Some pioneering efforts to redefine the categories describe themselves expressly as going "Beyond Genre," as Paul Hernadi put it, or as dealing with something beyond genre, as did Wladimir Weidlé, who calls his undertaking an analysis of "the two languages of the art of the word."[3] This refers to two basics, the specifically poetic and the specifically fictional elements of literary art. This, in spite of the different nomenclatures and in spite of the fact that the traditional three basic genre types have been replaced by four in the case of

Hernadi and two in the case of Weidlé.[4] Whatever such basic types are called, they are usually treated as forms of genre: the tradition of genre-criticism since Aristotle and Horace has proven too powerful to be done away with merely through the adoption of new names. It is no accident that one journal in the United States and one in Europe are devoted to nothing but genre-criticism.[5] Nor is it an accident that the most significant results of new approaches usually combine the new methods (in our time, for example, a structuralistic, pretentious vocabulary and linguistic one-sidedness) with traditional and established results, as in Klaus Hempfer's new theory of genres.[6]

Attempts have also been made to apply the method of information theory to genre-criticism.[7] Despite some new details or a greater precision of terminology, however, the basic criteria do not seem likely to change. There appears to be no question that genres are "literary" kinds, "not such subject-matter classifications as might equally be made for non-fiction."[8] Outer *and* inner form of the literary work, its aesthetic literary (not merely linguistic) structure, *and* its thematics will provide elements for its special genre-form and genre-unity. Finally, literary tradition as well as literary innovation will play an equally important role, and if in our time the statement was possible that the understanding of the structures of literary genres is probably of greater significance for literary communication or literary study than the most subtle interpretation of an individual masterpiece, then it must also be said that both kinds of comprehension rather complement than exclude one another.[9] This proves again the importance of genre-criticism. As Wellek and Warren phrased it: "Men's pleasure in a literary work is compounded of the sense of novelty and the sense of recognition . . . in the murder mystery, there is the gradual closing in or tightening of the plot—the gradual convergence (as in *Oedipus*) of the lines of evidence. The totally familiar and repetitive pattern is boring; the totally novel form will be unintelligible—is indeed unthinkable. The genre represents, so to speak, a sum of aesthetic devices at hand, available to the writer and already intelligible to the reader. The good writer partly conforms to the genre as it exists, and partly stretches it. By and large, great writers are rarely inventors of genres: Shakespeare and Racine, Molière and Jonson, Dickens and Dostoyevsky, enter into other men's labours."[10]

As far as generic criticism and theory of literary genre are concerned, it seems fair to say in general that the basic concept has suffered to some extent from Croce's opposition to it. There is, however, no doubt that it has gained a remarkable measure of renewed interest since Croce's day and that the popularity of Northrop Frye's *Anatomy of Criticism* has played a decisive role in winning a broader support for the concept of genre. Frye's approach was sharply criticized a short time ago by one of the few representatives of French structuralism who showed a certain practical interest in generic criticism.[11] David H. Richter made it clear that Todorov could and should be criticized by the same criteria on which he tries to attack Frye: "Having posited a 'conception of the work' from which his categories are to be naturally derived, Todorov suddenly finds that he must add a criterion of which his theory makes no mention. Prudence would dictate that Todorov expand his literary theory to account for the loose criterion, but since this expansion would force him to depart from the literature-language analogue upon which the theory was based and which had given it such coherence as it possessed, he must decline lest he destroy his original rationale."[12]

An even more serious objection to Todorov's triadic definition is that it is "easily reducible to a single element."[13] Generic criticism is definitely alive as long as such arguments are alive. Even more so: there is no question that the problem of literary genre and the theories dealing with it concern some of the most central and significant questions of literary criticism as well as of literary history, whether the subject or concept be called "genre" or not, whether it be believed possible to separate the systematic-aesthetic aspects and the historical aspects from each other or not, whether this basic significance of "genre" be admitted or not.

JOSEPH P. STRELKA

Notes

1. Gerhard R. Kaiser, "Zur Dynamik literarischer Gattungen," in *Die Gattungen in der Vergleichenden Literaturwissenschaft*, ed. Horst Ruediger (New York: De Gruyter, 1974), pp. 32–62.
2. Karl Viëtor, "Probleme der literarischen Gattungsgeschichte," *Deutsche*

Vierteljahrsschrift fuer Literaturwissenschaft und Geistesgeschichtes 9 (1931): 425–47; René Wellek and Austin Warren, *Theory of Literature* (New York: Harcourt, Brace, 1956), p. 227; Tzvetan Todorov, "Qu'est-ce que le structuralisme?," 2. *Poétique* (Paris: Seuil, 1968), p. 96.

3. Paul Hernadi, *Beyond Genre: New Directions in Literary Classification* (Ithaca: Cornell University Press, 1972); Wladimir Weidlé, "Die zwei 'Sprachen' der Sprachkunst," *Jahrbuch fuer Aesthetik und allgemeine Kunstwissenschaft* 12 (1967): 154–91.
4. The four basic types of Hernadi (cf. especially p. 166 in his book) may be seen as two times two special forms of the two basic kinds of Weidlé.
5. *Genre* has been published by the Department of English, State University College at Plattsburgh, Plattsburgh, New York, since 1968, and is edited by Donald E. Billiar, Edward F. Henston, and Robert L. Vales. *Zagadnienia Rodzajów Literackich* has been published by the Publishing House of the Polish Academy of Sciences, Warsaw, Poland, since 1958.
6. Klaus W. Hempfer, *Gattungstheorie* (Munich: Fink Verlag, 1973).
7. Jan Trzynadlowski, "Information Theory and Literary Genres," *Zagadnienia rodzajów literackich* 4 (1961): 45.
8. Wellek and Warren, *Theory of Literature*, p. 233.
9. Kaiser, "Zur Dynamik," p. 40.
10. Wellek and Warren, *Theory of Literature*, p. 235.
11. Tzvetan Todorov, *The Fantastic: A Structural Approach to a Literary Genre* (Cleveland: Press of Case Western Reserve University, 1973).
12. David H. Richter, "Pandora's Box, Revisited: A Review Article," *Critical Inquiry* 1, no. 2 (December 1974): 473.
13. Ibid.

BASIC THEORETICAL PROBLEMS

Henri Bonnet

DICHOTOMY OF ARTISTIC GENRES

The concept of genre is of great importance in the arts. As long as there is no distinction between the fundamental genres, there will be complete confusion in the field of aesthetics. Kant failed to cast any light on this subject in his monumental synthesis, *The Critique of Judgment,* and for a long time we have been satisfied with his distinction between the beautiful and the sublime, which are not true genres at all.

To see the matter more clearly, it is therefore necessary to return to the "things." There are two ways of knowing a thing, either empirically, in a manner that is more or less inexplicable but which has the advantage of being concrete, or "through a discourse which shows us why the thing exists"—that is, through an attempt to discover the essence or cause of the thing. This second way of knowing presupposes a belief in a world where everything has its own reason for existing, and one may raise the objection that this belief in a general rationality is precisely the one that has been rejected by modern irrationalism as we know it in the context of existentialism. But this rejection is of no great importance. It still remains purely theoretical, because as soon as we start expressing our thoughts, irrespective of the doctrine we advocate, we become dependent on both a personal experience and the logic of words that denote things and their relationships (unless we want to express plain absurdities).

All this amounts to saying that the raw material which has to be organized always comes from experience, and that the order to be imposed upon this material always comes from a certain logic inherent in our mind and in the things. That is exactly what I have shown in *Roman et Poésie* (1951), where I insist, above all, on the universal experience that arises out of fiction or poetry, an experience which gained its full value for me only when the concepts of fiction and poetry had clearly emerged in my mind through a progressive series of steps. This process is inevitable in the exercise of thought: we navigate between impressions and ideas, constantly fluctuating between them and reordering the former by the latter. We always have an idea as to what we are talking about, for example, and this is necessary, for without it we would not be talking. At the start of his investigations into the theory of poetry, Roman Jakobson possesses a very rich experience of the different art forms as well as a certain idea of what he calls the art of poetry. Unfortunately, he does not stop at the experience and the idea, but instead imprisons (so to speak) the art of poetry in linguistics. This is like trying to confine stone sculpture to mineralogy; thus Jakobson views the art of poetry as a form of communication—which it may very well be, but only accidentally and not essentially.

It is precisely in response to this utilitarian theory that I propose an existential one whereby poetry be considered as originating from the mind and not from the things. I do not apply this theory to poetry alone—even if understood in the broadest sense—but to the entire field of art. I consider art as a form of knowledge which can be defined by its object. It is exactly in this sense that art is disinterested, because we call any form of activity whose aim is knowledge "disinterested."

To be sure, words are meant for communication or usefulness. Whether they are meant for another purpose as well, for example, in the manifestation of a cry, is another question. Nevertheless when we read a great lyric poem, there comes a moment when we feel captivated by the images or the ideas and their association with the rhythms and sonorities. A miraculous metamorphosis takes place in which the words are transformed into images or ideas; the utilitarian element becomes disinterested expression. If one cannot disengage oneself from the useful, it simply means that the poetic essence has been neither discovered nor attained. The same is true for a novel. We see words substituted by characters whose idiosyncrasies we share to such an extent that we forget about ourselves. We are those characters just as the statue of Condillac becomes the fragrance of roses. The metamorphosis consists here of revealing to us an affinity to beings other than ourselves, whom we recreate within us. Like poetry, fiction is knowledge; but this knowledge, disinterested as any true knowledge is, carries us over into an existence other than our own.

Both examples I have given bring me back to the theory of artistic genres and the two fundamental artistic genres represented by fiction and poetry. One may ask, why only two? Does it not run counter to every tradition? Is it not true that we distinguish, especially in literature, among all kinds of genres, from the epic to the historic, from the tragic to the lyric, the rhetorical, comic, fable, short story, novel, and several others? The same applies to music, where we distinguish, say, between opera and operetta or symphony and chamber music. We are faced with such a variety that it seems to mock all our efforts at classification.

Actually, we are in the presence not only of essential genres, but of formal genres, of varieties which are nothing but species or hybrids. For instance, nothing essential distinguishes a short story from a novel, except the dimensions (as in a contrast of a short story by Maupassant or Hawthorne with a novel by Balzac or James). The theater is nothing but a mode of presentation of the fictional or poetical substance. This is true to such a degree that one can transpose novels for the stage, and Balzac was able to write a *Vautrin* for the theater. "The substance of tragedy," remarks Paul Bourget, "can be assimilated to that of the novel."[1]

History is not a literary genre. It is rather a narrative that aims at authenticity, a form of scientific truth. But when the historian is called Michelet, it happens that he may add a certain poetic charm to the veracity of facts; thus a sort of admixture takes place. But history in itself is by no means a literary genre. Similarly, we can say that the comic opera skillfully combines a kind of fiction (generally not very profound) with music and choreography. In 1972, the International Association of French Studies placed on the agenda of its annual meeting "the dialogue as a genre." The dialogue has never been a genre; it is a method, and this method can be adopted in a "philosophical dialogue" as in a purely literary work—in the drama, for instance, which hardly consists of anything more than dialogues, monologues, and conversations.

One can say the same about poetry and prose. They are nothing but various modes of expression. One can write novels in verse, as has been done quite often, especially in the Middle Ages. One can also write poems in prose or introduce in a work of prose essentially poetical passages, as Chateaubriand and Proust have done. Certainly verse is an instrument that fits perfectly the poetic expression, because it adds to the poetic image a musical element that stresses its expressive value.[2] And it is precisely this musical element, appearing in works of prose, that we call poetical, as in the prose of Flaubert, Barrès, or an orator such as Bossuet. But it is equally true that a novelist can do entirely without this musical element and be content with nothing but simple prose.

Only from that moment when we realized that pure products could exist did we begin to see some light. This began in the nineteenth century, with the appearance of new generations of poets on the one hand and with the extraordinary development of fiction in Europe on the other.

Romanticism is the first poetic revolution, a movement of liberation from a lyricism confined to conventions and classical models. With Baudelaire, and later with Mallarmé, a novel progress has been made. Both these poets advocated and realized a purely lyrical or poetic art, some examples of which had been given before by poets such as Goethe, Poe, Wordsworth, Shelley, Hugo, and Vigny, in whose works there was no place for didacticism. But no one probably went as far as Mallarmé and his disciple in France, Paul Valéry. Along with Valéry, the Abbé Bremond treated pure poetry to a great extent.

But, by analogy, fiction also originated in an almost pure form, exempt from any moral or moralizing purpose. It excluded above all this literature of the heart which Richardson, Rousseau, and Mme. de Staël had cultivated with success. The sentimental outbursts and effusions bowed not to insensitivity but to the truth within a certain objectivity as we see it in the works of George Eliot, Balzac, Stendhal, Tolstoi, Dostoyevsky, Flaubert, Maupassant, Hardy, Meredith, and James, to mention only the first and the foremost.

Thus fiction and poetry existed in fact simultaneously and separately in almost pure forms. Within the literary art (which we can no longer call *Poétique* without ambiguity), they are hardly confused any more—in spite of the very capacity of poetry to infuse itself into prose both under the guise of style and that of the prestige enjoyed in the eyes of the critics and amateurs by the so-called well-written novels, which represent a kind of mixture of both genres.

These forms consist of varieties, as the genera in natural history consist of species. With respect to the novel, we may refer to the excellent "Réflexions sur l'art du roman" by Paul Bourget (in *Études et Portraits*), which distinguishes the character novel, taking as an example *Le Rouge et le Noir*, from the novel of manners, as exemplified by *Madame Bovary*. In the novel of manners the characters represent a whole class, the average people. But "if the novel of manners thus seeks the complete detachment and the average," says Paul Bourget, "it is only logical that the character novel seeks, on the contrary, the outstanding trait and the exception." Indeed, in the realm of psychology the typical individual is the one who displays his character "to its highest degree of intensity." There remains what Bourget calls the supreme effort, the attempt to reproduce at the same time manners and characters which, he says, Balzac tried several times successfully. Bourget also proposes the addition of a third category to these two, "the novel of psychological analysis strictly speaking," represented by *La Princesse de Clèves, Dominique, Die Wahlverwandtschaften, Adolphe,* and even *Fanny.*"[3]

In a similar way, one could distinguish several varieties of poetry. From elegy to hymn, from Byron to Whitman, from Heine to Rilke, from "Tombeau de Baudelaire" by Mallarmé to "Cimetière marin" by Paul Valéry, or to the ironical "Complaintes" by Jules Laforgue, there are numerous nuances which can be classified by categories. This is a task that we do not intend to undertake here, but it shows that the poetic element—as well as the fictional—is not limited to one single form.

But what exists *de facto,* fiction on the one hand and poetry on the other, both in forms that are nearly pure (absolute purity being an ideal impossible to reach in our world of relativity), must be justified *de jure.* For this purpose it is indispensable to know in what way fiction and poetry belong to art—which is to ask, first of all, what they have in common. Only afterward shall we be able to ask in what ways they differ. Finally, there will remain only one problem to be resolved: why only two essential genres, fiction and poetry?

What they have in common is their mode of expression. The poet and the novelist are dominated by the preoccupation with the process of creating a work of art which must translate their feelings or their Weltanschauung. They may also be preoccupied with the public to which they are addressing themselves. This preoccupation can influence the work in one direction or another, but it is considered as a general rule to be accidental and harmful: harmful, since it is in bad taste and least honorable to flatter the public; accidental, because the essential thing is to express what lies deep in ourselves, and this essential element is precisely personal or in some ways individual. Art is therefore not essentially a means of communication, a telephone branched upon the external world, but a means of expression and a means of expression of the particular or the individual.

It is through this general purpose that fiction and poetry have something in common which is nothing but the object of the whole art. Marcel Proust fully understood this and expressed himself in this connection very clearly in *Le Temps retrouvé*. But *Le Temps retrouvé* is the end of a novel that describes the spiritual itinerary of a man who accedes progressively to a deep insight into art. Proust expressed himself in a didactic manner only once, in a review article ("La Chronique des Arts et de la Curiosité," 19 March 1904) where he writes: "We can hardly believe ... that science, since there is science of the universal only, may ever be confused with art whose mission it is precisely to gather the particular, this individual aspect which the syntheses of science let escape." We may add that in the remarkable passage on the Septet of Vinteuil which serves as a prelude in *La Prisonnière* to the chapter of *Temps retrouvé* entitled "L'Adoration perpétuelle," Proust says that the impression given by Vinteuil was different from any other, "as if the individual existed in spite of conclusions that seem to derive from science."

Actually, the object of art, compared to that of science, lies in the realm of an original mode of knowledge that uses appropriate means of expression. This mode of knowledge attains what Science will never reach and to what it has never claimed to accede, since science seeks to reveal the permanent, the recurrent—in short, the laws which rule the world—and to translate all that into a mathematical language, that is, in quantities and numerical relationships. But art is there to reveal to us precisely that which is unutterable in quantities or mathematical formulas; it is there in order to interpret the particular, the individual, the purely qualitative.

If poetry and fiction converge in the common purpose which is that of art—the expression of the individual in its quality or its originality—they nevertheless differ both in their particular object and in the means of expression. They differ in their particular object because the individual element is presented by the genuine poet in a subjective manner. It is the inner *self*, the nuances of the *self* which he translates. The novelist, however, gets away from the self, in order to reach the individual *in the others* or at least in an objective manner, as an independent reality of the self. We may observe that the power of the novelist comes to the fore only if he can detach himself from his case. The young writer feels extreme difficulties in freeing himself from his personal touch. That is why it is easier to be a poet than a novelist. That is the reason why we seldom have great novelists under the age of thirty, whereas there are several great poets between the ages of twenty and thirty.

We may also observe that the poet lives in his inner world, listening to what is going on within himself. Even in the case of a description, it is the impression felt, like that of Marcel Proust before the hawthorn bushes or the three belfries, to which he clings. The same thing happens to a musician, since the musical art is purely poetical, as we shall see later. The novelist, however, is facing the world. Accordingly, a demiurgic element appears even when in *Adolphe* or *Werther* he borrows his subject matter from his own substance. He is quite objective even if he uses the "I" as Proust does in *Le Côté de Guermantes* or in *La Fugitive*. It is of great significance that most of the novelists claim to be governed by their characters and confess not to know what they are going to do, being ignorant of the adventures in which they are going to be launched.

It is possible to be at the same time poet and novelist—at the same time, "but not simultaneously." When Victor Hugo is a poet, he writes "Les Contemplations." When he is a novelist, he writes *Les Misérables*. Paul Valéry is the example of a poet who remained rebellious to fiction. He refuses to write "the marquise left at five o'clock," because he finds no interest in particular facts such as these. He does not see that their addition may become *The Mill on the Floss* and that the marquise in question perhaps will be the marquise of Villeparisis.

The differences that exist between fiction and poetry also come to the fore when we consider the means or methods which they both employ to reach the individual element. The method used by the poet is style, that is, the cadences attached to the words, the choice of sonorities and images. The language is constituted of terms which, whether nouns, verbs, adjectives, or conjuctions, are all abstract and general terms with the exception of proper nouns (which by themselves do not express anything, if one does not know already those whom they denote). But these terms have a meaning that the poet sets in motion in order to suggest his subjectivity.

The means of the novelist are simpler. One may say that they are of historic nature. But "history," the novelist's narrative (or the description which is nothing but a fixed account of events), is not dominated by a preoccupation with authenticity as to the events related, but rather with an authenticity that reinstates the individual in its originality. The historian tells us what Caesar did in

Gaul, or how the Romans nourished themselves during the first century of our era. The novelist will be dominated by a quest for truth of another nature. Without necessarily neglecting the historic truth, and all the while using his own experience, he will cling to fiction, that is, to the characters and a world of imagination, even if he happens to mix with his heroes some characters that have really existed.[4] The value of fiction will derive from the truth of characters thus objectivized and from the world that surrounds them.

There is no fiction without unrolling facts and situations. Are there novels without characters? Are there novels without psychology? One may try to obliterate any psychological element in fiction. One may try to erase the characters, as Robbe-Grillet attempted to do in his *Jalousie*. But he has not been able to efface a certain unrolling of situations and facts which the reader necessarily relates to characters referred to in the work. Yet he eliminates everything, at least in his theoretical writings, even the narrative. But what becomes then of the novel for this brilliant theoretician of the "new novel"? Let us congratulate him for having refused to make any commitment, while we should observe at the same time that he has not rejected any philosophy, since he thinks that the world where we live excludes nineteenth-century humanism, qualified as "bourgeois," in favor of an irrationalism imposed upon us by the era in which we live. But one cannot do something with nothing. If the novel has no content, all that remains at the disposal of the novelist are words which he uses, and that is why, in the final analysis, for himself and for his rivals, the novel results from the mere use of written language.

If Robbe-Grillet had made the distinction between fiction and poetry, he would certainly not have committed this error, because poetry, as we have shown, is truly related to a specific process of using written language, that is, to the style. But it just so happens that Robbe-Grillet condemns one of the main elements of style, the analogical comparison, the metaphor.[5] He accuses the metaphor of bringing everything to ourselves, of animating the world, of placing man everywhere, and of subordinating everything to him. Indeed, this is probably the nature of the metaphor; Robbe-Grillet's analysis is good. But what he really reproaches to the artist of his time is the very vocation for an art whose aim is to interpret the subjective quality, and he is not sure even himself whether the pure and simple language can escape this subjective quality (for example, consider that the onomatopoeia from which we often derive it is analogical). It is true that the metaphor is charged with humanity, but it is by no means intended to fall into a narcissistic glorification of man; its only purpose is to express his inner riches whenever a true poet is capable enough to discover them.

The art of today, at least the one which claims to be "advanced," has found no better way to innovate and affirm its freedom than by trying to obliterate the past or confine it to a museum where admiration is permitted but restricted to the premises, and also by advocating an art deprived of almost all its essential means of expression, considered as traditional and outdated. It is true not only of the literature thus advocated, but also of the abstract painting which deprives itself of forms that Picasso had before dislocated and massacred. It is true of certain music where an analogous asceticism is rampant; but by dint of elimination, there comes a moment when there is not much left, as in the case of an abstract painter who asks us to admire the rectangular surface of a canvas uniformly painted in blue. When we have finally expurgated art from its constitutive elements, should we not wonder with Roland Barthes whether the promised land of literature is not a world without Literature.[6] This is an absurd hypothesis which does not shake the bold ones, but which can be explained by a general philosophy of despair, a relativistic skepticism, an anti-humanism which is above all the negation of values represented by man, where one substitutes another man who is nothing but a miserable shadow, incoherent, lacking in will power, and despondent. Actually, we are in the presence of a nihilism which, as any other form of nihilism, proposes nothing to replace what it destroys.[7] One claims to be revolutionary in order to destroy, but without any concern for constructing, as if destruction alone were capable of replacing what it obliterates.

For the endeavor which we condemn to be justified, man of today or of tomorrow should be absolutely different from the man of yesterday. The dissatisfaction of the new generations is not a valid proof in favor of this thesis, because this dissatisfaction is a common phenomenon with each succeeding generation. Certainly there is an evolution of humanity which is, above all, an evolution and a progress of techniques; essentially, man remains the same. If he evolves mentally, it can be only toward an intellectual progress. If this progress exists, it is not, however, visible on the scale of human time.

Now it remains for us to understand why the genres present

themselves under the dichotomic form: fiction and poetry. If art is truly, as we claim it to be, the expression of truth hidden by beings, viewed as individuals, then it is necessarily dual, as much as the individuals are dual. The individual—above all the human individual—shows, indeed, a dual aspect: corporeal and spiritual. He appears to us in an objective form, from the outside, governed by universal laws, as is visible in the novels of psychological analysis. He also appears to us in a subjective form, in each one of us, in a unique manner. The poet, like any other individual, is the only one to experience what he feels. When it is our turn to experience, in reading a poem, what the poet has felt, we do it subjectively, within us, and not otherwise.

The dichotomy, fiction-poetry, is therefore fundamentally linked to our individual condition. Art is dual because we are dual. It would be triple or quadruple, if we had a triple or quadruple nature. This does not seem to be conceivable, because we cannot imagine things beyond our own nature. That may be metaphysically impossible or possible, we do not have to preoccupy ourselves with that problem here.[8]

On the other hand, it is interesting to see what becomes of this dichotomy when we examine some art forms other than literature, specifically music and painting. In music, the dichotomy disappears; this marvelous art, because it interprets our feelings directly, is totally unable to express the objective. Certainly one can imitate the song of birds, the cries of animals, all sorts of noises; radio stations employ noisemakers who practice this sort of exercise. But the art of sound does not go further. One might object that musicians frequently choose themes from external objects. Ravel put to music the *Histoires naturelles* by Jules Renard; Saint-Saëns wrote *Le Rouet d'Omphale;* Beethoven composed the *Moonlight Sonata.* It is true that for Beethoven it meant nothing but the sonata in C sharp minor, and that the poet Ludwig Rellstab is the only person responsible for the title, because listening to the first movement he imagined a small boat in moonlight on Lake Lucerne. In the first two cases the object is nothing but a pretext to imagine a music which interprets the impressions of the musician but is incapable of describing the object. In the last case, the music acts upon the listener by eliciting in him a series of images about which the composer has never thought, and which can vary from one listener to another. It is a question of associations where the temperament of the listener plays a decisive role. To borrow a technical term, we are in the presence of a metonymy.

Music is an essentially poetic art. It is hidden in the subjectivity of feelings. The objective aspect of feeling, the one which interests the psychologist, does not concern it. Music places us in a total inwardness raised to the second power. Therefore the expression "pure music" is the equivalent of "pure poetry." "One cannot tolerate for a single moment," writes Henri Delacroix in his remarkable *Psychologie de l'Art,* "the thought that music expresses the all too familiar feelings of ordinary life. Such a hypothesis is excluded by the simple consideration of the world of sound and of musical forms. Music disengages and liberates itself from the common affectivity. Through music the feeling creates the paradox of freeing itself from the heavy burden of reality, without leaving the realm of feelings. Music breaks this blind domination of reality which prevented it from contemplating and expressing itself aesthetically." The same aesthetician adds here something that can be applied to the whole genre of poetry: "Music creates a novel emotional being. It does not come to terms with ordinary feelings which cannot enter its forms. Music refines them, abstracts, systemizes and simplifies them; it generalizes them.[9] Music reaches the great rhythms and the great undulations of the emotional absolute."

Painting is in a very different situation. The objective world cannot lie outside its realm. Art always uses sensitive matter in order to express itself. In the case of music, it was the sound and the sound forms. In painting, it is a question of colors and spatial forms. Sound forms integrate the sound just as spatial forms integrate the color. But whereas the sound forms find themselves in the realm of duration, that is, succession in time, the forms used by painters are located in motionless space. Now duration is subjective, whereas space is objective. Moreover, the spatial forms of the painter are borrowed from nature, which offers a variety of extraordinary abundance. It has been said that the painter is a being for whom the external world exists. He does not have to invent its forms: they are there, under his many-faceted eyes, always within his reach. How could that which we have called fiction not have its place in painting? Yet nothing is more disputed today, and for two reasons: the invention of photography and the development, during a whole century, of a purely poetic pictorial art.

Photography reproduces the exact natural forms. Why should the painter go to such pains to compete with a sure technique that makes constant progress? Thus we assist in the increasing decadence of the painted portrait and of drawing. But one forgets that the art of fiction cannot be reduced to photographic reproduction of things. We must recognize that the painter cannot profit, as the novelist does, from the availability of succession in time. He immobilizes in space what he paints, and captures only one instant of his subject. Nevertheless, it is true that in this moment alone—and Leonardo insists upon this advantage—the painter grasps an infinity of things and with such a power that defies any description by a novelist-man of letters. Above all, the great painter will express what photography, even in its artistic form, is unable to give us, to wit, the universal in the particular trait. Outside of conventional forms (in which the "pompiers"—stereotypes of all kinds—have lost themselves), this is exactly what has been expressed by a Leonardo with his Gioconda, a Jan van Eyck, a Dürer, a Van Dyck, a Vermeer, a Courbet, and by all those whom, along with Chardin, we call painters of reality, down to the Impressionists.

Just as the poets wanted to eliminate any element alien to the poetical one, in order to obtain a pure product, a certain number of painters wanted to eliminate from painting anything that smacked of photography. Drawing has lost some of its importance, it has changed its mission. The painter hardly cared any more about objective truth, about capturing the objects through the expert eye. Uneven quality has become the object of such a fetishism that the bad painting is no longer differentiated from what is truly good. One swallows everything, in one lump, upon the faith in a signature and a prestigious pricelist.

Most of the Impressionist painters have understood that they had to cultivate their idiosyncrasy—just as did the symbolist poets, their contemporaries. But this kind of originality, the quest for which is legitimate, can be obtained in two ways: either by a thorough work in depth (Mallarmé is the most conspicuous example of it in poetry, and Cézanne in painting); or by certain eccentricities (of which dadaism provides us with an amusing example in literature, and Dubuffet a disturbing one in painting). Then it just so happened that simplification as a methodical process has remained with some a simple method, corresponding to no real exigency. With others, it has brought about an impoverishment of the means of expression which has resulted in an abstract art having no more worth than decorative art.[10]

All that has resulted in an overestimation of not only primitive art, which has its own charm anyway, but of the naive and the kindergarten art that are without importance. A certain public, continually growing, has followed suit; some intellectuals have found a few justifications (like Paulhan for Dubuffet), and they have fallen into what Dunoyer de Segonzac called "the vanguard stereotypism" ("pompiérisme d'avant-garde"), which is in no way inferior to the "rear-guard stereotypism" that was prevalent at the end of the last century and which addressed itself to almost the same public—that of ignorant people, snobs, and various followers.

It seems to me certain that the decline of value judgments in painting which we now witness, even in spite of the lesson taught by the Impressionist and post-Impressionist painting at the end of last century and the beginning of this century, would not have taken place if we had realized that, beside a poetic form of art, a fictional form of art had kept its place in painting and was able to continue to thrive. This is proven by the paintings of Picasso[11] from his blue period, by the intense work of a Toulouse-Lautrec, or by that of a Suzanne Valadon and by the works of Manet, Degas, and Whistler. We should also mention the caricaturists, such as Daumier, as well as those who are still unknown; the revision of values yet to come in future centuries will put them in their proper place.

Immortality is granted only to that which is essential. It is not granted to the accidental. It is not because there was a war from 1939 to 1945, or because the atomic bomb destroyed Hiroshima, or because there was a general named De Gaulle, a revolutionary named Lenin, or even a dictator of sinister memory who wanted to exterminate the Jews that something essential has been changed.[12] Art, great art, has nothing to do with all those events which are nothing but accidents in spite of their traumatic nature. Art is affected by them only in mediocre works, works of circumstance.

The distinction between fiction and pure poetry is essential.[13] It will be perpetuated until the end of the world. The few threads that might allow us to distinguish forever a new form of fiction from all masterworks produced previously are ridiculous. It is not a question of denying the human mind the power to create novel works. The future riches are unforeseeable, like everything that is truly original. But they will be produced only be respecting those rules which cannot be transgressed, because they are in harmony with the very nature of things.

(Translated by Arnolds Grava)

Notes

1. *Etudes et Portraits* (Paris: Lemerre, 1889), p. 373.
2. We must observe that the French poets of today who disregard rhymes and classical forms feel the need to introduce certain rhythms in their works, especially under the guise of enumeration or of repetition.
3. We should note here that *Fanny* is by Ernest Feydeau, friend and rival of Flaubert.
4. We might as well talk of *deliberate* experiences, such as those to which Zola submitted himself. But we may quote here a great novelist, unjustly forgotten, J. H. Iouwick, who finds, in the geographical frame chosen by him, the source of inspiration for every one of his novels. His masterpiece *Mademoiselle Cornélie* (Paris: Plon), which has for background Albi in southern France, seems to me an excellent example of a pure novel.
5. Alain Robbe-Grillet, *Pour un Nouveau Roman* (New York: French and European, 1963), pp. 48–51.
6. *Le Degré zéro de l'écriture*, p. 108. The desire for purity in Mallarmé is misinterpreted by Roland Barthes. It does not tend toward annihilation but toward a greater intensity of expression, i.e., toward enrichment.
7. Pierre de Boisdeffre, in his article in *Nouvelles Littéraires* (4–10 March 1974), states that the New Novel does not bring us any truly valuable work.
8. By "metaphysically" I mean when we consider the nature of the World in its entirety. The Spinozist hypothesis, according to which matter and mind would belong to two Attributes of the Substance among an infinity of other Attributes real but unknown, allows for imagining the existence of beings very different from us. On the other hand, one can admit the existence of mixed genres, those where "the atmosphere" is superposed and rivals with the fictional element. Such is the case of what we call the epic, the sublime, the marvelous, the tragic, the comic.
9. *Psychologie de l'Art* (Paris, 1927), pp. 211–12. On this problem, which would deserve a detailed study, of the universal in the most qualitative of art forms, one finds quite interesting observations in the works of Marcel Proust.
10. See in this connection Robert Rey, *Contre l'art abstrait* (Paris: Flammarion, 1957).
11. The art of puzzle, which later will make Picasso famous, proves only one thing: the almost complete unanimity of contemporaries as to judgment does not prove anything in the field of aesthetics—or, for that matter, in many other fields.
12. According to the belief of André Malraux, who advocates, for our era, what he calls an art of destiny. See his Preface in the "Cahiers" of Mme. Van Rysselberghe, dedicated to Gide, and my response in *Les Nouvelles Littéraires* (1–6 May 1973), "L'Antibergottisme de Malraux."
13. It has not escaped Marcel Proust. In *Le Temps retrouvé* (Chapter: "L'Adoration perpétuelle") he has distinguished poetry, entirely qualitative, inherent in aesthetical impressions and involuntary memories, from the general truths which constitute the principal subject matter of his book and which are relative "to passions, characters, and manners."

Albert William Levi

LITERATURE AND THE IMAGINATION: A THEORY OF GENRES

Problems of the origin, validity, and expressive range of literary and poetic forms are open to at least three types of critical treatment: analytic, sociohistorical, and philosophical. The first, having roots in Aristotle's *Poetics,* receiving expansive development in the French classicism of the seventeenth century, and partially utilized by the New Critics of the twentieth, takes traditional literary forms like comedy and tragedy, epic and drama, ballad and sonnet for granted, and attempts to state the rules and principles governing each as if these rules are somehow essential to the literary universe as the principles of Newtonian mechanics were constitutive of the natural. Description and classification are important here, but the ultimate intent is normative: to lay down the characteristics of a "good" tragedy, of a "proper" epic, or of an "authentic" sonnet. It is the natural method of a secure tradition, a stable society, an orderly universe.

The second type—the sociohistorical treatment of literary genres—has been given enormous impetus by the currently fashionable Marxist perspective. Lucien Goldmann's study of the tragedy of Racine marks a high water mark of care and sensitivity in this tradition, although the usual aesthetic texts current in the countries of eastern Europe (for example, the *Grundlagen der marxistisch-leninistischen Aesthetik,* a work of cooperative Russian authorship published in Moscow in 1961) are coarse and mechanistic in their transcription of the theory of class struggle into aesthetic terms. But even non-Marxists like Erich Auerbach have felt the force of the sociological challenge and have persuasively examined the forms of European literature in terms of class stratification and perception. It is this tradition which has provided some of the most serviceable clichés of contemporary criticism: for example, that the epic form is the natural literary expression of an aristocratic society, and that the novel of the eighteenth and nineteenth centuries is but the mirror image of a rising commercial bourgeoisie—its values, its tragic dilemmas, its authentic mode of perception. This type of criticism also has its veiled value judgments hidden beneath the cloak of social factuality; for example, such a critic may claim the contemporary bourgeoisie is no longer "worthy" of tragedy, in fact that the tragic impulse is *unzugänglich* in a bourgeois age and is necessarily giving way to the more metaphysically superficial forms of irony, parody, and caricature.

It is not the validity of these judgments but their sociohistorical presuppositions which are important, and here the sociological axioms are the direct opposite of those which govern the analytic method outlined above. For the forms of literary presentation—the genres—are for the analyst somewhat like the Platonic ideas, beyond time and change, permanent archetypes of literary possibility, whereas here they are only the offshoots of human praxis, of the complicated processes of social life, and thus all distinctions between different literary forms influencing the practice of novelists and poets are essentially relative and impermanent. Indeed there is almost a certain preestablished harmony between the sociohistorical perspective and the conditions of the "throw-away" society. In an age like our own where authoritative tradition has vanished, constant and accelerated change has become the rule, and life itself seems scandalously provisional, the very fixity implied in the concept of a "genre" is called into question, and all sharp lines of literary demarcation are wrapped in the mists of ambiguity. The anti-novel comes into being. The stage is given over to burlesque (tragicomedy). Musical composers are given fellowships for choosing silence!

The classical French commitment to *clarté* with its formality and its repugnance for the obscure was fertile soil for the growth of a theory of genres. The modern world celebrates its complete inversion since most of the contemporary arts have relinquished the guideposts of strict formal categories. The sonata form beloved of Haydn and Mozart has passed out of existence; the clear boundary between easel painting and sculpture (already compromised by the thick impasto and textural experiments of the Fauvists) no longer holds; the invention of "happenings" and the invitation to audience participation in "living theater" have purposely annulled the distinction between art and life. This is the direct consequence of theories of aesthetic liberation, for an increasing number of practitioners consider the very concept of a sonnet, a two-dimensional oil painting, or binary form in music as an intolerable constraint on the freedom of the artist. In this perspective the very notion of genres, standard literary forms, becomes reactionary and repressive.

That a theory of genres has its critical utilities, nevertheless, seems to me beyond doubt. It is only necessary, I think, to pass from an analytic or a sociohistorical to a philosophical perspective. The analytic mode implies a logical fixity outside of temporal determination which is so abstract as to be unpersuasive to any but the most recalcitrant of Platonists. The sociohistorical mode in turn corrects this abstractness, but at the cost of making all artistic form subject to such temporal contingency as to reduce it to the sociologically accidental. But the philosophical mode is at once empirical and necessary, for it attempts to ground perceived aesthetic diversity in the categories of the mind and in the formal possibilities inherent in our sensory and conceptual equipment. In short, it marks a return to the modes of thought characteristic of Kant and Hume, and, in fact, of the entire eighteenth century—to an attempt to analyze literary forms as necessary outcomes of divergent modes of perception; to trace the forms of literature to ultimate "propensities" or "faculties" of human nature; to ground aesthetic possibility within the structure of the human imagination. There is fixity here to be sure, but it is epistemic rather than logical. There is an invitation to empirical inspection also, but the reference is to psychological, not sociohistorical, fact. This critical perspective is the focus of the examples which follow.

What are the possibilities for the novel? The analyst answers this question by placing it within the received topography of forms, sketching its family resemblances as well as its essential differences from, let us say, the epic and the novella. (The Germans have an entire quantitative spectrum for this elaborate game: *Skizze, Märchen, Erzählung, Novelle, Kurzroman, Roman, Epopöe,* etc.) The historicist indicates the conditions of the novel's origin in the rise of an authentic commercial bourgeoisie in the seventeenth century, and charts its formal shifts as it affirmatively undergirds that rise (as in *Moll Flanders* or *Tom Jones*) or marks its critical decline (as in *Buddenbrooks* or *À la Recherche du Temps Perdu*). But the philosopher tends to assimilate it to the epistemic structure of the natural flow of human experience as anatomized in our common distinctions between internality and externality, inward looking and outward looking, subjectivity and objectivity.

If, for example, I say that Hemingway is a disciple of John Locke whereas Proust was a Cartesian (understanding that neither may ever have read one word of philosophical prose), the intention is clear. *The Sun Also Rises* is an uncomplex presentation of *life as sensation,* whereas *À la Recherche du Temps Perdu* is a reading of human experience based on *the subjectivist principle.* Obviously the novelist is as such no theorist. He does not define or explain; he *presents,* but the presentation hinges upon a subconscious and unformulated epistemology. Like Locke, Hemingway relies on the morality of the right sensation. Like Descartes, the wonderful work of Proust is constructed on the epistemic motto *Cogito ergo sum.*

Thus there is implicit in the novel a metaphysics and an epistemology expressed less in material content than in narrative form. We can do no better than to accept Erich Auerbach's thesis that in *the form of a story* lies a peculiar representation of reality, which is completely congruent with Sartre's insistence that divergent philosophies lie concealed within the majestic flow of fictional time. Consider for a moment the contrast between the oysters of Stepan Arkadyevitch and Pyotr Stepanovitch's beefsteak.

Early in *Anna Karenina* Levin is carried off by Stepan Arkadyevitch Oblonsky for dinner at a famous and fashionable Moscow restaurant, the England. After the usual appetizer of fish and vodka, the waiter announces that fresh Flensburg oysters have arrived, and then, although Levin says that he would just as soon have cabbage soup and porridge, Stepan Arkadyevitch ceremoniously orders an elaborate dinner: three dozen oysters, clear soup with vegetables, turbot with thick sauce, roast beef, capons, sweets. The waiter repeats the whole menu to himself according to the bill of fare: "Soupe printanière, turbot, sauce Beaumarchais, poularde à l'estragon, macédoine de fruits ... etc.," and then rushes off to fill the order.

> And the Tatar ran off with flying coat-tails, and in five minutes darted in with a dish of opened oysters on mother-of-pearl shells, and a bottle between his fingers.

Stepan Arkadyevitch crushed the starchy napkin, tucked it into his waistcoat, and settling his arms comfortably, started on the oysters.
"Not bad," he said, stripping the oysters from the pearly shell with a silver fork, and swallowing them one after another. "Not bad," he repeated, turning his dewy, brilliant eyes from Levin to the Tatar.
Levin ate the oysters indeed, though white bread and cheese would have pleased him better. But he was admiring Oblonsky. Even the Tatar, uncorking the bottle and pouring the sparkling wine into the delicate glasses, glanced at Stepan Arkadyevitch, and settled his white cravat with a perceptible smile of satisfaction.

The scene is characteristically Tolstoy, for although it is used to contrast the rough, simple, and unpretentious Levin with the good-natured, sophisticated, and epicurean Oblonsky, the complicated richness of this aspect of the sensual life is made superbly manifest. The dinner is not assumed, it is detailed. The gourmet attitude receives exquisite documentation through loving attention to the *objects* toward which it is directed. The oysters in their mother-of-pearl shells, the silver fork, the starchy napkin, the delicate glasses, the sparkling wine—all are described, and they provide a backdrop of externality, of *things* and their opulence interesting in themselves against which the comfortable dialectic of character can work.

In Dostoyevsky it is profoundly different. Late in *The Possessed*, just before the murder of Shatov, occurs a curious scene between Pyotr Stepanovitch Verhovensky, leader of the conspirators, and Liputin, one of his accomplices. Pyotr is, as usual, high-handed and overbearing and Liputin hates him for it. Shatov's contemplated murder is on the minds of both as they trudge through the town.

Suddenly Pyotor Stepanovitch halted in one of the principal thoroughfares and went into a restaurant.
"What are you doing?" cried Liputin, boiling over. "This is a restaurant."
"I want a beefsteak."
"Upon my word! It is always full of people."
"What if it is?" . . .
Pyotr Stepanovitch went to a room apart. Liputin sat in an easy chair on one side angry and resentful, and watched him eating. Half an hour and more passed. Pyotr Stepanovitch did not hurry himself; he ate with relish, rang the bell, asked for a

different kind of mustard, then for beer, without saying a word to Liputin. He was pondering deeply. He was capable of doing two things at once—eating with relish and pondering deeply. Liputin loathed him so intensely at last that he could not tear himself away. It was like a nervous obsession. He counted every morsel of beefsteak that Pyotr Stepanovitch put into his mouth; he loathed him for the way he opened it, for the way he chewed, for the way he smacked his lips over the fat morsels. He loathed the steak itself. At last things began to swim before his eyes; he began to feel slightly giddy; he felt hot and cold run down his spine by turns.

How differently function the oysters of Stepan Arkadyevitch and the beefsteak of Pyotr Stepanovictch Verhovensky! There is food and drink here in Dostoyevsky to be sure: the beefsteak and the mustard and the beer, yet they do not work as objects, but as the symbols or tokens or correlatives of the interior state. Pyotr Stepanovitch, Dostoyevsky tells us, is "capable of doing two things at once—eating with relish and pondering deeply," and since in this case the pondering deeply is a rehearsal of Shatov's murder, the eating with relish while planning murder expresses calculated cruelty. The intrinsic innocence of a beefsteak and a glass of beer is transmuted into an image of nausea and disgust reflected in Liputin's loathing. Each morsel of steak is a register of guilt and complicity, so that when Verhovensky smacks his lips over the fat morsels, it is as if he is smacking his lips over a corpse. Incarnation is symbolically at work. It is the obscenity of the meaning of what is perceived and a latent consciousness of his own implication in Verhovensky's voracious cannibalism (and not simply the accumulated impatience, resentment, and anger) which drive Liputin toward nausea, so that he feels giddy and things begin to swim before his eyes.

Oblonsky's oysters are interesting in themselves and as the voluptuous furniture of life. Verhovensky's beefsteak is but an image of the murderous devouring, simultaneously occupying the mind and the teeth. This contrast between two "restaurant scenes" in Tolstoy and Dostoyevsky is characteristic of the differences between the two men and of the two uses of the novelistic imagination which they respectively exemplify.

Tolstoy is an objectivist, even an Aristotelian. For him the world consists of a plurality of primary substances, solid, resistant, distinguishable by adjectives. Dostoyevsky is dominated by the subjectivist principle; he suggests more what might have been produced by the interval in modern philosophy from Descartes to Kant, a world of flux where violent acts are prepared in the grotesque theater of the mind. Characters for Tolstoy are what they *are* and what they *have;* for Dostoyevsky they are what they *do,* but chiefly what they *think.* Dostoyevsky's novelistic imagination always crystallizes around a nucleus of violent action: murder, rape, suicide, or bloody accident. Tostoy operates within a solid world of objects—a universe fitted out like a St. Petersburg drawing room, with its necessary accessories of silken drapes, crystal chandeliers, thick Chinese carpets, and insubstantial French furniture. Time in Dostoyevsky moves swiftly, and although there are long interludes of breathtaking dialectic, there are moments when no speech is swift enough and we have the sudden substitution of the dramatic gesture like the stunning blow in the face which Shatov gives Stavrogin, Sonya's kneeling before Raskolnikov, Father Zossima bowing to the earth before Mitya, Prince Myshkin's sudden epileptic fits. Time in Tolstoy unrolls slowly, like the budding of the seasons and the stately transformations of nature, and the inner metamorphoses of persons are finely registered in the bodies which house them (objects also): in the loss of vivacity in a step or sparkle in an eye, in the appearance of heaviness in a middle-aged body or wrinkles in a forehead hitherto smooth and untroubled.

In general Dostoyevsky's characters live in a purely interior world of moral and religious significance, full of anguish and decisions, horrified contemplation and philosophical problems. They do not eat or dress, relax in the parks or pay money for bread and cheese. The commonplaces of existence may be presupposed, but there is no romance of the quotidian. But in Tolstoy the commonplace is the frame of life; whether the landowner doing his daily accounts, the urban nobility with its endless dinners and card playing, or the domestic routines of instructing the servants and caring for the children. This is why the contrast in the novelistic imagination illustrated by the two restaurant scenes could be duplicated for any aspect of life whatsoever.

Objectivity as in Tolstoy and subjectivity as in Dostoyevsky are then two possibilities of technical accomplishment which exemplify two types of latent philosophy expressing themselves as modes of literary imagination. It is a matter of philosophic commitment which goes back to ancient dualisms between things and ideas, bodies and minds, materialism and idealism. Whether one takes as point of primary reference the furniture of the world or the encapsulated area of mind has novelistic implications. In Tolstoy and Dostoyevsky the contrast is dramatized by the attitude toward objects—contempt in Dostoyevsky and basic respect in Tolstoy.

The historicist is tempted to read this polarity in terms of social categories—to find in Tolstoy's commitment to place the traditional anchorage of the old landed aristocracy, in Dostoyevsky the wandering and restless homelessness of the urban proletariat. It is true that there is a congruence between novelistic accomplishment and life history. Dostoyevsky's rootlessness is registered in the gambling rooms of Wiesbaden, the boulevards of Paris, and the house in Florence just across from the Pitti Palace where most of *The Idiot* was written. Tolstoy's life, on the other hand, is meaningless apart from the rolling fields and ancestral memories of Yasnaya Polyana. When Dostoyevsky in his *Winter Notes on Summer Impressions* describes his European wanderings, he sounds like some ill-natured and dyspeptic tourist. The Cologne Cathedral impresses him as a lace paperweight five hundred feet tall. In London he sees only the monstrous buildings and the painted women in the Haymarket, and the Parisian bourgeoisie fill him with contempt. But Tolstoy's books and his diaries are filled with the solace of the countryside near Moscow and his writing is full of the deep satisfactions of the soil and of the life of nature. Tolstoy's rootedness and Dostoyevsky's restlessness are less emblems of class affiliation than of cognitive modes of perception. This is directly relevant to that other dualism with which we have been concerned, for there is a sense in which even attitude toward place is but a metaphor embodying a basic metaphysics. The rootedness of things is due to the fact that they have definiteness of location in space. The restlessness of ideas lies in the limitless ways in which they rove the corridors of time. Concentration upon the inner or upon the outer in the methodology of the novelist reflects less the historical accidents of social class membership than two ultimate and permanently available propensities of the human imagination.

What are the possibilities for poetry? The analyst answers this question by recourse to the logical distinction between structures of linear expression. He is concerned with syllabic stresses and strains, measures of breath, accents, rhythms. From this he constructs the metrical measures and types which permit the creation of the poetic line in terms of standardized units and leaves him in the end in possession of the vocabulary of quatrains and sprung rhythm, of couplets and terza rima, of heroic verse and Alexandrines. The historicist, on the other hand, is concerned with how epic form grows out of the ambience of Greek primitive kingship, to be reconstituted in the situation of rigid medieval class stratification, and of how the lyric impulse feeds the agonistic requirements of Greek life (as celebration of martial victory or preeminence in the Olympic contests) only centuries later to become sublimated into the delicate expression of courtly love. But the philosopher seeks the conditions of poetic possibility in the perceptual dimensions of mind and in those modes of apprehension inherent in our epistemic equipment.

One such persuasive phenomenology of human perception has been presented by the great American logician Charles Sanders Peirce. In investigating the most universal and pervasive features of those experiences which come before the mind he was led to distinguish immediate qualitative character, the sense of activity or tension, and the symbolic conveyance of meaning. The color magenta, the odor of attar, the sound of a railway whistle, or the taste of quinine are examples of the first—all, in short, in our perceptual experience which is immediate, novel, spontaneous, and vivid. It is our perception of activity, of tension, of things opposed to one another or pushing against one another or causing one another which constitutes the second—all sense of action and reaction in bodies as of strain and muscular tension in our own. This is the realm of antagonistic juxtaposition, sudden movement, gesticulation, shock, surprise, and violence. Finally, when things stand for something beyond their immediate presence, point to something beyond, transcend their own local particularity by symbolizing or having meaning, then we are in the realm of the third.

If Peirce is indeed correct, and these are categories presupposed in all perceptual experience, then they must likewise find their expression in the arts, and the ultimate characteristic of any painting or sculpture, any work of literature or of the drama, and above all of any poem will be that its threefold function is the presentation of qualities, the delineation of movements, and the expression of meanings. The creative imagination in its productive activity will always be consciously or unconsciously directed to one or all of these three tasks. Indeed, since it is unlikely that it is possible to achieve excellence in all three simultaneously, it is probable that there will be a narrowing of intent toward one in particular which is dictated by that mode of perception which uniquely defines the mentality of the poet. In this respect three of the greatest poets of the recent past, Wallace Stevens, Ezra Pound, and T.S. Eliot, may be illuminating examples.

The poetry of Wallace Stevens deals with surfaces, with the structure of appearance, and his aesthetic attitude frequently is elicited through the exciting properties of sensory qualities themselves: sounds, tastes, vivid colors. His lyrics are always a firm celebration of the presentational immediacy of experience.

Here is the disclosure of what a taste may be:

> Like Candide,
> Yeoman and grub, but with a fig in sight,
> And cream for the fig and silver for the cream,
> A blonde to tip the silver and to taste
> The rapey gouts.

And here the reflective elaboration of a world of smell:

> Tilting up his nose
> He inhaled the rancid rosin, burly smells
> Of dampened lumber, emanations blown
> From warehouse doors, the gustiness of ropes
> Decays of sacks, and all the arrant stinks
> That helped him round his rude aesthetic out.
> He savored rankness like a sensualist.

And here is sound presented through the onomatopoeic strategy which animated so much of his verse:

> To a chirr of gongs
> And a chitter of cries
> And the heavy thrum
> Of the endless tread
> That they tread.

But Stevens's point of view is essentially that of a man whose center is painting, and this is manifest in his acute sensitivity to the vocabulary of color. In this respect his inspiration is Chinese. Fenollosa noted that Chinese poetry always speaks with the vividness of painting, and he attributed this to the metaphorical character of the Chinese ideogram—its push toward concreteness. Our scientific sophistication causes us to press "red" ever further toward the abstract universal "redness." But for the Chinese "red" becomes the accumulated storehouse of cherry, rose, sunset, iron-rust, flamingo, ox-blood, and the like. Fenollosa could have been speaking of the poetic strategy of Wallace Stevens.

> The sun, in clownish yellow, but not a clown,
> Brings the day to perfection and then fails . . .
> . . . A big bird pecks at him
> For food. The big bird's boney appetite
> Is as insatiable as the suns's. The bird
> Rose from an imperfection of its own
> To feed on the yellow bloom of the yellow fruit
> Dropped down from turquoise leaves. In the landscape of
> The sun, its grossest appetite becomes less gross. . . .
>
> The sun is the country wherever he is. The bird
> In the brightest landscape downwardly revolves
> Disdaining each astringent ripening,
> Evading the point of redness, not content
> To repose in an hour or season or long era
> Of the country colors crowding against it. . . .

The "sun in clownish yellow" dominates the poem, as it does the landscape which is the poem's stage, and the yellow of bloom and fruit, of glitter and brightness cast their glow here as they do over the harvest fields of Arles on the canvases of van Gogh. What is more initially abstract than the common name for a quality like yellow? But if each of its uses is grounded in sensory particularity—the yellow of Aix, the yellow of Stockholm, the clownish yellow of the sun, the yellow bloom, the yellow fruit, the yellow bird—then the meaning becomes richer from line to line and from poem to poem. Thus within the context of Stevens's poetry experienced as a corporate body, the abstract yellow acquires a luminosity of painterly accretion which through its compounding finally simulates the immediacy of the direct sensory experience of real yellow objects.

By poetry devoted to the realm of taste, smell, sound, and above all color, Stevens celebrates the immediacy of the perceptive act. But the magic which informs the poetic creation is the product of an acute imaginative intelligence, with its power not only to possess the moment it perceives but to render it permanent through language. There is no gaunt world of reason here, nor of reflection apart from the perception which sets it in motion. The pleasure of the poet as imaginative man, said Stevens, "is the pleasure of powers that create a truth that cannot be arrived at by the reason alone, a truth that the poet recognizes by sensation. The morality of the poet's radiant and productive atmosphere is the morality of the right sensation."

As Stevens is the poet of qualities and sensations, Ezra Pound is the poet of movements and oppositions. His *Cantos* are written in ten languages. There are passages in Latin, Greek, French, German, Italian, Spanish, and Provençal. There are occasional phrases transliterated from Hebrew. There are innumerable Chinese ideograms. There are notations in Arabic. There is a subtle typographical calligraphy. The poet presents his message in the image, the meter, the look of the page. But despite the cosmopolitan culture, the presence of the entire "Penelope web of European awareness," there can be little doubt that the key to Pound's achievement in *The Cantos* lies in their moral intent. Their central subject is integrity. They assert that integrity is the right guide of men and states, and they assert this in two demonstrations—one direct, the other indirect. The direct demonstration (with its culmination in Cantos XIII and LIII) exhibits the life of perfect integrity according to the canon of Confucius. The indirect demonstration (with its culmination in Cantos XLV, XLVI, and LI) exhibits the absolute lack of integrity in the idea of usury and its working out within society.

For Stevens reality is to be *enjoyed,* and this response to the world is the clue to his presentation of sensuous immediacy. But for Pound reality is perpetually to be *judged,* to be submitted to the principles of moral choice. In this ethical response he utilizes all the devices of his poetic equipment: vigorous insistence, strained language, muscular effort, polarity in presentation, shock, sudden changes, antagonistic juxtaposition, in short, the whole paraphernalia of moral struggle sublimated into the texture of his verse.

The voice of Stevens is suave and well modulated. Pound thunders with the accents of a Dante inveighing against Florence, or of a Jeremiah crying out against the iniquities of his people.

> The ant's a centaur in his dragon world.
> Pull down thy vanity, it is not man
> Made courage, or made order, or made grace,
>   Pull down thy vanity, I say pull down.
>   . . .
> Thou art a beaten dog beneath the hail,
> A swollen magpie in a fitful sun,
> Half black, half white

> Nor knowst'ou wing from tail
> Pull down thy vanity
>   How mean thy hates
> Fostered in falsity,
>   Pull down thy vanity,
> Rathe to destroy, niggard in charity,
> Pull down thy vanity,
>   I say pull down.

Despite Pound's commitment to Confucius, his affirmative presentations of the moral life are less insistent and emotional than his negative demonstrations. One part of his epic poem (Cantos XIV and XV) is constructed in conscious imitation of Dante's *Inferno* and includes the politicians, the profiteers, the financiers,

> And the betrayers of language
>   ... and the press gang
> And those who had lied for hire;
> the perverts, the perverters of language,
>   the perverts, who have set money-lust
> Before the pleasures of the senses,

as well as the bigots, the vice-crusaders, the English, the liars, the saccharescent lying in glucose, the pompous in cotton wool, the slum-owners, the panders to authority, the obscurers of texts with philology, the monopolists, the obstructors of knowledge, the obstructors of distribution, the Fabians, the conservatives, the backscratchers, the litigious, the news-owners, and the whole lot *nulla fidentia inter eos*. It is a heterogeneous group, given unity in Pound's eyes by a common treason to natural society, and it remains the butt of his constant poetic invective.

Very early Pound said: "I believe in technique as the test of a man's sincerity." He also said: "There are only two passions in art; there are only love and hate." Love and hate rule Pound's perception and the technical devices which are the test of his sincerity are used for their reinforcement. Two of these devices are recurrent: the contrast and shock of juxtaposed segments of material within the poetic narrative and the enthronement of verb forms in the syntactical structure of the verse. The last provides Pound's dynamism:

> And the *running* form, naked, Blake,
> *Shouting, whirling* his arms, the swift limbs,

> *Howling* against the evil,
>   his eyes *rolling*,
> *Whirling* like *flaming* cart-wheels,
>   and his head held backward to gaze on the evil
> As he ran from it,
>   to be hid by the steel mountain,
> And when he showed again from the north side;
>   his eyes *blazing* toward hell mouth. . . .
>   [Italics added]

The first is Pound's mode of exhibiting the constant dialectic of values within the universe:

> "Beer bottle on the statue's pediment!
> "That, Fritz, is the era, today against the past,"
>
> Greek rascality against Hagoromo
>   Kamasaka vs/vulgarity
>
> God bless the Constitution
>   and *save* it
>   . . .
> And god damn the perverters

An empty beer bottle at the foot of the monument to a war hero, past against present, human rascality and vulgarity against Japanese aesthetic perception, bless the Constitution and damn the perverters: these contrasts in the imagery are the simple analogues of the love and hate which rule Pound's perception. Their infinite repetition in *The Cantos*—his acute awareness of the contrast between fact and value, the fake and the fine, the cheap and the beautiful, Kung and Herr Krupp, modern hypocrisy and Homeric truth, Ch'ing Ming and contemporary advertising, *neschek* and *ethos*, St. Trophime and the Albert Memorial, John Adams and Franz Joseph, a concentration camp near Pisa and the Tempio Malatestiano—show Pound to be less lyricist than moralist, and so of a totally different poetic species than Wallace Stevens.

If Stevens is the poet of qualities and sensations, and Pound of movement and oppositions, T.S. Eliot is the poet of symbolic references and transcendent meanings. Just before beginning *Four Quartets* Eliot spoke of "a poetry so transparent that in reading it we are intent on what the poem points at and not what is in the poetry; this seems to me the thing to try for. To get *beyond* poetry as Beethoven in his later works strove to get beyond music." To get beyond the poem is to visualize it as a symbolic mechanism pointing to experiences beyond itself (largely religious in Eliot's case) and it is to forsake qualities and tensions for conceptual feelings. In *The Waste Land* Eliot asks:

> What are the roots that clutch, what branches grow
> Out of this stony rubbish? Son of man,
> You cannot say, or guess, for you only know
> A heap of broken images, where the sun beats,
> And the dead tree gives no shelter, the cricket no relief,
> And the dry stone no sound of water. . . .

This at first sight seems an imagery of natural qualities. But it is clear that the stony rubbish, the heap of broken images, and the dry stone mean allegorically more than themselves: they mean an actual drought in the landscape of the poem, but more importantly they symbolize a spiritual drought within the modern psyche, where Christian revelation haunts the scene but at such a distance that the dead tree of the Cross provides no sheltering comfort.

Ash Wednesday is the transitional poem in Eliot's development, falling between the earlier *The Waste Land* and *The Hollow Men* (which register Eliot's dark night of the soul) and the mystical message of *Four Quartets*. It marks his emergence from despair into an ambience of grace. It is a deeply religious poem, renunciatory and penitential, using the ritual language of the Christian Church to explore the imagery and the urgent sincerities of the religious life. Its dominating figure is a Lady (reminiscent of Dante's Beatrice), lovely, bright, and pure, who "honors the Virgin in meditation." He speaks of her in the fourth episode as one

> Who walked between the violet and the violet
> Who walked between
> The various ranks of varied green
> Going in white and blue, in Mary's colour,
> Talking of trivial things
> In ignorance and in knowledge of eternal dolour
> Who moved among the others as they walked,
> Who then made strong the fountains and made
>   fresh the springs

It is an instructive passage to compare with the Stevens poem about yellow, instructive particularly for the contrast with which the two poets use color adjectives. The adjective in Stevens is a device of presentational immediacy, used exclusively for the pictorial representation of vivid surface quality. But in Eliot it is used allegorically, for the elucidation of meanings which have spiritual reference. His violet is the violet of penance. His green is the green of hope. His white is the white of purity. His blue is the blue of Heaven. Just as in the paintings of Fra Angelico, here too any sensory vividness of color is used in the service of religious communication.

While Wallace Stevens celebrates the sensual appearances of the natural world for their own sake, and Ezra Pound explores all the byways of Western culture and Chinese wisdom to sustain his own particular brand of moral judgment, T.S. Eliot presents those inner states of consciousness and meditative wanderings which illuminate the Christian message. He both engages in a reflective elaboration of the materials of ordinary perception and presents poetic "propositions" which then contribute their insights in the pursuance of the religious life. However much his imagery is seasonal, occasional, and directly focused on natural objects, its purpose is to illuminate a series of truths which lie beyond perception. His poetry emphasizes the limitations of natural life and the higher purposiveness of the familiar. But this is only to say that his verse is reflective by temperament, concerned with meanings as to motive, and transcendental in its intent.

Eliot's images are drenched in mysticism, and in this he differs profoundly both from Stevens and from Pound. The universe of Stevens reflects a Platonism in which the items of experience disclose myriad and interesting resemblances. The universe of Pound reflects an ultimate Manicheaism where all things may be grouped in polar oppositions and where there is no escape from antagonistic moral tensions. But the universe of Eliot is ultimately *one*—God's universe—and therefore contains objects which point beyond themselves to become emblematic of the divine intention.

These are profound metaphysical differences, due less to differences in *theories* systematically held than to an intrinsic difference in *types of imagination* illustrated in three separate forms of poetic perception. Actual differences in poetic practice resulting in different poetic *forms* thus stem from differences which are philosophical, and they can be explored best through a phenomenology of the imagination.

What are the possibilities for drama? The analyst answers the question by means of a terminology at least as old as Aristotle's *Poetics,* distinguishing dramatic forms from lyric and epic and defining the two branches of the dramatic as comedy and tragedy. Along with the greater refinements of classification introduced since the eighteenth century, the analyst may spend considerable ingenuity distinguishing the proliferation of types determined according to content and intention such as the drama of ideas, of manners, of political insistence, or of ironic commentary. The historicist, however much he depends on this prior classification, will interpret the historic occurrence of these various forms in value-centered terms, discussing Roman and Restoration comedy as indexes of social decadence, and finding the moments of the historical flowering of tragedy to be particularly symptomatic of sharpened conflict situations with respect to the leadership patterns of society. For this mentality the story of Oedipus or Agamemnon is a meditation upon the usurpation of power, and the tragedy of Richard II that of feudal patterns of order compromised by an emerging class ambiguity. But the philosopher finds the rhythm of tragedy emblematic of the general form of psychological experience and will distinguish within the form two characteristic types expressive of the general moral dilemma of human existence.

It is wholly characteristic of Aristotle's naturalism that he should find the origin of the arts in a quality of human nature, that he should find the successful reception of the skill of creation entrusted to the exercise of a natural power. Thus the instinct to imitate and the desire to know inspire both poet and spectator. The urge to mimicry, the impulse to copy, represent, transform, caricature, exaggerate, reenact, is an original impulse making for drama, and is equaled only by the passive pleasure which we feel as spectators. Built into human nature, therefore, are the conditions of theater, alternatively histrionic and participative. As the *Politics* envisages the political process as that of now "ruling," now "being ruled," so the *Poetics* envisages the imagination as now "playing the part" and now "witnessing the performance."

Both are governed by the rhythmic flow of natural experience based on the mechanisms of tension and release. This is why the organic unity of the tragic plot consists in the fact that it has a beginning, a middle, and an end—a cliché of experience which is at the same time the first principle of the dramatic imagination. For this cliché makes a deeper reference to passion, involvement, and concern. The beginning of the play means the rousing of excitement, the middle of the play its maximization, the end its dwindling. In Aristotle all of this psychological suggestiveness is presupposed, but expressed in the idiom of tragic plot construction. Every tragedy has three parts: the complication (*desis*), the dénoument (*lusis*), and the turning point or climax (*metabasis*) which separates them and falls in between. Complication winds up the emotions like a tautened spring, climax brings maximum excitement, and dénouement assures that return to the plateau of ordinary emotion which rounds off the dramatic experience. Each of these stages makes reference to the modalities of belief. In the beginning everything was possible. In the middle certain things have become increasingly probable. At the end, everything has become necessary. From the conflict between Bolingbroke and Mobray in the first act of *Richard II* anything can follow. By act 3 even Richard himself senses the probable passage "From Richard's night to Bolingbroke's fair day." In act 5 Richard's murder by Exton has become inevitable. The tragic rhythm of action is the point of intersection of art and natural existence.

Since Aristotle, no ancient drama has been so persistently taken to represent the Greek approach to the problem of destiny as *Oedipus Rex*. Since Goethe and Coleridge, no Renaissance tragedy has so consistently occupied the Western consciousness as *Hamlet*. But it has seldom been remarked how the natural psychological mechanisms of tension and release in both have produced two dramas with an identical tragic rhythm of action. In each of these two plays a pollution of the natural order or a violation of the traditional ethos presents its consequences in sickness, blight, and the uncanny intervention of supernatural powers; and the ultimate "solution" is a "ritual cleansing" which accomplishes itself through mutilation, banishment, or a stage yielding a rich harvest of corpses in the final act.

The dramatic strategy of *Hamlet* and *Oedipus Rex* are alike. Both begin with a trouble in the state. This is indicated by the eruption of the unnatural (in *Oedipus* the plague, in *Hamlet* the ghost), whereupon a movement of destruction begins (in *Oedipus* to seek the culprit, in *Hamlet* to seek revenge). And when the culprit has been revealed and the revenge (with all its secondary consequences) has been secured, then (with Oedipus exiled to Cithaeron and the sovereignty of Thebes in Creon's hands, and with Gertrude, Claudius, and Hamlet dead, and the power of Denmark passed at last to Norway's Fortinbras) we have the restoration of order. Purgation has been accomplished. The slate has been wiped clean. Life (natural and political) can begin again.

Hamlet and *Oedipus Rex* are both tragedies of purgation and as such they share a common structure of dramatic action fed by characteristics deeply rooted in human psychology. But if they are similar in this respect, they are very dissimilar in others, and these dissimilarities are equally instructive in helping us to understand the paradox of the dramatic imagination and how it eventuates in different types or genres of tragedy.

Their profound differences we feel at once. Hamlet is a secular drama; it contains perhaps an epistemology, but hardly a metaphysics. *Oedipus Rex,* on the other hand, presupposes a cosmos. Its universe is total with a sustaining nature below the level of human action and an actively interested Olympian hierarchy above. Its chorus has one eye on the tragic action within the *polis* and the other focused on the divine order and the immortal gods, so that its privileged commentary is equally balanced by doubts about the human action, modulating references to the decrees of Fate, and intermittent invocation to Apollo, Artemis, and Athena.

In Shakespeare there is none of this. There is only the world of human society magnified to the proportions of Elizabethan pride. It is as if the notion of the total cosmos eludes him, as if he feels no metaphysical need to frame and explore this cosmological idea. Of course he depicts human life itself in all its richness and variety, but leaves it without a cosmic or religious setting, and this has consequences for the theory of human action which his plays embody. The difference in this respect between the Sophoclean and the Shakespearean tragedy was clearly enunciated by August Wilhelm Schlegel and later by Oswald Spengler in his historical distinction between the philosophical presuppositions of the classical and the Faustian worlds:

> What happened to Oedipus—unlike the fate of Lear—might just as well have happened to anyone else. This is the Classical "Destiny," the *Fatum* which is common to all mankind . . . and in no wise depends upon incidents of personality. . . . Consider Oedipus once more: that which happened to him was wholly extrinsic, was neither brought about nor conditioned by anything subjective to himself. This is the very form of the classical myth. . . . Compare with it the necessity . . . that resides in the destiny of Hamlet, of Don Quixote, of Werther. It is . . . the difference of situation-tragedy and character-tragedy.

Spengler grounds his distinction on historicist principles, but he could have done the same only by reference to the functioning of the human imagination as we have done in treating of the novel.

Character and fate are two polar concepts which have their historical incidence respectively in the Renaissance and the Classical world, but they represent possibilities which are inherent in the human mind. *Oedipus Rex* (like the novels of Tolstoy) is a product of the objective imagination where objects, body, the fixity of the cosmos, and fate determine action. *Hamlet* (like the novels of Dostoyevsky) is a work of subjectivity where meaning, inwardness, reflection, meditation, and character are everything.

It would be foolish to raise again the purely formal issue of the ancient quarrel between character and plot. It is obvious that the Aristotelian distinction cannot be made into an absolute separation. *Character in a pattern of action* is the primary datum of the tragic drama, but dramatic practice necessarily varies in its relative emphasis. Aristotle's assertion that "plot is the principle and the soul of tragedy" is both a perfect exemplification of the actual drama of the ancient world and of the objective imagination. A.C. Bradley's statement that in *Hamlet* "the whole story turns upon the peculiar character of the hero" represents the claims of the subjective imagination as well as the historically grounded and morally oriented conception of man which the Christian community has inherited from *The Confessions* of St. Augustine.

Of course from the modern point of view the character of Oedipus is underdeveloped. He has little inwardness or reflective inclination, and his destiny has little to do with psychology or with ethics. For the interest of Greek tragedy lies in the progressive revelation of the separate strands which are *unalterably* interwoven in the web of Fate. In this complex net Oedipus is fixed like a struggling creature. His efforts to escape fail. His undoubted virtue and sense of responsibility as King of Thebes are of no help. Any attempt to establish a relation between his guilt and his misfortune (a common error of those under the spell of Christian moralism) is irrelevant, for the Greeks see fate as a structure of the world, singularly like that of their Euclidean geometry. Like the deduction of a theorem, fate embodies a geometrical necessity. No human force can change the pattern, and therefore the plot of *Oedipus Rex* unrolls with the swift and dreadful motion of a logical entailment.

The ambience of unavoidability which permeates *Oedipus Rex* and *Agamemnon* is a far cry from the realm of human free will, of the voluntary and purposive choices of a Hamlet, an Iago, or a Richard III. There is a nemesis in both, but in the first case it is that of an impersonal structure of the universe while in the second it follows from the conventional workings of the system of human justice. Thus it becomes clear that the antinomic character of the dramatic imagination not only allows for, but actually demands alternative interpretations of Aristotle's *hamartia,* or tragic flaw, and that the ambiguity of the dramatic event hides two conflicting dimensions of the problem of evil—one metaphysical, the other moral. Tragedy as an artistic form, as an aesthetic convention, is the perfect expression of an imagination anchored at one extreme in cosmology, and at the other in ethics, and this duality expresses itself perfectly in questions concerning the primacy of "justice" or of "fate."

If there is a determining force in the universe to the explication of which the tragic poet sets his talents, is this in the end a factor of natural necessity or of moral retribution? To this persistent question, despite their opposing emphases, neither the Greeks nor the Elizabethans could give absolutely unambiguous answers. Aeschylus performs at once as cosmic moralist and metaphysician; in the *Oresteia* fate and justice seem inordinately close. Shakespeare is primarily a humanist, expressing explicitly that men are the masters of their fate, yet from time to time noting uneasily the claims of a necessity from outside and treating the dislocations of character as alternatively fated and humanly self-produced. "His plays," said Goethe, "all hinge upon that mysterious point ... in which the peculiar property of our ego, the assumed freedom of our will, comes into conflict with the necessary course of events." The modern consciousness finds this conception hopelessly but at the same time tantalizingly confused. Freedom and determinism are opposites. Yet the ancient tragedians through the device of the chorus made explicit what Goethe only suggests. The Greek dramatists retained the interest of an audience which knew in advance the fate of a Creon, an Ajax, or an Agamemnon, and the chorus was the dramatic agent of this prior knowledge. Thus in the classical drama, the alternating appearance of protagonist and chorus, the one acting with a self-delusive freedom, the other pondering and commenting upon the causality of inevitable decree, superbly presents the antinomy of the dramatic imagination, the mutual implication of participant and spectator, free will and fate, without at the same time exploding the dramatic arena into a thousand fragments of skepticism and improbability.

Any critic interested in the problem of types of tragedy must inevitably distinguish between character drama and situation drama, the tragedy of free will and the tragedy of fate, but these distinctions arise neither from the mere contingency of history nor from an abstract awareness of mere logical possibility. They are distinctions which are empirical in the sense that they characterize the dramatic imagination, but a priori in the sense that they are simultaneously dimensions of our epistemic equipment, and they show how the problem of genres is rooted in a philosophy of human nature.

In choosing to deal with literary genres from the philosophical rather than the analytic or sociohistorical perspective, I have not meant to deny the considerable utility of the latter two. Analysis of the norms of literary expression will always be valuable as a survey of the given terrain, and the effort to show how they are rooted in the historical experience of people living under determinate cultural conditions adds a necessary dimension of temporal uniqueness and sociological concern. But the further attempt to ground them in the continuous operations of the imagination emphasizes the human center of creativity—its possibilities, its limits, its necessary principles of performance. From Descartes to Kant philosophers saw their task as that on inquiry into the origin, the extent, and the validity of human knowledge. A comparable task for the contemporary literary critic might be that of an inquiry into the origins, the extent, and the validity (functional utility) of the human imagination.

Such an inquiry always necessarily begins from empirical materials. That is why in asking certain general questions about genres—What are the possibilities for the novel? What are the possibilities for poetry? What are the possibilities for drama?—I have settled on the novels of Tolstoy and Dostoyevsky, the poetry of Stevens, Pound, and Eliot, and the tragic drama of Sophocles and Shakespeare. For my concern has been less a complete architectonic of the imagination than a consideration of certain restricted modes of its functioning, and my attention to internality and externality in the novel, sensory quality, movement, and meaning in poetry, and freedom of character as opposed to the determinism of situation in the tragic drama has meant to be merely suggestive of the type of critical enterprise which I would recommend. Carried to completion it would require not only a complex web of individual literary inquiries but, finally, a generalized theory of the imagination itself. This, as I have indicated, is a return to various modes of traditional eighteenth-century philosophic perception.

Forms of literary criticism have their conceptual styles and their seasons. The aesthetics of the ancient world is built around the concept of *imitation*, that of the eighteenth century around the concept of *imagination*, that of the contemporary world around the concept of *communication*. This should be eminently clear by a comparative reading of, say, Aristotle's *Poetics*, Kant's *Critique of Judgment*, and Dewey's *Art as Experience*. Problems in literature and the arts can be alternatively stated as problems of imitation, imagination, or communication. My own inquiry takes the concept of imagination as central and as such finds its chief theoretical resources in Kant, Dilthey, and their contemporary followers. But it finds important confirmations in Aristotle and Dewey also; for the naturalism in which they share suggests important ways in which the functioning of the imagination is geared to the rhythms of human experience. Both imply that there is an inherently dramatic quality in all experience, so that drama is less a fortuitous human artifact than the characteristic expression of the histrionic sensibility native to the human species.

The drama as a literary form implies a composition arranged for reenactment. But it draws on real events in human experience—its vivid gestures, expressive movements, unexpected conjunctions, intense oppositions, striking resolutions and conclusions. These in turn are subject to the rhythms of organic existence and to the inescapable polarities of which they are constituted: action-fatigue, hope-despair, waking-sleep, hunger-satiety, love-hate, curiosity-knowledge, desire-appeasement, emotion-relaxation, striving-contentment, anxiety-peace. Experience *means* temporality, change and development, vivid contrast. It is inherently dramatic because it comes in blocks or quanta having incipience and finality, tensions and climaxes, recognitions and reversals, beginnings and endings. The dramatic poet in his numerous guises merely adapts for his purposes those structures of lived experience which are common to us all.

But the imagination which, creatively utilized, provides the repertory of literary forms is not only dramatic, it is also *teleological*. Closely associated with the myth-making faculty in man, it creates a special world in accordance with its own needs, which are less rooted in an uncritical intuition of the magical force inherent in all things than in the impulse to find purposiveness in all the accidents of nature and human life. It is one thing to distinguish the perceptual space of physiological optics from the abstract space of Democritus, Newton, and projective geometry; it is quite another to distinguish both of these from the mythical space through which Homer charts the navigations of Odysseus—a space that is like a magnetic field filled with nameless dangers which is nonetheless a line of direction through which a course of action must be charted and pursued. This space is neither neutral nor abstract, for it is related to fearfulness and peril or to safety and returning home. It is charming and beautifully beside the point that Victor Bérard spent his life in charting the navigations of Odysseus through the literal geography of the Mediterranean world as we know it, and we are indebted to him (as any scientific age must be) for showing the rugged contours of fact emerging from the mists of myth. But in fact it fitfully distracts our attention from the teleological quality of the Homeric narrative in which the weary human adventurer seeks his home. Homeric space is no Democritean void or Newtonian matrix of mathematical relations. It is a plenum of magical powers—friendly in Aeolus, cruel with Scylla and Charybdis—but meaningful because heavily laden with value properties and infinitely relevant to the purposes of the hero.

There is something deeply cognate in the teleological imagination and the myth-making faculty in man, and to this intimacy we owe the novel, the drama, and poetry in all of their infinite forms. Even if the operations of this faculty seem not to assist the understanding in its work, but rather to seduce the intelligence away from its natural operations, this too has its higher utility in humanistic terms. Bergson spoke of the myth-making faculty as a defensive reaction of nature against the dissolvent character of the intelligence. He was speaking of the life-furthering powers of illusion against the consciousness of ultimate death and the ever present probability of human unhappiness. Wallace Stevens without this evolutionary pragmatism comes to conclusions which are very similar. He sees the literary artist as giving to life the supreme fictions without which we are unable to conceive of it. "It is a violence from within that protects us from a violence without. It is the imagination pressing back against the pressure of reality. It seems in the last analysis to have something to do with our self-preservation: and that no doubt is why the expression of it, the sound of its words, helps us to live our lives." The teleological imagination is the impulse pressing back against the pressure of reality, and if we wish to understand the luxurious proliferation of literary forms and genres, which are its instruments, we must not simply analyze them and provide their historical documentation, but appreciate the psychological and philosophical necessities from which they spring.

Adrian Marino

TOWARD A DEFINITION OF LITERARY GENRES

The main question is to find a satisfactory *method* of analysis and definition of *literary genres*. For obvious reasons such a method cannot be logical or historical or categorial. Abstract classifications are empty of meaning, a historical study does not reveal aesthetic structures, the typology of the creative act is usually drawn up in accordance with the constitutive instances of art in general.[1] People frequently speak of "lyrical genres" and "dramatic genres," without referring to literature only; for example, when one speaks of an "epic" painting the concept of genre and that of aesthetic category are taken to be one and the same. But no one can explain why the *lyrical* and *epic* genres should not be included in the same category as the *comic, tragic, sublime, graceful*, thus extending the restrictive list to be found in prescriptive aesthetic treatises. Nor are all aesthetic criteria equally adequate. The classification by content, for instance, can be extended ad infinitum. There are as many literary contents as there are genres.[2] The division into "poetic" and "nonpoetic," "fictional" and "nonfictional" must also be dropped as all genres acquire a right to aesthetic existence precisely through their "poetic," "fictional" character. Likewise unacceptable are the criteria sometimes put forth by the Russian formalists for defining genres in terms of *secondary features* and *dimensions* of genres; some are unessential and others plainly empirical or conventional. "Short" genre, "long" genre—what could be more relative and arbitrary? Classification in accordance with the practical use of the genres—poetic, scientific, utilitarian—should be discarded because of the very extra-aesthetical, predominantly heteronomous criteria adopted.

However outdated and ambiguous the age-old theory of imitation may be, it does provide some solutions. In accordance with the role played by imitation in literary creations, Plato distinguished between those genres in which one could speak of full imitation, in the form of fiction (the tragedy and the comedy), those in which the poet spoke only about himself (the dithyramb), and those which combined both modalities (the epic). One might nevertheless say that although poetry is by definition imitation, there are some genres which are more "imitative" than others. While sometimes it is the poet himself who speaks, sometimes he speaks on behalf of his heroes, whom he only imitates (*The Republic*, III, 393a–c; 394b–c). At any rate, this is an anticipation of the no less traditional discrimination between subjective and objective genres: those in which the subject is present throughout the narrative and those in which the subject is absent or dissimulated in the course of the fictional discourse. Aristotle accepts this discrimination which, with various qualifications, has been preserved in the most up-to-date classifications: "Indeed, with the same means, the same models, one must also speak of imitation when one tells a story—under guise of some one else, like Homer, or preserving his own unchanged self—and when the story shows those imitated in full operation and movement" (*Poetics*, III, 1448a).

The whole "modern" study of the relationship writer/personage, direct/indirect style, first person present tense/third person past tense, does not go far beyond these simple and basic distinctions. Their continuity can be traced uninterruptedly ever since the Alexandrine period (Diomedes, *Ars Gramatica*: "Genus Activum vel Imitativum, ennarativum, commune") and the Renaissance,[3] through divisions in accordance with the degree and modality of imitation: *narrative* poetry—mere imitation of history (in fact of the representations of memory); *representative*—the image of present actions; *allusive*—using parables and symbols as with Bacon (*Of the Advancement of Learning*, II, IV, 3, 1605). This pattern continues with direct visual representation (the drama), indirect, narrated (the epic genre), in conformity, for instance, with the qualification made by people like Batteux (*Principes de la Littérature*, sec. I, ch. 2, 1746), or the modern Northrop Frye, in whose work the drama is "an external and the lyric an internal mimesis of sound and imagery." At any rate, this is a less arbitrary distinction than Frye's *thematic* (lyrical) and *fictional* (comic and epic) genres (*Anatomy of Criticism*, 1957). The great and eternal difficulty lies in the very understanding of the concept of "imitation" itself: is this a process of imitation, representation, creation, or fiction? There will always be room for fresh interpretations.

Formal-expressive categories—the stylistic, linguistic ones—speculate on identical relations translated into various languages of communication: "narrative" means the direct intervention of the poet, "representative" means the poet "does not speak" but only evokes; the distinction is Aristotelian in origin, and Guarini takes it over in the Renaissance. The lyrical genre therefore should be considered "narrative" as it "narrates" the poet's inner self. The classification is discarded in the classical age, which delimits the two genres as follows: the epic is a narrative told by the poet, while the dramatic conveys the substance of the discourse through the personage's "mouth" (Rollin, *Traité des études*, I, 2, ch. 3, art. III, 1726). There would be therefore two types of discourse (expositive and in dialogue), to which a third should be added: the descriptive. All this is finally linked to the purpose of communication: private or public; *reading* in the former case, *declamation* in the latter. Everything would therefore boil down to the specific character of the communication between the poet and his ideal audience: acted, spoken, written, dramatic, lyrical, epic—a kind of literature meant for the spectator or the listener or the reader; in the modern approach these are performed, uttered, written.[4] But in this case, if the theater, the speech, and the printing press are the only means of expression, I do not quite see where one could place, for instance, the lyrical genre which can be equally "oral" or "written." If by genres we really mean existential attitudes, the lyric can be equally well expressed through all the above three. The various levels are neither reconciled nor overlapping; the typological criteria do not coincide with the formal ones. "The content" does not correspond to the "form" and vice-versa; this is a fundamental obstacle to any dualistic classification of the literary genres. It becomes simply impossible, artificial, arbitrary from the point of view of form or of content whenever the organic unity of the literary work is broken in one sense or another.

The purely linguistic solutions, though more consistent, are no less formal. At the level of language, a number of "situations" and "primary speech patterns," along with a series of "universals" covering the corpus of folk literary productions, can be typified on the basis of schemata and stereotype situations (myths, legends, proverbs, riddles, witticism).[5] Nevertheless, as soon as one finds a direct expression of an emotion within these communication clichés, the tracks begin to get blurred, the genres overlap, and finally they can be reduced to songs, tales, and shows, or to the old threefold distinction—lyrical, epic, and dramatic—without any real progress. Another attempt, based on the concept of the work's time and space (*Zeit-im-Werk* and *Raum-im-Werk*), admits the existence of a time of reading, of recitation, and of performance. An action which lasts two hours in terms of the "work's time" requires only ten minutes in "reading time."[6] The dimensions of space representations also differ; this is a commonly accepted thing. Nor is this conducive to any real progress. The criterion remains abstract, extraliterary, and brings us back to traditional observations.

The expository and interlocutory genres are the only genres that can be used with little difficulty to formalize the outcome of indirect speech in the third person (epic) and of direct, first person speech (lyrical, dramatic, oratorical), in conformity with Roman Jakobson's classification (accepted by other specialists as well),[7] and possibly qualified by underlining the participation of various functions of the language besides the dominant, poetic function. Epic poetry, centered around the third person, widely uses the referential function of the language, while lyrical poetry focuses on the first person and is intimately linked to the emotional function.[8] Yet it is not clear to which genre poetry written in the second person, "dominated" by the connotative function, oriented toward the interlocutor (of appeal, supplication, or exhortation), corresponds, although probably it is the dramatic one.[9]

The inclusion of the literary discourse into a specific "duration" makes it possible to classify the genres in accordance with the grammatical and temporal dimension. The authors and the heroes can be differentiated by their positions toward time, by facts being evoked in the present (lyric genre), in the past (epic genre), or in the future (dramatic genre). Jean-Paul Richter seems to be first to adopt this trichotomy whose modern modified version Emil Staiger discovers in "recollection" (*Erinnerung*), "representation" (*Vorstellung*), and "tension" (*Spannung*), the corresponding forms for the past (lyrical), the present (epic), and the future (dramatic).[10] The only objection is that at the level of linguistic expression tenses differ, as it seems more legitimate for lyrical poetry to cultivate the first person present tense, and for the epic the third person past tense, a fact pointed out by the Russian formalists.

Any work belonging to any genre has two tenses: the present (of immediate lyrical expression, of the narrative, of the dramatic presentation, actualized, made "present" for the duration of the recitation, the reading, the performance), and a sort of time which is peculiar to each work taken separately (it may be present, past, or future). There is also a lack of scientific criteria in this type of classification, in contradiction to the poetic character of the language, which puts together lyrical, epic, and dramatic situations through its expressive, image-building, rhythmical potentialities.[11] Language is at the same time metonymy (epic), metaphor (lyrical), enthymeme (intellectual), in accordance with the recent structuralist classification initiated by Roman Jakobson.

The concept of *form* may be useful in defining genres provided we discard all artificial dualism. If form contains and expresses its own content,[12] the obvious consequence is that there are as many genres as identifiable forms, but one key question remains: What is the meaning of "form" with reference to literary genres? In a first sense, form is an essential, typological mode of creation, independent of the spirit and the phenomenology of the genre which bears its name. The metahistorical category of "lyrical form" goes far beyond the literary history of the lyrical genre. Its transtemporal existence projects it into universal time and space. The genre can be equally thought of as "inner form," an active principle which organizes a group of literary works in a unitary manner from within. This also justifies the existence of the "outer form" including stylistic, technical, formal components (eternal and metahistorical); for instance, the same poetical rhythm can be found in various epochs used by *different* and even *all* genres.

The classical formal classification (verse, prose, dramatic genres) proves external for the same reasons[13] and was rejected even in the Renaissance (Sir Philip Sidney, An Apologie for Poetrie, 1595). Verse can express, in itself, any kind of "content." Lyrical instances can be found in verse, in prose writings (nonversified), in dramatic dialogues. A dramatic conflict may have epic segments and lyrical moments. Nor is the notion of "style," "trend," or "school" more satisfactory. Not every genre has its own style, but every genre may be present in various styles, trends, schools. The adoption of strictly formal criteria (stanzas, meters, "fixed forms") ignores the existential and typological substance of the genres. It is a matter of common belief that formal characteristics correspond more closely to the species and subcategories than to the main genres. Since, however, some works may be included in certain genres without having marked formal characteristics, this dissociation also fails. Too broad a definition of the form of genre does not say anything. Too narrow a definition tends to admit as many genres as distinct, individualized forms can be observed. In fact, the strictly formal meaning of genres is adequate only with regard to the "fixed forms," so that the only well-identified genres would be the sonnet, the rondel, and so on. The conventionalism of such a conclusion is obvious.

To the extent to which we admit that literary genres accept specific types of literary organization, the definition of *structure* remains far more acceptable. The genres are structures in the sense of being unitary modes of literary construction, the principle on the basis of which Aristotle himself pointed out that the poet "was not allowed to apply an epic structure to tragedy" (*Poetics*, XVIII, 1456a). There is an internal, radical incompatibility between the two genres or species, yet one which it is difficult to study because of a widespread fallacy.

The most frequent study technique is to select a group of works previously defined as lyrical, epic, dramatic, then to try to identify the structure previously defined as lyrical, epic, dramatic. This a priori (though inevitable) approach spoils the whole technique. Instead of proceeding objectively, through inference by *first* identifying the structures we are going to define a posteriori as lyrical, epic, dramatic, we use only preconceived notions which we ascribe a priori to the structures discussed, which ought to be recognized and named *after* such an examination. There is no theoretical justification for the identification of a type of structure with the lyrical or epic genres, which are simple linguistic signs, either conventional or arbitrary. The only justified conclusion is the identification and objective description of the structures which we will later call "lyrical," "epic," or "dramatic"—not on the basis of deduction but on the basis of ascription, of conventional categorial definition. In this light (though the study of genre structure is still in a primary stage) the genres may be seen as "composition units," metahistorical, somehow "natural" (in the sense that Goethe gave the word), suggesting an internal cohesion, a functional interdependence, a specific "systematic" character. The genres then might be considered "systems" of characteristics and common devices whose *dominant* note justifies the formation, the delimitation, and the definition of each genre. There are latent, immanent affinities among various devices as a result of which the latter are structured into internal constellations (constructions, architectural structures, and so on) which are specialized and differentiated.[14] This mutual dependence makes it possible for some themes to lend themselves better to being used in certain situations (heroic, tragical), while others seem less suitable for it. This accounts for deeply rooted (yet insufficiently studied) incompatibilities between the lyrical and the grotesque, for instance. The epic requires relations of succession, the dramatic only relations of contiguity. In fact, these features can be identified, and described, but can hardly be explained. They are intrinsically structural. Yet a systematic description of the genres, completed by a semantic study in the nature of meanings, has not been written. Even the traditional, didactic definitions recognize the existence of a "group of works," which have "common features," "a set of characteristic features," *Ordnungsprinzipien*, etc. The trouble is that in all these definitions, the criteria—most of them bearing on content—are a jumble.

The only fully justified solution to this question of literary genres would be their definition as types of creativity, identified within the very process of creation, as the most specific attitude of the creative self, which is *self-reflection* and *detachment*. Hence a first conclusion: since the creative self adopts a unique literary attitude—the only possible one—literature must have essentially one genre, *mono*-logue and *self*-logue, corresponding to the "lyrical," unique category of emotion and perception. In this sense of the necessary fundamental self-reflection, the theory of the "lyrical" character of literature is undoubtedly justified, on condition we exclude any practical sentimental interpretation, any idea of self-expression, of "sincerity," or other psychological parameters. The consistent adoption of this point of view solves many difficulties of defining literary genres.

The controversial problem of *typology* can be similarly solved by identifying the existing types of distancing and self-reflection: the self which contemplates itself in the act of self-expression defines the *lyrical* genre; the self which reflects itself for the whole duration of the subjective or objective narrative defines the *epic* genre; the self which reflects itself in its internal tensions or external conflicts defines the *dramatic-tragical* genre; the self which reflects itself in the critical, ironical, ridiculous attitudes defines the *comic* genre. In all cases, the same existential situation is to be found in differentiated technical hypostases: substantial lyricism, declared lyricism, narrative lyricism, conflictual lyricism, burlesque lyricism. The spirit expresses itself in succession, in contradiction, and in caricature.

The unity of these situations is ensured by one and the same lyrical participation; specialization derives from the possible directions of this participation, somehow a peculiarity which leaves open the "list" of literary genres. If the established inventory is correct, their number is narrowed down to four. This interpretation stresses the identification of natural forms of self-conscious expression, whose literary manifestations—more or less adequate—acquire the traditional and conventional name of *lyrical, epic, dramatic, tragical, comic*. For the rest, the transition from the genre to the species is a question of a naturalistic classification, meaningless from our point of view. As a matter of fact, the catalogue of "literary species" is not yet complete; what some people consider to belong to the "genre," others consider to be a "species." What is "the novel"? Is it a genre or a species? According to some it is a "genre" just like all the "subdivisions" of the "fundamental" categories or genres, a definition which others reject.

If the self-scrutinizing (autoscopic) ego consititutes the "lyrical" condition of literature, all the modalities and hypostases of this "self-scrutiny" become essentially "lyrical," "poetical." Hence literary genres are virtually unique: one substance, one created impulse with various phenomenological manifestations. The intrinsic (not the historical) origin of the genres can be explained in the same way: all genres can be only primary, "primitive." They appear well-delimited in the productions of those peoples who have not yet outgrown the stage of folklore and absence of alphabet. Finally a very important consequence: literature—being the product of only creative self, the "author" of a basically unitary kind of literature—is at the same time lyrical, epic, dramatic in a circular movement. Any literary utterance virtually includes every genre, and therefore all possible genres.

The *fundamental solidarity* of situations implicitly of literary genres thus receives the fullest confirmation. The creative self passes successively or alternatively through all the literary moments, whether they be lyrical, epic, dramatic, as demonstrated by the evident continuity and genealogical potential of literature. The same event may be sung, narrated, presented as a core of tensions and conflicts. The same emotion can be translated and transferred in any type of human situation or relation. Being integrated with the sequence of history, we are implicitly "epic." Since history is dialectical, we become no less "dramatic." When the same history fills us with enthusiasm we cannot help being "lyrical." The epic passes into the dramatic, the dramatic into the lyrical, the lyrical into the epic, each genre being the anticipation or the conditions of the others, a rotation which is reflected also in the ambiguity of definitions. We can feel, narrate, dramatize, burlesque anything, and anything can be defined as such. Hence the hesitations, the nuances, and the infinite paradoxes of literature, which cannot be reduced to stable or univocal formulas. The major, essential genre of the creative self is therefore by definition the *poly-genre*. This conclusion rejects the whole traditional theory of literary genres.

Nevertheless, in its internal or historical development the unity and the categorial solidarity of literature does not exclude moments of instability and unbalance, expressed by strong accents in one field or another. The conclusion is that literary genres have only a transient, fragmentary, and hierarchical existence. The appearance of certain works in which the lyrical moment is predominant justifies their recognition, definition, and inclusion into the "lyrical genre." This circumstance does not exclude the coexistence within the same work with other genres which are relegated to the background, to a secondary position and dimension. Literary genres therefore have a prevalent reality, not an exclusive one.

Under the circumstances, to what extent can one refer to the "laws" of literary genres? First, one may speak of internal development, in accordance with the tendency of literature to become reintegrated into its original unity. The latent movement of the genres being considered the recovery of primary solidarity, their intrinsic logic rejects strict divisions or stagnation in an excessive specialization. This feature explains the permanent aspiration toward regrouping, the tendency to remove barriers between genres, the insistence upon intermediary, graduated nuances and tinges. Such "pictorial" analyses were made as early as the eighteenth century, when Lord Kames observed that no one can tell where a species ends and where another begins.[15] Moreover, the same tendency can be identified among other arts through significant metaphors: pictorial narration, musical dramatism, the forerunners of the modern "correspondences"; when they approach music, the genres become "warm," "full of passion"; when they approach geometry, they become "transparent," "empty," and "cold."[16]

A similar two-stroke movement of contraction and dilatation can be detected on the historical plane, where a constant movement from dogma-ridden approaches to liberal approaches, from rules to challenges and individualized expression is noticeable. The genres begin to be recognized, defined, and theoretically classified by various dogmatic legislators and end by being combined or simply negated by the writer. In Rumanian criticism Titu Maiorescu is the representative of "the first necessity: clearly to mark the frontier between poetry and the other literary genres."[17] Al. A. Macedonski illustrates the second: "a poem... must include everything: sorrow, suffering, tears, despair, disappointment, skepticism, philosophy, faith, irony, love, wisdom, madness,"[18] briefly, all the genres, *toute la lyre*!

The inconsistency of dogmatism, and generally of the traditional conception about literary genres, thus becomes self-evident. It can be reduced to several rigorous principles and codes broadly mapped out by the rhetoricists and the grammarians of the Alexandrine epoch,[19] reaching full maturity in the Renaissance and strictly delimited by the whole of Neo-Classicism in Europe. The great admiration for Classical works and principles turns into norms and constraints, the view that poets "have to" observe and cultivate the following principles, logically derived from one another:

1. Each genre has its own laws, ideals, beauty (Boileau, *L'Art Poétique*, II, v. 139), and mixing must be prohibited. The mixing of comic and tragical elements is excluded (Horace, *Ars Poetica*, v. 89–92).

2. The rigorous separation of the genres obliges each poet to keep within the strict limits of the genre adopted.

3. Thus each genre maintains its unadulterated "purity," its "unity" of tone. The genres are *bien tranchés* or they do not exist at all.

4. Conformity with the internal and formal norms of each genre leads to the achievement of the work. The fact is not possible without compliance with the precepts of criticism.

5. There is a hierarchy of genres (including higher and lower genres, "great" and "petty") essential for the scale of values in literature.

All these are, without exception, either false or highly exaggerated.

Unitary in its aesthetic essence, literary art evinces in each and every work the same basic characteristics, the same specific techniques. One and indivisible, literature is the expression of a unique principle, identified according to circumstances, as "the sublime" (a traditional concept, extended and frequently used in the eighteenth century, for all the genres),[20] "poetry" or "lyricism" in conformity with the German romantic conception (F. Schlegel, *Gespräch über die Poesie*, 1800), or with Croce's radical distinction between "poetry" and "literature." "The poetic genres being poetry itself," the typical literary "genre" becomes poetry, and lyricism is the core and the initial impulse of every genre. Identifying three literary genres: ideology, poetry, and literature, M. Dragomirescu is the first of the Rumanian aestheticians to take this stand, and L. Rusu seems to be a supporter of the idea of a fundamental "lyricism."[21]

Literary works, unique and irrepeatable in essence and definition, therefore "original," defy rigorous subcategorization and all leveling pigeonholes. They form distinctive structures, irreducible to the category of a genre, which is always denied by the particular coefficient of invention, specific to every genuine creation. In fact, people know only about tragedies, not about *tragedy;* about novels, not about *the novel*, both being theoretical abstractions, while each and every work is an absolute, incomparable individuality. The romantics (A.W. Schlegel, Schleiermacher, Wackenroder, Ugo Foscolo, Fauriel) reject the theory and the classification of the genres on this ground too and so do many "new critics."[22]

In this way, each literary work can be written *only* "in its own genre," belongs to its own genre, and starts a *new genre*. To admit that each genre is achieved in a lump through adaptation to its internal norm means an unacceptable aesthetic finalism. First a new, original, uncommon work appears, and then the concept of the corresponding genre is created, as a sort of subsequent justification. In response to the Renaissance play *Orlando Furioso* Giraldi Cintio coined the term "Romanzo" and theorized upon it, illustrating one such situation. There are as many true genres and species as there are true poets—very much as Giordano Bruno put it in *Degli Eroici furori* (1585). The whole history of literature unfolds between one genre and an infinity of genres—each novel, each poem in Schlegel's phrase "a genre in itself" (*eine Gattung für sich*). There are as many genres as there are literary "natures" (Condillac). The entire traditional aesthetics of inspiration, the genius and creative fancy, is fundamentally hostile to the theory of the genres.

All these latent realities and historical truths are more or less clearly intuited as early as antiquity, so that the dogmatism of the rules meets vehement opposition in all epochs through an interrupted dialectical action and reaction. The other side—and the inevitable shadow—of each classical and dogmatic approach is the opposition of the critical spirit, the *polemics against precepts* (contested as early as Quintilian's time), the instinctive reaction of the genuine creator who knows, as Giordano Bruno states, that "poetry is born out of rules only through very fortuitous accidents." He refuses "to ape other people's Muses," definitely opposing the idea of imitation, genre, serial production. Questioning positions are formulated in various ways, with various nuances: lampoon-like (with V. Gravina, scornful of "ambitious and miserly" precepts), ironical (in Corneille's style: "It is easy to understand Aristotle"), burlesque (Pope, "A Receipt to Make an Epick Poem," 1713, similar to the modern Rumanian writer I.L. Caragiale's *Magic Salve*). These protests, more and more frequent in the eighteenth century (Dubos, La Motte Houdard, Voltaire), in the Sturm und Drang, and in French Romanticism, can all be traced back to the same principle of the liberty of creation and the freedom of the literary personality with full rights to initiative, invention, and therefore nonconformism with aesthetic dogmas. In Rumanian literature, Bolliac rejected "the prison rules," "Mr. Boileau's rules," as early as 1845–46.[23]

As any work somehow violates the conventional rules of one genre or another, the frontiers between genres become increasingly artificial and unnatural. "To create in accordance with one genre means to extend this genre," Thibaudet observed. Their fate is to be dilated, violated, totally annihilated, often proclaimed with pompous declarations of satisfaction: "Fall, fall down you walls that separate the genres!" (Sébastien Mercier, *Du Théâtre, ou nouvel essai sur l'art dramatique,* 1773). In the romantic perspective of abolishing any distinction, "all classical literary genres are ridiculous in their strict purity" (F. Schlegel, *Lyceum Fr.,* 60). Victor Hugo's preface to *Cromwell* develops the same idea, a genuine commonplace of romanticism, complicated in modern literature by the Baroque tendency of the collaboration or fusion of poetry with the other arts.

The theoretical wiping out of the "impenetrable magic circles" drawn by dogmatic critics around the genres is fully anticipated in each and every epoch by the existence in practice of "mixed," "bastard," "hybrid," "frontier" genres—a phenomenon of current interference present at all times, ever since the Renaissance.[24] Such are the "tragical-comical-historical-pastoral scene individable, or poem unlimited" of which Polonius spoke in *Hamlet* (II, 2), the Baroque ballet-comedy, the "larmoyant" comedy and the "bourgeois" drama of the eighteenth century, the poetic theater and the Romantic melodrama and so on. Baroque literature and especially Romanticism cultivated and theorized precisely these interferences, retrospectively identified and praised (Homer, The Bible, Dante), and anticipated the synthesis of life in the visionary perspective of a total art. The romantic aestheticians (the Schlegel brothers, Schelling, Hölderlin, Schleiermacher) always lay stress on this transformation which is not mere evolution but metamorphosis. There are no pure genres but only intermediary forms, ambiguous categories. Where does a genre begin, and where does it end? The genius combines all the genres. Each genre can comprise in various proportions all possible forms of self-imitation, inspired from all situations and "experiences" of life. Hence it may be concluded that precise classifications are not only absurd but are impossible. In the sixteenth century the French Protestant poet Du Bartas said about himself that he was "partly panegyric, partly prophetic, partly didactic." To deny the mixture of tragedy and comedy meant—in the words of Ogier, a critic of the classical age—"to ignore the conditions of the life of people," a modern argument or a romantic one. For Cervantes, the romance "allows the author to show the epic, the lyrical, the tragical and the comic parts as well" (*Don Quixote*, I, ch. 47), an attribute ascribed by F. Schlegel to the novel as a whole and greatly praised as such. In modern literature, all literary genres seem to coincide with the concept of this genre which would include them all. But *Faust* can claim the same merits. The same is true about Wagner's *gesamt Kunstwerk*. The assertion can be proved at the level of an author's whole work, which is difficult to include in only one genre. But to study it separately, sliced up in compartments (novel, drama, poetry), means to break its unity, to overlook inner coherence; yet this is unfortunately a frequent sight in everyday literary histories, crammed with "many-headed monsters."

The principle of dividing the genres into major and minor also proves to be mistaken, as it establishes a relative, transient, extraaesthetic scale of values, of a purely historical significance. In ancient times the tragedy and the epic vied for supremacy largely by using the same arguments (Aristotle, *Poetics,* XXVI; Horace, *Satires,* I, 4, v. 39–69). In the Renaisance, the "great genres" are the epic, the ode, the epistle, the satire, the sonnet; the minor ones are lyrical poetry, the epigram, the pastoral. Through Boileau, classicism sanctioned the same traditional hierarchy and the major genres became the tragedy, the epic, the comedy; the minor

ones were the idyll, the elegy, the song, the satire, the sonnet, the epigram, the rondel, the vaudeville. The same broad repartition was maintained in the eighteenth century: the epic, the ode, the tragedy, the epistle, the satire, the essay.[25] The order was broken only by the ascent of the novel, a "minor" genre during the Enlightenment, reinstated in its rights and strongly promoted during Romanticism (F. Schlegel) and predominant in the literature of the last two centuries. This phenomenon confirms the theory of the Russian formalists regarding "the canonization of the lower genres," the popular ones. There are classical examples in the nineteenth century as well: Pushkin exalts gallant poetry; Chekhov—the sketch, the farce; Dostoyevsky—the detective story.[26]

This argument turns against hierarchy as it is enough for a great creator to appear in order that the previous order might be overturned. Then again, "canonization" is not an operation made by the writers themselves but by the critics who only come to sanction new creations, substantially equal to the previous ones, creation actually being anywhere and at any time of only one rank. Voltaire is right: "All genres are good except the boring ones." The frequency and reputation of a genre is not one and the same thing as the value of individual achievements because in this case the statistic criterion would be superior to the aesthetic one. If "lyricism" is the essence of literary art, the epic does not necessarily become inferior, nor does the mixed genre become necessarily superior because the former allegedly lacks the substance of the fundamental genre while the latter, on the contrary, allegedly contains all of them. To the extent to which they fulfill the condition of art, all genres are or become "lyrical" in a variable proportion. As in the case of classifications the hierarchy of genres also starts from the generalization of some fragmentary, unessential characteristic.

Finally, let us permanently bear in mind that the definitions of literary genres—like those of literary concepts—are historical, therefore mobile, transient, *conventional*, therefore approximative, nominal, relative, therefore not entirely adequate, vacillating as contradictions and discrepancies can be observed between a conceptual label and the literary reality. Between the essence of genres (defined by literary *notions* and *ideas*) and the phenomenon of genres (expressed in literary *forms*) experience very often discovers flagrant incompatibilities. Under these conditions it is rash and unwise to dogmatize one definition or another. If literature itself is sometimes ahead of definitions and sometimes behind them, it is absurd to try to immobilize it in a *ne varietur* formula. As long as the consciousness of the literary genre does not perfectly coincide with its existence, no fixity is possible.

Notes

1. Tudor Vianu, "Genurile artistice," in *Estetica* (Bucharest, 1939), p. 193.
2. The proof: R. Dovadă, *Glossaire des genres littéraires* (82!), in *Histoire des littératures* (Paris, 1957), 2: 1731–34.
3. J.E. Spingarn, *La Critica letteraria nel Rinascimento* (Bari, 1905), pp. 60–61.
4. Northrop Frye, "Theory of genres," in *Anatomy of Criticism* (Princeton, N.J., 1957), pp. 247–48.
5. André Jolles, *Einfache Formen, Legende, Sage, Mythe, Rätsel, Spruch, Kasus, Memorabile, Märchen, Witz* (Halle, 1929); "Gattung," in *Kleines literarisches Lexikon, Sachbegriffe* (Bern, 1966), pp. 140–42; "Gattungslehre," in *Das Fischer Lexikon* (Frankfurt am Main), II, 1, pp. 237–40.
6. Frank C. Maatje, "Versuch einer Poetik des Raumes, Der lyrische, epische und dramatische Raum," in *Zagadnienia Rodzajow Literarickich* [Les problèmes des genres littéraires], T.XI, nr.1/1968, pp. 5–23.
7. Radu Manoliu, "Genurile literare," in *Convorbiri literare* (Bucharest, 1933), pp. 837–38.
8. Roman Jakobson, "Linguistique et poétique," in *Essais de linguistique générale* (Paris, 1963), pp. 209–48.
9. Edward Stankiewicz, "Poetic and Non-Poetic Language in Their Interrelation," in *Poetics* . . . (Warsaw, 1962), 1:46.
10. Max Wehrli, *Allgemeine Literaturwissenschaft* (Bern, 1969), pp. 75–76.
11. Karl Vossler, *Aus der romanischen Welt* (Leipzig, 1940), 2:141–42.
12. In the field of theory of literary genres this correspondence seems to be established for the first time by F. Schlegel, cf. Peter Szondi, "La Théorie des genres littéraires chez Fréderic Schlegel," *Critique*, no. 250 (1968), 276–77.
13. Paul Van Tieghem, "Genres et styles," in *La Littérature comparée*, 4th ed. (Paris, 1951), pp. 70–87.
14. B. Tomachevski, "Les Genres littéraires," in *Théorie de la littérature* (Paris, 1965), pp. 302–3.
15. Kames, Henry Home, Lord, *Elements of Criticism* (Basel, 1795), 3:145.
16. Abbé Batteux, *Principes de la littérature* (Paris, 1774), 3:215.
17. T. Maiorescu, "Conditia materială a poeziei," in *Critice* (Bucharest, 1967), 1:31.
18. Al. A. Macedonski, "Poema poemelor," in *Literatorul* 21 (1880).
19. Augusto Rostagni, "Il 'Sublime' nella storia dell'estetica antica," in *Annali della R. Scuola Normale Superiore di Pisa*, vol. 3, fasc. I–II (Bologna, 1933), p. 107.
20. Norman Maclean, "From Action to Image: Theories of the Lyric in the Eighteenth Century," in *Critics and Criticism*, ed. R.S.Crane (Chicago, 1965), p. 421.

21. M.Dragomirescu, "Les Principes de l'esthétique intégrale," in *Deuxième Congrès International d'Esthétique et de Science de l'Art* (Paris, 1937), 1:30; *La Science de la littérature* (Paris, 1928), 2: 24,146; Liviu Rusu, "Teoria genurilor literare," in *Estetica poeziei lirice* (Bucharest, 1969), p. 81.
22. René Wellek, *A History of Modern Criticism* (London, 1961), 2: 50, 266, 305; Mario Fubini, "Genesi e storia dei generi letterari," in *Tecnica e teoria letteraria* (Milan, 1959), p. 66; Fauriel, foreword to *Parthénéide* of Baggessen, 1810, in Roger Fayolle's *La Critique littéraire* (Paris, 1964), pp. 252–53; Maurice Blanchot, *Le livre à venir* (Paris, 1959).
23. Cezar Bolliac, *"Răspuns la articolul 'Poezie',"* in *Foaie pentru minte, inimă și literatură*, no. 8 (1845), and "Poezia," no. 27–30 (1846).
24. *Der Briefwechsel zwischen Schiller und Goethe*, eds. Hans Gerhard Gräf and Albert Leitzmann (Leipzig, 1955), Goethe, 23 December 1797, 1: 452f.
25. Paul F. Leedy, "Genres Criticism and the Significance of Warton's Essay on Pope," *Journal of English and Germanic Philology* 45 (1946): 142.
26. Tomachevski, *Théorie de la littérature*, pp. 304–5.

John Reichert

MORE THAN KIN AND LESS THAN KIND: THE LIMITS OF GENRE THEORY

Let us begin with an elemental distinction between genre criticism and genre theory. Let us regard genre criticism as discourse which makes use of the fact that literary works can be classified or separated into groups or genres on the basis of similarities found within them, and let us consider genre theory—a subcategory of genre criticism—as the attempt to use the existence of such genres to construct a theory of criticism or a special and perhaps privileged method of criticism. Genre theory in this sense is of special interest because since the 1950s a number of critics—particularly those with a strong penchant for methodology and system building—have sought, in the fact of literary kinds and kinships, the solution to several traditional literary problems, problems having to do with the genesis of literary works and with their interpretation and evaluation.

This paper is concerned with the theoretical weight that the genres have been asked to bear, and more particularly with the theories of the Chicago critics—R.S. Crane, Elder Olson, and later Sheldon Sacks—of Northrop Frye, and most recently of the Bulgarian structuralist Tzvetan Todorov.

These critics might justly resent this association, even if only for a short time, in the confines of a single essay. But they are all given to using generic and classificatory schemes, whether or not they share a single point of view or definition of "genre." If my broad definition of a genre as any group of works selected on the basis of some shared features would not do full justice to the nuances of any of their positions, it nevertheless embraces them all, and each of them is subject to the logical implications of classifying things in general.

Since much of what gets said here will be of a skeptical cast, I want to make it clear that I believe that genre criticism—apart from genre theorizing—is usually a good and necessary sort of criticism. Whenever we try to communicate our understanding of something to someone else (and this is surely an important aspect of criticism) we make use of generic language, saying what kind of a thing something is, and perhaps how it differs from other things of the same kind. As E.D. Hirsch and others have pointed out, the very act of reading—of coming to know a novel, poem, or play firsthand—involves generic conceptions and expectations.[1]

Furthermore, genres constitute a natural object of historical inquiry. The critic may select a group of roughly similar works (say Jacobean and Restoration comedy, or the novel of manners from Fielding through Austen to James) and use the shared features as a framework within which to detect and narrate chronological change and development. Or he may note the presence of similarities among works vastly separated chronologically or culturally and try to account for the similarities. How did they get there? How did the genre come to be? He may, that is, embark upon a causal explanation of whatever features define the genre he has construed.

Having said this much, however—having allowed for the omnipresence of generic thinking in literary studies—we have scarcely touched upon the ways in which generic concepts have proven to be problematical, or upon the difficult methodological tasks which they have been asked to perform. It is into this field that we must now make our way, charted by a series of more or less traditional questions.

DO GENRES "EXPLAIN" LITERARY WORKS?

We have already seen that in one very important sense they do. Along with analogies, paraphrases, and plot summaries, which they closely resemble, descriptions of a genre, or references to a well-known genre, can render a work intelligible, clarifying the relations among its parts, and perhaps helping to fit it into a larger historical framework. For example, merely to say that a work is to be read ironically (i.e., as one reads works of an ironic

THE LIMITS OF GENRE THEORY 59

kind) is to offer a new way of making sense of what might not otherwise seem sensible. Similarly, the scientist explains a complicated structure or mechanism to a novice with the aid of physical models, or by placing it (verbally) in a class of things with similar but better known structures. One way to render something intelligible is to ask: "How shall we regard this sort of thing?"

But "explain" also has other meanings, and genres are sometimes treated as explaining *why* a work is as it is, or, in Northrop Frye's words, "how the structure came to be what it was."[2] Consider the following two passages, both from Frye:

> The conventional comic form is in *Pride and Prejudice* somewhat as the sonata form is in a Mozart symphony. Its presence there does not account for any of the merits of the novel, but it does account for its conventional, as distinct from its individual, structure.

> In drama, characterization depends on function; what a character is follows from what he has to do in the play. Dramatic function in its turn depends on the structure of the play; the character has certain things to do because the play has such and such a shape. The structure of the play in its turn depends on the category of the play; if it is a comedy, its structure will require a comic resolution and a prevailing comic mood.

The first of these passages is more blatantly tautological than the second. What can "account for" mean in the proposition that the presence of the conventional comic form in the novel *accounts for* the conventional structure of the novel? (If there is a distinction intended between form and structure it is certainly not hinted at in the essay from which the passage is taken.) Let us assume that our description of the conventional comic form includes a plot that moves toward marriage or some socially harmonious analogue of it, a certain kind of mood, and the presence of certain kinds of characters rather than others; and let us assume that *Pride and Prejudice* embodies these three characteristics. If "account for" means simply "describes," then of course the genre description describes the work; if it didn't, the work wouldn't belong to the genre. But the class doesn't tell us why any individual is a member of the class, any more than a list of the features shared by vertebrates tells us why any individual vertebrate has these features.

The second passage is more complicated. Though it is not,

strictly speaking, tautological, it is misleading, as can be shown by the fact that what truth it contains is preserved in a sequence of clauses reversing all its terms, thus:

> The category of a play will depend on its structure; if its structure requires a comic resolution and a prevailing comic mood, it will be a comedy. The play will have such and such a shape because of what the characters do. And what a character does in a play—the function he performs—will depend on what sort of a character he is. Function depends on characterization, in drama.

The truth inscribed on both sides of this reversible coin is that certain aspects of a literary work are related to each other, perhaps "functionally" related. It is true that what a character does is related to what he is, for what he does is our chief means of knowing what he is, and, if he is a consistent character, what he does may be seen to be the result of the kind of person he is. But anything that may be said about the function of different parts of a work may be said without reference to any genre, though of course genre may provide a convenient short cut. To explain how any elements came to be present in the work requires an appeal to something other than the class to which the work belongs, an appeal, say, to the ideas or feelings the author wished to express, to the effects he wished to achieve, or to audience demands for certain kinds of consistency, and so on. It might appeal even to the author's decision to write a conventional comedy, which would in turn be related to preceding reasons or causes. The possession of a certain trait is a reason for assigning a work to a particular category, but a category is simply not the sort of thing that, by itself, can be a reason for, or cause of anything. A sentence like "It has a happy ending because it's a comedy" either is tautological or assumes a reference to some real but unmentioned causal agency. Similarly, the famous syllogism that concludes in Socrates's mortality explains why Socrates dies only to those who know in advance why all men must die.

DOES THE GENRE OF A WORK LIMIT THE INTERPRETIVE PROCEDURES APPROPRIATE TO IT?[3]

In the 1950s R.S. Crane and Elder Olson developed Aristotle's remarks on tragedy into a general theory in which works are classified according to their final causes ("principles of construction," "unifying ideas," "distinctive powers"). Starting with two very general classes—the mimetic and the didactic—they characteristically zeroed in on a work by locating it in increasingly narrow subclasses, employing other Aristotelian terms as they went, but subordinating these always to the discovery and description of the "real final cause" of the work.[4] One of the goals of the theory was a means of determining which interpretive questions could legitimately be asked of a work, and which could not.

Thus a didactic work, the final cause of which is, by definition, to persuade us of some doctrine, would next be classified as either exemplum, allegory, or parable, depending on whether its thesis is implied by induction, deduction, or analogy. A mimetic novel or drama, the final cause of which is the production of a specific emotional response to the characters and their fates, must have one of three kinds of plot: a plot of action, of character, or of thought. Crane, for example, in his famous essay on the plot of *Tom Jones*, first classified the work as a mimetic novel with a complex, comic plot of action. Then he attempted to describe the particular comic effect—comprised of certain kinds of attitudes, expectations, fears, and satisfactions—which one must assume Fielding to have aimed at producing.[5] While the analysis of the work thus achieved was specific insofar as it distinguished the novel from others of its kind, it was also exclusive, since the various acts of classifying along the way eliminated certain possible approaches or questions. This exclusion, of course, was intentional, designed to prevent the critic from "reading into" the work qualities or kinds of meaning that it does not possess. Thus Crane's original decision to treat *Tom Jones* as a mimetic work was meant to exclude the discovery (or invention) of any themes or doctrines.

Perhaps the most interesting feature of this theory is the initial assumption that there are two classes, the mimetic and the didactic, into which all literary works fall, and whose "basic principles of construction," according to Crane, are "sharply distinct."[6] Mimetic works are "so constructed as to give us a specific pleasure by arousing and allaying our emotions." Didactic works, on the other hand, "must always either propound a doctrine or determine a moral and emotional attitude toward a doctrine in such a way as to command action in accordance with it.... The principle of didactic poetry, therefore, is its doctrine or thesis."[7] In a mimetic work any doctrinal or intellectual content that is introduced has as its purpose not the reader's acceptance of that content but rather the enhancement and qualification of the pleasure the work aims at. *Oedipus Rex,* Shakespeare's tragedies, Gray's "Elegy" are mimetic works; *The Divine Comedy, Absalom and Achitophel, 1984* are didactic.

Crane's and Olson's theory has been extended further into the field of prose fiction by Sheldon Sacks, in *Fiction and the Shape of Belief.* Sacks's purpose is "to explore the possibility that the variant principles of organization of coherent prose fictions limit the way in which a writer may embody his ethical beliefs, opinions or prejudices in them." In order to make certain that our questions about a work of fiction are "asked in a legitimate manner," Sacks offers definitions of three classes of prose fiction: the satire, the apologue, and the "represented action" or novel. His definitions, like Crane's and Olson's, state the principles according to which the various parts of the works so classified have been organized:

> A satire is a work organized so that it ridicules objects external to the fictional world created in it.
> An apologue is a work organized as a fictional example of the truth of a formulable statement or a series of such statements.
> An action is a work organized so that it introduces characters, about whose fates we are made to care, in unstable relationships which are then further complicated until the complication is finally resolved by the removal of the represented instability. (p.26)[8]

As his primary examples of the three genres, Sacks examines *Gulliver's Travels* (satire), *Rasselas* (apologue), and *Joseph Andrews* and *Tom Jones* (represented actions). The evidence offered for the claim that Swift's great work *is* a coherent satire is, first, the success with which its parts can be understood in the light of the definition, and second, the demonstration that certain parts must seem ill-contructed if examined in the light of either of the other definitions. The same general method is then applied to the fictions by Johnson and Fielding. Thus the existence of the three classes and the membership of these works in the classes is demonstrated simultaneously.

The term "coherent" is of great importance in Sacks's theory. The conclusions about a work deduced from the definition of its class obviously depend for their cogency upon *all* of the parts of the work having been organized to contribute to the principle defined. "Unless all the elements of a work make such a contribution, we will temporarily refuse to classify it as a coherent satire" (p.7). At the same time, "all relevant works of prose fiction are organized according to one of the three mutually exclusive types" (p.25). One implication of this stress on total coherence is the possibility that there may be no works whatsoever that belong to any of the three types. Accident, confused or mixed aims, or unconscious determinants at cross purpose with the author's plan might easily disqualify a work from membership.

If certain questions are to be ruled out of order for a given work, the generic categories must be shown to be, in Sacks's own words, mutually exclusive. Sacks, and Crane and Olson before him, clearly think that their categories fit this bill. Sacks writes: "Satire exists as a literary fact ... as the existence of mammals is a 'fact' of the physical world" (pp. 5–6). And: "One cannot create an action which is also a satire any more than he can write an active sentence which is also a passive sentence in English" (p. 46).

But is there anything in the nature of Sacks's three definitions that makes them mutually exclusive, or that would prevent a writer from composing a work that is both a coherent satire and a coherent action? One can imagine classificatory schemes that offer such exclusiveness, such as the class of works narrated by the protagonist, as distinct from the class not narrated by the protagonist, or the class of works whose heroes undergo a change of character as distinct from the class in which they do not. Similarly, of course, animals that have hair and suckle their young are distinct from those which do not. In these instances, however, the classes are distinguished by the absence or presence of a single characteristic or set of characteristics.

But such is not the case with Sacks's definitions. Satires are defined in terms of the attitude they are designed to evoke toward something external to the work. Apologues are defined in terms of their logical relationship to a general statement. Actions are defined, first, in terms of the attitudes they are designed to evoke toward characters within them, and second, in terms of the nature of the changing relationships among characters. As Sacks defines these three classes there is no more reason to suppose that a satire could not also be a represented action *and* an apologue than to suppose that a pencil could not be both long and wooden, or that a professor could not be a citizen and a husband as well. To put the matter differently, there is nothing illogical about imagining a work that simultaneously ridicules hypocrisy, exemplifies general statements about how hypocrites and honest men behave, and makes us care about the fates of the characters who represent these kinds of men. It may be that in a given work one of these purposes will predominate, but that fact should not deceive us into thinking that everything in the work exists *only* for the sake of that predominant purpose.

The same objections hold, I think, in the case of Crane's and Olson's mimetic-didactic opposition. There is nothing in the history of literature or in the nature of audiences and readers or in the way the two definitions are formulated that makes the arousing and allaying of emotions and the propounding of a doctrine mutually exclusive ends. Hence the danger is that the placing of a work in one class or the other may well distort it.

Ironically, the first critic who comes to mind as sponsoring the view that a single work can be mimetic and didactic at once is Aristotle. While Crane and Olson accept the mimetic nature of Greek and Shakespearian tragedy as axiomatic, Aristotle clearly saw excellent tragedy as dependent upon the protagonist's ambivalent stature as both individual and representative: "Pity is occasioned by undeserved misfortune, and fear by that of one like ourselves" (*Poetics*, 1453a). Pity is a response to a character seen as an individual distinct from one's self, fear (the tragic fear that we might fall victim to a fate like the protagonist's) is a response possible only when we see that individual as belonging to a class of people to which we also belong. For Aristotle fearing *is* learning. To the extent to which a tragedy evokes fear, as Aristotle presents it, it exemplifies a general statement the particularization of which is the protagonist's fate in the play.

The practical dangers of the assumption that genres can direct and restrict our modes of inquiry are, then, the assigning to a work the traits of a genre prior to the demonstration that the whole work really belongs to it, and the ignoring of effects achieved in the work but not anticipated by the definition of the genre. I have tried in " 'Organizing Principles' and Genre Theory" to show how Sacks falls victim to these dangers in his discussions of Swift, Fielding, and Johnson. It will be sufficient here to suggest that no preconceived unifying principle that a reader carries with him to a work will be, in the last analysis, satisfactory. I do not mean only that the last analysis must be more specific than any of the models he brings to the work; the theories we have explored allow for specificity of a kind. I mean rather that no preconceived unifying principle will be sufficiently inclusive. The definitions we have explored throw certain features of a work into high relief—and they are useful in that respect—but they inevitably throw others into the shadows. Thus to treat *Tom Jones* as a satire is to emphasize its more allusive passages, its type characters, their traits, and so on. To treat it as an apologue is to emphasize the way its repeated narrative patterns encourage the reader to draw general inferences from it. Martin Price has written of the "central theme" of Fielding's work: "The opposition between the flow of soul—of selfless generosity—and the structures—screens, defences, moats of indifference—that people build around themselves."[9] His remarks are useful and valid, however useful and valid Sacks's treatment of the novel as a represented action may also be. They are valid because in some respects *Tom Jones* is organized around recurring themes. To treat the novel as a whole would involve the posing of several questions, a confluence of generic possibilities, including those we have been considering and others as well.

If we return to the question we began with—does the genre of a work limit the interpretive procedures appropriate to it?—we might risk the following generalizations:

First, of course, it is misleading to speak at all of *the* genre to which a work belongs. The placing of a work in one genre can never rule out the interpretive questions raised by some other genre to which it may also belong.

Second, if one were to define a group of genres in such a way that they were indeed mutually exclusive, they would in all likelihood be trivial (e.g., all novels over a given length), or nearly empty classes (e.g., all works whose *sole* aim is ridicule), or so general as to dictate no particular critical approach. Drama, for example, though a fairly well-defined genre with few troublesome borderline cases, is hardly a category that narrows significantly the number of interpretive procedures relevant to it.

Third, it would seem that the only way to test the legitimacy of a critical question for a given work—questions like: What is the author trying to tell us? How does he want us to respond emotionally? What is he ridiculing?—is to try to answer it, and then to test the answer against whatever else one knows about the work. Try reading *Tom Jones* as an apologue and see what happens. Its thematic aspect will emerge if it has such an aspect. It is unfortunately true that one may "discover" themes or symbols or objects of ridicule whose existence is doubtful. This is the curse that all teachers and students of literature labor under: that when asked what *XYZ* symbolizes in a poem or novel they are more tempted to construct an answer than, after consideration, to reject the question. But the question cannot be dismissed out of hand on the basis of a prior act of classification; it can only be rejected after due competition with other ways of making sense of *XYZ*.

ARE THERE "PURELY LITERARY" GENRES?

In his *Introduction à la littérature fantastique*, Tzvetan Todorov outlines a plan for studying the literary genres that is ambitious and rigorous in its methodological demands.[10] One of his demands is that the criteria by which we define the genres should be *literary* criteria. He berates Frye, who made much the same demand, for having in fact drawn his key distinguishing terms (isolation and integration, superior and inferior, real and ideal, introverted and extroverted, personal and intellectual) from philosophy, psychology, and social ethics. "For a distinction to be valid in literature," Todorov writes, "it must be based on literary criteria" (p. 161).

There is one sense in which it is easy to speak of purely literary genres: "A poem is a literary work in which . . . "; "A tragedy is a play in which . . . "; "A picaresque novel is one which. . . . " Most descriptions of kinds of literature begin by offering as genus either literature itself or some obvious subcategory thereof. Indeed it is difficult to imagine a critic proceeding otherwise if he is actually trying to distinguish among kinds of literature. It is rarely a question of the critic actually confusing literary works with nonliterary objects or events. It seems to be, rather, for Todorov, a question of discovering terms that would apply to *nothing but* literature.

There are also many genre definitions in which not only the genus but the differentiae are admittedly literary: "An Italian sonnet is a poem consisting of 14 lines of iambic pentameter, rhymed. . . . " It is not that numbers of lines, metrical patterns, and rhyme are purely literary properties. But the combination of properties that the definition predicates of the Italian sonnet would scarcely be found outside of literature. They denote a conventional form that poets and poetry-readers alone employ.

There remains some question, however, whether the methods of classifying literary works that critics have found most useful and most important are purely literary in the sense that the definition of the Italian sonnet is literary. And is there any reason to demand that they be so? Is it a flaw of Frye's scheme that his differentiating terms are extraliterary? My answer to both these questions is *no,* and an exploration of Todorov's own scheme will show why.

In the course of his study of the literature of the fantastic, Todorov discusses the literary situation in a number of useful ways—always with allegedly "literary" terms. As for the fantastic itself, Todorov defines the genre by describing its effect on the reader, and by distinguishing it in this respect from certain related genres. The fantastic is that sort of literature which is designed in such a way that the reader will hesitate between a natural and a supernatural explanation of the events presented in it. Usually, but not always, the reader's hesitation will be shared by a character in the story with whom the reader will identify. The book which "inaugurated the epoch of the fantastic tale" was Jan Potocki's *Saragossa Manuscript* (1804). It includes such works as Nerval's *Aurélia*, Nodier's *Ines de las Sierras*, James's *The Turn of the Screw*, Mérimée's *La Vénus d'Ille*, and it more or less faded out of existence after Maupassant.

This hesitation, as Todorov points out, can be a very ephemeral effect, and only a limited number of works sustain it throughout. If, on the one hand, the causes of the events are only apparently supernatural, and the reader is led to settle on a naturalistic explanation, then we are dealing not with the fantastic, but with *the strange*. If, however, the reader is led to accept the supernatural as the only possible way of explaining the events, then we are in the world not of the fantastic but of *the marvelous*. The boundaries between these three genres are not firm, but fluid, and many works evoke the essential hesitation only momentarily.

Since this hesitation over the causes of the narrated events is the defining characteristic of the genre, it is essential that the reader's attention be directed toward those events. "The text must oblige the reader to consider the world of characters as a world of living people" (p. 37). This attention is destroyed by a text which calls attention to itself, to the words of which it is composed, rather than to the events. That is, the fantastic belongs to the larger genre of *fiction* rather than to the genre of *poetry*. Fiction Todorov defines as literature which is "representative" of events, literature which leads us to speak of characters, action, atmosphere, and so on. Poetry, however, calls attention to itself as a "pure semantic combination," and we speak of it in terms of rhyme, rhythm, rhetorical figures, and the like (pp. 64–65).

Another distinction is brought into play here: the distinction between *allegory* (e.g., animal fables), which explicitly invites the construction of a second, nonliteral meaning, and the *literal*, which does not. Of two general classes into which literature can be divided—*the literal* and the nonliteral or *allegorical*—the fantastic belongs to the first.

Again, the fantastic belongs, along with the detective story, to a class of works bound by the convention of the "irreversibility of time." They demand a sequential reading "from left to right":

> One ought to read an ordinary novel (nonfantastic), a novel by Balzac, for example, from beginning to end, but if by chance, one reads the fifteenth chapter before the fourteenth, the loss one suffers is not so great as with a fantastic tale. If one knows from the beginning the end of such a tale, all the fun is lost, for the reader can no longer follow step by step the process of identification; but following it is the first condition of the genre.... The first and second readings of a fantastic tale give very different impressions (much more so than with another type of tale); in fact, in the second reading, identification is no longer possible. (p. 95)

Finally, taking together all those works which treat of the supernatural, including the strange and the marvelous as well as the fantastic, one can subdivide them into two groups according to their thematic content. Todorov labels these two thematic systems (*réseaux*) "themes of *I*" and "themes of *thou*." The themes of *I* include metamorphosis and "pan-determinism." Metamorphosis refers to changes in states of being: from animal or statue into man, or vice-versa, from the individual into his double, from genie into old man, from real to "suspended" time, and so on. Pan-determinism is the assumption that all events have causes, and are not to be attributed to chance or coincidence. Hence if an event occurs for which one can discover no cause, one assumes the existence of one even if it must be "supernatural" (p. 116).

Themes of *thou* include various forms of sexuality ranging from intense heterosexual passion to homosexuality, incest, promiscuity, necrophilia, and sadism. These two thematic networks, Todorov claims, are never found in the same work, and he attempts to give an explanation of the opposition between them.[11]

We have, then, several generic categories—sometimes overlapping—employed to help "place" the fantastic. Let us summarize them by indicating the criterion used to define each one:

1. *The fantastic* obliges the reader to hesitate over whether the events are to be accounted for by reference to natural or supernatural causes.

2. *The strange* inclines the reader toward certainty that the causes are natural.

3. *The marvelous* inclines the reader toward certainty that the causes are supernatural.

4. *Allegory* explicitly invites the construction of a second, nonliteral meaning.

5. *The literal* does not so invite.

6. *Fiction* represents events and calls the reader's attention to those events.

7. *Poetry* calls attention to the language of the text itself.

8. *The time-bound* necessitates a left-right reading.

9. *Themes of I* represent events that exemplify metamorphosis and assume a belief in pan-determinism.

10. *Themes of thou* represent events exemplifying varieties of extreme sexuality.

These groups of literary works are certainly purely literary in the sense first defined, just as Frye's are, or those of any other genre critic. We know that Todorov is talking about fantastic *literature*, so no confusion is likely between real-life events that oblige one to suspect supernatural causes and a tale that relates such events. But the terms by which the groups are distinguished among each other *cannot* be thought of as purely literary. Hesitation, metamorphosis and transformation, intense sexual desire—these are obviously no more literary than Frye's various dichotomous terms. As for the criteria of categories 4 through 7 (allegory, literal, fiction, poetry), they may at least be said to be linguistic, though not purely literary. The preacher's exemplum and the wit's ironic remark both call attention to a nonliteral meaning, and the accidental rhyme, the unintentionally rhythmical sentence, the apt figure of speech all direct the listener's ear and mind toward language.

Let me emphasize that I do not consider the nonliterary nature of Todorov's criteria in any sense a weakness or flaw in his theory. Far from it; indeed the book as a whole would have benefited from a less timid approach to the connections between literature and the rest of life. Why does the critic, unlike the biologist or the physicist, the linguist or the historian, think it in any way necessary or desirable to eliminate what Todorov calls "borrowed terms" from his descriptions of his subject matter? Todorov speaks of wishing to preserve the "autonomy" of literature (p. 20). Whatever that overworked phrase refers to, surely his own borrowed terms do not threaten it. Indeed the critic who restricted himself to terms that can refer only to literature would find his commentary arid and his readers few.

ARE GENRE STUDIES SCIENTIFIC?

The question is too large in scope for this paper, but the analogies, both pre- and post-Darwinian, that are often drawn between the major literary genres and the biological species, as well as the more recent influences of the "scientific" methods of structuralism, force to our attention the issues adumbrated by the larger question.

Now the genres, like anything else, can certainly be studied or investigated scientifically. One can ask why a certain genre fell into or out of favor at a certain period, or why it acquired certain characteristics and dropped others as it developed during a particular span of time, and the criteria for judging the validity of one's answers to such questions would be the same as those for answering similar causal-historical questions in any field, from political history to biology, geology, or astronomy. It is the genre itself—its presence, absence, or development—that is being explained by means of something like scientific methods. But this is not the sense in which a structuralist like Todorov speaks of genre studies as scientific. For Todorov the knowledge that one attains about a genre is in some sense, ipso facto, more scientific than the knowledge one can attain of an individual work. Like Frye before him, he emulates "scientific method" (p. 8) and holds out for genre studies the possibility of a higher degree of "certainty" and "objectivity" than other approaches to literature are capable of (p. 149). At one point he describes the genre theorist as one who investigates "a relatively limited number of occurrences, draws from them a general hypothesis, and tests it on other works, thereby either correcting or rejecting it" (p. 8).

It is not altogether clear what procedures in *Introduction à la littérature fantastique* could be described in these terms. The word "hypothesis" is used hardly at all. At one point, however, after discussing the notions of metamorphosis and pan-determinism, he offers the following conclusions:

> One can say that the common denominator of the two themes, metamorphosis and pan-determinism, is the rupture ... of the boundary between matter and spirit. Now at last we are au-

thorized to advance a hypothesis as to the generative principle of both the themes in this system: *the passage from spirit to matter has become possible.* (p. 120)

This is very puzzling, however, for the hypothesis is merely a vague and metaphorical redescription of the two themes, which have already been described as presenting the intrusion of a supernatural or spiritual order into a natural one, and as signifying that "the limit between physical and mental, between matter and spirit, between the thing and the word, ceases to be water-tight" (p. 119). (The basis for saying that metamorphosis entails a transgression of the separation between matter and spirit—which may not be obvious—is that some metamorphoses may be seen as literal versions of figures of speech, e.g., "he fights like a lion.") By what stretch of the imagination can the "common denominator" of two concepts be regarded as their generative principle? One requirement for a hypothesis surely is that it add something *new* to the data it is supposed to explain; Todorov's merely summarizes it. Its tautological nature is demonstrated by the impossibility of testing it. A work that Todorov's hypothesis failed to account for would not call the hypothesis into question; it would simply be a work which contained neither theme.

At the very end of his study, however, Todorov advances what looks much more like a genuine hypothesis, a hypothesis concerning the "social function" of the literature of the supernatural during the period which he considers to have been its heyday. Noting the presence of "taboo themes" in the works he has treated, and of modes of thought which society judged psychotic or juvenile, he speculates that "the function of the supernatural [was] to protect the text from the action of the law and by that means to transgress it" (p. 167). *Function* presumably implies the function for the authors and for their readers, and the law is both the written law of society and the individual's internalized censor. Now Todorov, apparently under the misapprehension that the hypothesis is self-evidently true, fails to offer any justification for it. It is, nevertheless, a perfectly reasonable hypothesis, capable, if not of neat and final confirmation or disconfirmation, at least of some testing against relevant aspects of nineteenth-century literary and social history, and against what we know about the authors in question.

A further clue to what Todorov means by calling genre studies scientific may be seen in the following passage:

> We postulate that the whole literary text functions in the manner of a system; which means that there are necessary, not arbitrary, relations between the constitutive parts of the text. Cuvier, one recalls, aroused the admiration of his contemporaries by reconstructing the image of an animal on the basis of the single vertebra which he had at his disposal. Knowing the structure of the literary work, one ought to be able, knowing a single trait, to reconstruct all the others. The analogy is valid, moreover, precisely at the level of the genre: Cuvier, too, claimed to define the species, not the individual animal.... It is not possible for one of the traits of the work to be fixed without all the others being influenced.... If the literary work truly forms a structure, we should find, at all levels, the consequences of the reader's ambiguous perception by which the fantastic is characterized. (pp. 80–81)

The comparison between the genre critic and a paleontologist like Cuvier must be treated cautiously. The scientist may be able to make an intelligent guess about the structure of an animal on the basis of a single vertebra if he knows enough about the function of bones in vertebrate species, and about the area where the specimen was found. But when is the literary critic—with the rare exception of the discoverer of a fragment—engaged in a comparable guessing game? If we are in such a position midway through a book, waiting for all the facts to come in, we can also finish the whole work, or examine, as it were, the whole animal.

More important, every trait that Todorov assigns to the fantastic, apart from its defining characteristic, is, as he acknowledges, shared by works in other genres as well. (Even the defining characteristic—the hesitation or ambiguous perception—is found in countless works written long before and long after Todorov's historically chosen set of works. Whether they belong to the genre or not is a question that Todorov doesn't discuss.) Consequently, the knowledge of a single trait would hardly enable us to say whether the work belongs to the fantastic or not. There is a bit of sleight of hand employed when Todorov writes, "knowing the structure of the literary work, one ought to be able, knowing a single trait, to reconstruct all the others." But Cuvier did not know both the structure of the animal *and* a single trait (or bone). It was the structure of the animal which he guessed at, using the bone, his knowledge of various possible vertebrate structures, and other environmental information as well. If by "structure" Todorov means the way the defining characteristic necessitates the presence of certain traits, then his claim is obviously and tautologically true.

Knowing the structure in that sense, he would not need to have even a single trait present to know *all* the traits. They would be implicit in his knowledge of the structure. But knowing a single trait (e.g., literalness, time-boundedness, sexuality) *without* knowing the structure would get him nowhere.

On the other hand, there is a sense in which it is very reasonable to speak about the relations between the various aspects of a work, and about the "consequences" of the defining characteristic of the genre. Like Aristotle and the Chicagoans, and (for once) unlike Frye, Todorov defines his genres primarily in terms of their effects on audience or reader. At their best, both Aristotle's and Todorov's treatises can be regarded as conditional arguments of the following form: *If* a work is to have these effects (pity and fear in the case of tragedy, hesitation in the case of the fantastic), then it must possess these traits, and it must not possess those others. To make such arguments, one must rely on a commonsense psychology of reader- or audience-response. Aristotle, for example, assumes that certain kinds of characters and events are likely to evoke moral repugnance, others sympathy, or wonder, or the like. Todorov relies on assumptions about how readers are likely to respond to certain sorts of narrators, events, stylistic devices, and so on. The sort of knowledge that would enable a novelist or dramatist to arrange his fable with an eye to certain effects enables the critic or reader to draw inferences about the effects that certain kinds of works are likely to produce.

Todorov is at great pains to avoid reader psychology, for the same reason that he hoped to avoid nonliterary terms in differentiating the genres (pp. 39–40, 98). He attempts to get around it by speaking always of a reader "implicit in the text," whose perceptions are "inscribed in the text with the same precision as the movements of the characters." This concept creates some peculiar puzzles: Does the implicit reader enjoy the time-bound text less on his second reading of it? And it fails to sidestep psychology, since the same psychological assumptions would be needed to speak of the implicit reader's responses as to speak of the responses of any appropriately informed and attentive "real" reader. But what good reason is there, after all, to exclude reader-psychology from criticism or poetics? Where, if not in the responses that it evokes, does the primary interest and value of literature reside?

These speculations about the relations between the features of a literary work and its effects, whether or not they are scientific in any strict sense, at least have the virtue of being open to debate and rebuttal. They might be confronted by an alternative psychology, as Aristotle's rather kindly view of audiences might be challenged by the views of La Rochefoucauld or Hobbes or Freud; or by references to the experiences of real audiences or readers; or, most readily, perhaps, by different claims about what is actually occurring in the text.

DOES THE GENRE OF A WORK HELP TO DETERMINE ITS VALUE?

No one is likely to take seriously the notion that the mere possession of the traits by which a genre is defined is sufficient to guarantee the goodness or value of a work, except in those cases where the defining traits are themselves evaluative, or in the weak sense in which a work may then be said to be a good example of its kind. The closest link between genres and genuine evaluation was established by the neoclassical critics, who took a different tack. For them, membership in a genre was related to value because the genres themselves were described and ranked according to their merits, and proper arguments about the worth of a genre lay behind the assessment of an individual work. Thus Addison's exhaustive exploration of the heroic features of *Paradise Lost* was a perfectly logical mode of assessing the poem given prior arguments by Addison and most of his literary predecessors about the supreme value of the genre. As he pointed out, "It will be sufficient to its Perfection, if it has all the Beauties of the highest Kind of Poetry."[12] Conversely, Johnson's curt dismissal of *Lycidas*—"Its form is that of a pastoral, easy, vulgar, and therefore disgusting"—was founded on his developed and consistent stance with regard to the nature and shortcomings of the genre, including the two *Rambler* papers (Nos. 36,37) where he not only offers reasons for placing *Lycidas* low within the genre, but describes those slight charms which, to his mind, the pastoral possessed.[13]

It is, after all, as possible to justify a high evaluation of a *kind* of work as it is to justify a high evaluation of a particular work. Aristotle clearly regards the effects he assigns to tragedy as valuable, though in the form in which the *Poetics* has come down to us the arguments justifying that assessment are missing. It is likely that Aristotle could have given, and did in fact give those arguments, perhaps along the lines suggested by Castelvetro, and more recently by Gerald Else, presenting the catharsis of pity and fear as an answer to Plato's attack on the emotional effects of literature.[14]

What continues to haunt criticism, however, is the suspicion that one ought to appraise something according to its nature, in terms or criteria appropriate to the kind of work it is:

> A great romancer should be examined in terms of the conventions he chose. William Morris should not be left on the side lines of prose fiction merely because the critic has not learned to take the romance form seriously.... If Scott has any claims to be a romancer, it is not good criticism to deal only with his defects as a novelist.[15]

Frye's remark is appealing. It makes good sense. But then so does Wayne Booth's more toughly reasoned answer:

> How can we apply to any one novel the standards appropriate to any one defined type without a divine decree authorizing us to consider *this* novel as of *this* type? Are elements of fantasy inappropriate in "the novel" but acceptable in "the romance"? Very well. I note that *this* novel indulges in fantasy. Shall I call it a botched novel or a successful romance? To do either, I must appeal to standards not derived from within my classification.[16]

What truth can we rescue from Frye's observation, and what does that truth have to do with genres? Certainly the presence of conventional elements in a novel does not guarantee that they have been used *well,* or *to good purpose.* To determine that, we would have to appeal, as Booth points out, to some further standard. Nor need we examine or judge a writer in terms of the conventions he chose. We can judge him in whatever terms we can justify as relevant to a reasoned assessment of his work. We might, for example, argue that his conventions (those of the romance, say) are trivial or worse, yet judge his work highly for the possession of qualities only loosely related to the conventions.

Nonetheless, what one rightly wishes to avoid is the *ignoring* of any virtues that the work may possess. One does not wish to be blinded by narrow conceptions, foolishly dismissing the work while missing its point. That, it seems to me, is the strong side of Frye's remark. It is related to genre theory in the following way: the genre theorist is committed to diversity, to a recognition of a plurality of possible literary forms and aims. Hence he is least likely to fall victim to what Crane used to call "critical monism," the application of a single standard to all works, the search for one and only one sort of point.

This is a practical matter, not a logical one. Any judgment that can be made of a work, like any description of it, can be made and substantiated without reference to any genre whatsoever. If the heroic qualities Addison finds in *Paradise Lost* are valuable, they are so whether or not there are any other works possessing those qualities. But studies that attempt to enumerate "the" genres of literature have the merit of expanding our sense of the variety of what we may look for. Thus anyone who gives the *Anatomy* or any of the other studies we have considered a generous reading, whatever he thinks of its "first principles," will come away armed with new expectations, new ways of seeing, reading, and making sense of literary texts, and, finally, of assessing them.

These observations suggest that the value of genre theorizing—at least if our theorists are representative—is chiefly preparatory, heuristic, pedagogical. (I regard these as highly laudatory terms, though I realize that many readers would disagree.) If genre theory solves few of the problems it pretends to solve—if it can neither establish rules for interpreting or evaluating texts, nor explain how a work came to be what it is, if it offers no unusually objective or scientific alternative to other forms of criticism—it *can* provide us, as we have just seen, with a healthy counter to literary singlemindedness.

Perhaps, indeed, there would be some merit in reconstruing the genre theorist's task. It may be that the notion of generalizing about literary classes is less descriptive of what, at his best, he does, than the notion of analyzing paradigm cases—works which illustrate with unusual clarity some possible form, effect, theme, and so on. If one looks again, from this standpoint, at the various genre definitions our theorists put forward, one may see them frequently as describing not "properties" that works either do or do not possess, but rather the ends of a spectrum, the limits of a tendency. Sometimes it is as if the theorist were conjuring up, in his definitions, an imaginary work, purified of all gross elements, but neatly illustrative of some structural principle that is hard to untangle from the knotty substance of a real work. Take Frye's notion of comedy and tragedy as presenting, respectively, the integration of the hero with, and the exclusion of the hero from, society. If these two formulas oversimplify almost any work one can name, they nevertheless designate tendencies within a relationship the importance of which in any plot is undeniable. They call attention to significant literary variables.

Much the same could be said for the Chicagoans' mimetic-didactic distinction. Though these two aims do not cancel each other out and though they often cooperate in a single work, they do receive varying degrees of emphasis from one work to another. There is something to be learned by operating with the fiction that a work is constructed with a single and clearly conceived aim in view, provided one knows when to drop the fiction before making the work seem simpler than it is. Again, Todorov, as we saw, distinguished fiction from poetry on the basis of whether our attention is drawn to character and event or to language. Since we cannot understand the language in a work at all without supposing a character who is using the language to some end, I find it difficult to imagine a single example of pure poetry according to his definition, or to think that his distinction has much to do with what we ordinarily think of as poetry and fiction. Yet we can usefully isolate two aspects of a text upon either of which we may wish, for some reason, to dwell. (This holds, I think, for all his dichotomies.)

Aristotle has often enough been chided for basing his account of tragedy so insistently on *Oedipus Rex*. But such chiding is the fruit of expecting results which *no* classificatory scheme or study could provide. If one sees him instead as speculating on the best ways for producing certain ends, articulating the consequences of one possible literary aim, then his emphasis on a single exemplary work is fully warranted. Similarly, one might chide Todorov for neglecting many fantastic works—both ancient and contemporary—that lie outside his narrow historical range. It could be argued, for example, that some of Shakespeare's tragedies belong to the genre as he defines it. The audience often hesitates between natural and supernatural explanations of the tragic events, and so do some of the characters with whose points of view the audience is likely to sympathize. ("Is there any cause in nature that makes these hard hearts?" "Is this the promised end?") But *King Lear* and *Macbeth* would hardly do as introductions to the genre. They are too rich, too multiple in their effects, to serve as instructive paradigms. Nor would they fit very well into the other categories that Todorov uses to describe his lesser, simpler, but pedagogically more useful members of the genre.

I am not, I should insist, advocating a new School of Paradigm Case Studies, or the founding of a journal by that name. The field already exists, and is the healthier for being anonymous. But if it is true that we often expect the wrong sort of results from genre studies, it is also important to affirm that their contribution to criticism has nevertheless been substantial, and to understand why this is so.

Notes

1. *Validity in Interpretation* (New Haven: Yale University Press, 1967), ch. 3.
2. Northrop Frye, "The Archetypes of Literature," in *Fables of Identity* (New York: Harcourt, Brace, 1963), p. 9. The following quotations are from "Myth, Fiction, and Displacement," ibid., p. 34, and *Anatomy of Criticism: Four Essays* (Princeton: Princeton University Press, 1957), pp. 171-72.
3. This section condenses some material from my article " 'Organizing Principles' and Genre Theory," *Genre* 1 (1968): 1-12.
4. See Olson's contributions to *Critics and Criticism*, ed. R.S. Crane (Chicago: University of Chicago Press, 1952), esp. pp. 65-68 and 588-94. Crane explores the idea in detail in his *The Languages of Criticism and the Structure of Poetry* (Toronto: University of Toronto Press, 1953), pp. 140-83.
5. *Critics and Criticism*, pp. 620ff.
6. *The Languages of Criticism and the Structure of Poetry*, p. 158.
7. Olson, *Critics and Criticism*, pp. 66-67.
8. Page numbers given in parentheses are from Sacks, *Fiction and the Shape of Belief* (Berkeley, University of California Press, 1964).
9. *To the Palace of Wisdom* (Carbondale: Southern Illinois University Press, 1964).
10. Paris: Editions du Seuil, 1970. The translations are my own. Page numbers are given in the text.
11. Approximately one-third of Todorov's study is devoted to these two sets of themes. While the truth of Todorov's remarks about the works he cites is not pertinent to the theoretical bias of this essay, it should be pointed out that his claim about the mutually exclusive character of these two themes is, so far as I can make out, distinctly untrue. For example, "The Second Kalendar's Tale" from *The Thousand and One Nights* is his paradigm of a tale illustrating the "themes of I." While it does portray a variety of rather comical transformations, it is also true that the hero is invited to live with and make love to a woman, and that the genie who "owns" her falls into a jealous rage, strips her, ties her to the ground, tortures her, and removes her hands, legs, and head. Metamorphosis and sexual passion, the themes of I and Thou, commingle. Conversely, the first and third Kalendars' tales, which Todorov cites as

illustrating the "thou" themes of incestuous and promiscuous love, respectively, are also tales of metamorphosis. In the first the brother and sister are transformed into charcoal; in the third a house sprouts wings, forty maidens "fly away like birds," and a variety of lesser events occur illustrating most of the characteristics of the themes of I. To turn to a more sinister tale, Todorov's prime example of excessive sexuality is Gautier's *La Morte amoureuse,* the story of a priest seduced by a vampire. But it also embodies notions of "the double," of transformations of time and space, and of metamorphosis, all of which Todorov locates in the *I* category. Much the same could be said for *The Saragossa Manuscript,* which Todorov also places in the *Thou* category. Why, after all, would one expect these two sets of themes to be incompatible one with the other? Todorov promises an explanation, but offers instead a series of far-fetched analogies between these themes and the experiences of psychotics, children, and drug-users. But it is no wonder that the incompatibility resists explanation: it doesn't exist.

12. *The Spectator,* ed. Donald F. Bond (Oxford: Clarendon Press, 1965) 2:538.
13. Samuel Johnson, "The Life of Milton," in *Lives of the English Poets,* ed. George Birbeck Hill (Oxford: Clarendon Press, 1905).
14. See the introduction to Else's translation of the *Poetics* (Ann Arbor: University of Michigan Press, 1967), pp. 2–7, and Castelvetro's commentary on the *Poetics,* Section VI.
15. Frye, *Anatomy of Criticism,* p. 305.
16. *The Rhetoric of Fiction* (Chicago: University of Chicago Press, 1961), p. 37.

Ernest L. Stahl

LITERARY GENRES: SOME IDIOSYNCRATIC CONCEPTS

One of the principal difficulties in defining and delimiting literary genres is that the works belonging to them are organic structures as well as artifacts. They are man-made but are also subject to processes such as genesis and evolution which are parallel to, but of course not identical with, biological processes of growth and change. The analogy is terminologically explicit in German, but not to the same extent in English. Whereas the words *Gattung* and *Art* are used both in biology and in poetics, in English usage *genus* and *species* are reserved for the former, while *genre* and *kind* are the equivalent of *genus* in poetics, the word *kind*, however, also pertaining to biology. This disparity is enhanced by discrepancies within German usage. The words *Gattung* and *Art* have often been used indiscriminately. Grimm's *Deutsches Wörterbuch* contains the following statements on *Gattung*:

> In das abstracte *art* übergehend; die beispiele aber zwischen diesem und dem vorigen alle scharf zu scheiden ist nicht möglich. a) schon im 16. jahr.: gattung, *genus* . . . b) später wurden *gattung* und *art* logisch so unterschieden, dass man jenes für *genus*, dieses für *species* brauchte . . . c) dass aber noch nach 1770 jene unterscheidung nicht allgemein war, zeigt folgendes, wo *gattung* und *art* umgekehrt gebraucht sind.[1]

Interchangeability in the use of the two words continues into the present century, at least in defining and delimiting literary genres. Thus Karl Viëtor, one of the most distinguished recent writers on the subject, dissociates himself from current practice and adopts the terminology contrary to it. In doing so he arrives at the concept *Grundhaltungen*, fundamental human attitudes in literary production without reference to the actual works thus produced or to the reaction of the reader and the audience to them. Since that concept is one of the most idiosyncratic in the history of the subject, it is worthwhile quoting a considerable portion of the opening paragraph of Viëtor's essay "Probleme der literarischen Gattungsgeschichte":

> First a word of explanation of terminology. In the scholarly debate which has arisen in the last decade over the nature and relationships of the literary genres, the concept of "genre" is not used with the uniformity that would be necessary if progress is eventually to be made in this difficult area. Epic, lyric, and drama are spoken of as the three great *genres*, and at the same time Novelle, comedy, and ode are also called genres. A single term is used for two such disparate things. In order to be unambiguous and logical, however, we must restrict the term to one of the two. Thus if the lyric as a whole is to be called a genre, then elegy, hymn, song, ode, sonnet, etc., should be called "kinds," just as in science since the eighteenth century a distinction has been made between the "genus" as the higher unit and the "species" as the subunit. In my opinion, however, it is clearer and more correct to restrict the term "genre" to these "kinds" just as Linnaeus designated the "species" as "genus" in his scientific systems. The epic, the lyric, and the drama, after all, are not artistic structures, or works, or creations, but are, so to speak, ultimate creative fundamental attitudes. . . . The three great areas of literature, they are rooted in three natural and basic fundamental attitudes of the poet: attitudes not toward the aesthetic object and the public, but of a more basic nature: fundamental human attitudes to reality, to the mastering of reality in their effect and countereffect.[2]

These are authoritative statements, yet their chief burden fails to carry conviction. Viëtor confuses the issue by asserting: "Epik, Lyrik, Dramatik sind doch keine Kunstgebilde, Werke, Gestaltungen." This is logically no more defensible than saying that "Botanik ist doch keine Pflanze." A great deal of confusion has been caused in discussing the problems of literary genres by terminological shifts from the words "epic," "lyric," "drama" to "the epical," "the lyrical," the "dramatic," from "Epos," "Lyrik," "Drama" to "das Epische," "das Lyrische," "das Dramatische." The tendency inherent in making this shift entails preferring the general to the particular, attitudes of mind to concrete literary works, or, as Viëtor puts it, "Grundhaltungen nicht dem ästhetischen Gegenstand und dem Publikum gegenüber, sondern elementarer: Grundhaltungen zur Wirklichkeit." In the last resort it amounts to a shift from interest in literary works themselves to the psychology involved in their production. The interest in such fundamental attitudes is valid and the result can be valuable, but it may be doubted whether it is an adequate approach in the study of literary genres, which, at least by implication, primarily concerns literary *works*.

Friedrich Schiller inaugurated discussion on the topic of poets' "Grundhaltungen," but he did this without confusing fundamental attitudes with literary genres. *Über naive und sentimentalische Dichtung* is the seminal work in this context. Here his use of the terms Gattung and Art is determined by his distinction between the two "ganz verschiedene Dichtungsweisen, durch welche das ganze Gebiet der Poesie erschöpft und ausgemessen wird." He also uses the terms *Empfindungsweisen, Dichtungsarten, Gedichtarten,* and *Formen* with cogency and precision. Quotations from the long note at the beginning of the section on "Idylle" explain his terminology:

> I must repeat once again that satire, elegy, and idyll, as they are here laid down as the only three possible species of sentimental poetry, have nothing in common with the three particular genres of poem which are known by these names, other than the *modes of perception* which are proper to the former as well as to the latter. . . . Anyone who could now still ask me to which of the three species I assign the epic, the novel, the tragedy, etc., would not have understood me at all. For the concept of these last, as individual *genres of composition*, is either not at all or at least not solely determined by the mode of perception; it is clear, rather, that they can be executed in more than one of the species of poetry I have established . . . but this much we learn from experience, that in the hands of sentimental poets (even the most outstanding) no single type of composition has ever remained entirely what it was among the ancients, and that often very new types have been executed under the old names.[3]

Schiller's approach differs from Lessing's in *Laokoon*. Lessing's distinctions are based not on Empfindungsweisen but on categories of perception within time and space. Nor was he primarily concerned in *Laokoon*, as he was to be in *Hamburgische Dramaturgie*, with the problem of a literary genre, even when he demarcated poetry and music from painting and sculpture. Later, Herder came nearer to dealing with genres in refining upon Lessing by postulating the differences between painting and sculpture, on the one hand, poetry and music, on the other. Instead of adducing the space-time categories alone, he cited energy as the power operative in producing poetic effects. But like Lessing he refrained in this connection from embarking on the problem of Gattungen and Arten.

Schiller was aware that in *Über naive und sentimentalische Dichtung* his approach did not cover the normal division of poetical works into kinds. In the note at the beginning of the section "Elegische Dichtung," he speaks of that type of idyll "welche eine Spezies der sentimentalischen Dichtung ist" and concludes with the following remark:

> Finally, I would still observe that the division attempted here, for the very reason that it is simply based on the distinction of mode of perception, should by no means whatever determine the division of poetry itself nor the derivation of poetic genres; since the poet is in no way bound, even in a single work, to the same mode of perception, that division therefore cannot apply, but must be taken from the form of the presentation.[4]

The principal contribution that methods of inquiry like Schiller's make is the act of focusing attention on archetypal patterns of production and on the typology of creative writing. The main interest is, in the widest sense of the term, anthropological, and Schiller was quite consistent in concluding his treatise with an account of the broader equivalents of *naive* and *sentimental* poets—the realist and the idealist. In this context he extended the use of the terms Gattung and Art by calling the naive and the sentimental poets Arten of the Gattung poet. "Thus the naive poetic genius" he says, relies upon support from "nature instinct with form, a poetic world, naive humanity." "If, however, this assistance from without is not forthcoming," he continues, "he finds himself surrounded by a spiritless matter, and only two things then occur. Either he abandons his species if the genus predominates in him, and he becomes sentimental if only to remain poetic; or, if the characteristics of the species retain their predominance, he abandons his genus and becomes common nature if only to remain nature."[5]

On the other hand, Schiller prefers Formen when referring to modes of literary presentation. At the end of the section "Die sentimentalischen Dichter" he says: "The varied impression of naive poetry depends . . . solely upon the various degrees of one and the same mode of feeling; even the variety of external forms cannot effect any alteration in the quality of that aesthetic impression."[6]

In the note at the beginning of the section "Idylle," Schiller asserts the equivalence of the "dreifache Empfindungszustand" with his "Gedichtarten," "Satire," "Idylle," and "Elegie," "sobald man sich nur an die Stimmung erinnert, in welche die unter diesen Namen vorkommenden Gedichtarten das Gemüt versetzen, und von den Mitteln abstrahiert, wodurch sie dieselbe bewirken." While envisaging the reader's or listener's attitude as well as that of the poet, he diverts attention from the means by which the relevant *Stimmung* is produced. Viëtor goes farther in asserting that the poet's attitudes are "Grundhaltungen nicht dem ästhetischen Gegenstand und dem Publikum gegenüber." This means that in his kind of inquiry not only the work in its concrete particularity but also the complex of discussion on audience reaction, which traditionally belongs to the subject of defining literary genres, forfeits its central significance.

The difference is evident when one recalls Lessing's argument in *Hamburgische Dramaturgie* where he defines tragedy with the participation of the audience in mind by insisting on the arousing and the purging of the strictly circumscribed and closely related emotions of pity and fear, as well as their catharsis, not in the dramatic characters, but in the audience. He pointedly distinguishes *vorgestellte* from *erregte Leidenschaften* and restricts the process of catharsis to the latter, whereas earlier (and some later) critics hold that purgation involves the passions displayed by the characters of a tragedy as well. For Lessing tragedy is the only literary form that is capable of realizing the particular effects envisaged by him, representing, as it does, an immediate and living enactment in the presence of an audience. In his usage tragedy is the word for a literary kind. It does not exist outside the confines of that kind: in particular, it does not carry the meaning given to it by the exponents of *Pantragismus* from Schopenhauer to Eduard von Hartmann.

Lessing belongs to the European tradition of criticism which, with many variations, subsisted from the Renaissance until the emergence of the Romantic movement. This tradition was progressively altered and then abandoned by new developments already inaugurated in Lessing's time. Concerning audience participation a significant change can be observed in the theory and practice of comedy. Lessing modified the traditional view by advancing the notion that the purpose of comedy is to evoke laughter (*Lachen*), but not malicious laughter through excessive ridicule (*Verlachen*), just as for tragedy he advocated the moderate passion of *Furcht* against the more radical *Schrecken*. His major concern in both cases was to enlist a sympathetic response in the audience. A much more striking change occurred in German literature at the beginning of the Romantic movement when, in Tieck's comedies, the audience, so far from being intended to sympathize with dramatic characters or even taking sides against them, became the butt of satire and ridicule through the device of a *Spiel im Spiel* which aimed at confusing the real audience in the theater by denigrating its analogue on the stage. Another extreme in changing the traditional approach is Brecht's *Verfremdungseffekt*, with its design to supplant the audience's empathy by inducing it to practice critical detachment and independent judgment.

The invention of a new medium accounts for the introduction of a distinct species in the dramatic genre. Radio plays may be compared with novels in that both owe their development to technical innovations, the wireless and the printing press, respectively. In the case of radio plays (*Hörspiele*) concentration on auditory phenomena (noise and music as well as speech) to the exclusion of visual impressions considerably alters the range of appeals by comparison with those of a theatrical performance. The genre is also affected by the absence of an audience, a group of people gathered together in one and the same place. This is a feature that may be well worth investigating from the point of view of mass psychology insofar as it has aesthetic significance. The question may be asked whether the classical dramatist's aim to arouse and purge the tragic emotions and Brecht's Verfremdungseffekt can be achieved without the existence of such a mass audience, and, if not, how the difference between performances of radio plays and of dramas for the stage affects the structure of works in the genre as a whole.[7]

Changes of a different kind were brought about as a result of intellectual developments since the eighteenth century. New theories in poetics were formulated by adherents of leading philosophers from Kant to Heidegger. The latter's influence on Emil Staiger's *Grundbegriffe der Poetik* intensified a trend in the definition of literary genres which has already been noted. Here the starting point of classification is the acknowledgment of the three *Grundelemente*, the lyrical, the epical, and the dramatic, categories which transcend individual literary works assignable to them. Staiger's treatment is perhaps the most idiosyncratic in the whole range of approaches to the subject. He links the three fundamental modes to the three dimensions of time: the lyrical to the past, the epical to the present, and the dramatic to the future; moreover he coordinates them respectively with the terms *Erinnerung, Vorstellung, Spannung;* with *Stimmung, Verfallen, Verstehen;* with the three ages of man; with three of man's faculties; and finally with three linguistic forms: syllable, word, and sentence.

Such attempts at systemization can be paralleled, if not to the same extent for the literary genres, elsewhere in the history of the subject, for example, in Hegel's *Aesthetics.* They are fascinating exercises in contrived ingenuity and they present many illuminating interpretations. But they tend to remove discussion from an adequately representative collection of texts, so that in the end the contribution of this kind of approach is extraliterary and not sufficiently specific.

In an often quoted passage Goethe uses the term *Naturformen* for the three genres, avoiding the word *Gattungen:* "There are only three genuine natural forms of literature: the straightforward narrative, the enthusiastically excited, and that expressed through the actions of dramatic characters: the epic, the lyric, and the drama. These three modes of literature can operate either combined or separately."[8] Viëtor, quoting this passage, wrongly calls Goethe's categories "menschliche Grundhaltungen zur Wirklichkeit" and confuses the issue by also referring to them as "natural and basic fundamental attitudes of the poet."[9] Goethe's natural forms and modes of literature, unlike Schiller's categories, are not expressions of fundamental human attitudes; they are designations of purely literary forms, although Goethe himself may be said to have caused confusion by using the term Naturformen beside *Dichtweisen.*

Another complication has been pointed out by René Wellek. Goethe, he says, "introduced the totally different criterion of tone, excitement, enthusiasm in order to accommodate" the lyric and to distinguish it from the "clearly telling epic" and the "personally acting drama."[10] The referential shift from the objective criteria narration and action to the subjective criterion emotion has been common practice in dealing with the "triadic division" of the literary genres,[11] and throughout, the coordination of the lyric with the epic and the drama has presented difficulties. The lyric has traditionally been the odd genre out, partly because it was not widely recognized as a genre at all until the eighteenth century. Discussion centered on the Arten (ode, elegy, sonnet, etc.), and when the generic qualities of these Arten met with recognition, their characteristic feature was held to be subjectivity in contrast to the objective criteria of the epic and the drama.

This division is anomalous because it inserts the poet's personality into the definition of just one of the three traditionally acknowledged genres. It prevailed as long as the principle of imitation (in a mistaken interpretation of Aristotle's term "mimesis") guided the production and the judgment of literary works. The tag "imitation" could obviously be applied most convincingly to the drama and the novel, but hardly at all to lyric poetry, unless it was postulated that in writing such poetry the poet was imitating his emotional experiences by "recollecting them in tranquillity." In fact, not until imitation ceased to be *the* critical precept could lyric poetry be taken into the same fold as the other genres.

The change occurred when imitation gave way to principles like expression, creation, and presentation in determining the nature and the purpose of art. The transformation can be traced in German writings on aesthetics during the second half of the eighteenth century, with particular reference to the emergence of the term *Darstellung,* which came to be used increasingly in place of *Nachahmung.* The emphasis on the presentational rather than the imitative character of poetry is notable in the aesthetic and critical writings of Kant, Klopstock, Schiller, K.P. Moritz, and many other theoreticians in the Classical and Romantic eras, as is the case in England, particularly in Coleridge's critical treatises.[12] Acceptance of this new principle largely accounts for the revised interpretation of the nature of lyric poetry and its alignment with the other genres. Henceforth poems could be regarded as artifacts no different *qua* literary products from dramas and novels, works that do not require for their understanding primary correlation with the writer's personal experiences, even in the case of such manifestly "autobiographical" novels as Goethe's *Die Leiden des jungen Werthers.*

Revised estimates of the nature of lyric poetry vis-à-vis the other genres also came about through changes in the hierarchy of literary forms. As may be seen in compendia on poetics throughout Europe from the Renaissance to the eighteenth century, including Opitz's *Buch von der deutschen Poeterey* and Gottsched's *Versuch einer critischen Dichtkunst vor die Deutschen,* the epic took pride of place, to be supplanted, as the eighteenth century progressed, by the drama, and by tragedy in particular. Then, increasingly with the growing preponderance of Romantic ideas, the more art was held to aspire to the condition of music, the more poetry came to be considered the primary literary form. This process was partly inaugurated by Lessing's rejection of the plastic arts as models for literature, especially the downgrading of descriptive poetry as a result of his repudiation of Horace's *ut pictura poesis* principle and his alignment of poetry with music, the two forms which accomplish their effects through *"das Nacheinander in der Zeit."*

One eventual consequence was the grading within poetry itself. The *Lied* came to be regarded as the dominant form. Other kinds, such as the ode, declined in the nineteenth century, and although the elegy and the sonnet remained in favor, they could not vie in prestige or frequency of composition with the Lied. This situation prevailed until the second half of the century saw the appearance of *Dinggedichte* with Mörike's "Auf eine Lampe," C.F. Meyer's "Der römische Brunnen" and, as a culmination, Rilke's *Neue Gedichte*. These works represent a return (in novel form) to descriptive poetry and the disavowal of purely emotional values, as well as the restriction of the "musical" texture of lyric poetry.

During the nineteenth century critical grading of the literary genres in another field followed the decline of the epic and the rise of the novel, together with that of the distinctive shorter narrative form, the *Novelle*. The relations between the epic and the novel and between the novel and the Novelle present special problems. Adequate recognition of the novel as a genre in its own right was delayed by its being identified with the epic in kind and considered a mere successor to the epic in time, even by such pioneers as Blankenburg (*Versuch über den Roman*, 1774) and Lukács (*Theorie des Romans*, 1920). Terminological inadequacies in critical idiom still bolster up this deficiency when the novel is classified as belonging to the epic genre, instead of being firmly treated as an individual narrative genre.[13]

The Novelle has likewise been inadequately characterized as a shorter version in the craft of fiction not in any fundamental sense structurally different from the short story. In fact, Novellen, in some important respects, are more closely related to dramas than to novels. They have similarly tense actions and movements rapidly propelled toward culminating points.[14] It is true that the classical prescriptions of dramatic structure on the sequence of exposition, development, climax, dénouement are no longer stringent, and that in particular the position of the climax can be greatly varied. This is equally the case for the *Wendepunkt* of a Novelle. Therefore it is often notoriously difficult to distinguish a Novelle from an ordinary short story or *Erzählung*. The writer's own nomenclature, for example, Heinrich von Kleist's, is no reliable guide to the difference. Nor is there a good reason why he should not exercise his right to choose his own terms. But in critical discourse it seems equally reasonable to insist that some kind of Wendepunkt in the action of a Novelle forms its distinctive structural feature.

The structure of Novellen may be accounted for to some extent by another feature they share with dramas. Several outstanding collections of them were conceived with a kind of listening audience built into the works. In the best known examples—*Decamerone, Canterbury Tales* (the verse form is infrequent but not exceptional), *Unterhaltungen deutscher Ausgewanderten*—identical situations prevail. Each member of a group of persons having an interest in common with the other members tells a tale in order to entertain and, specifically, to divert attention from an unpleasant event or irksome condition, in Boccaccio the plague, in Chaucer the tediousness of the journey, in Goethe the strain caused by a tactless remark. *The Arabian Nights* is a first example, in a singular form: there is only one listener and his position is different from that of the audiences in other collections of tales, although he too craves diversion and it is the single storyteller alone who has to try to avert an impending dire event.

In such typical Novelle situations the purpose envisaged is attained by a special form of entertainment. The people involved forget their unpleasant situation while listening to accounts of arresting events or to amusing anecdotes: many critics have pointed out the anecdotal quality of Novellen. The distraction thus provided is best achieved by continuously aroused expectancy and, eventually, by a surprising turn of events or by the point of the story. In this consists the dramatic quality inherent in the structure of Novellen. Their entertainment value differs from that of novels which may include the reader in their "intentionality,"[15] but normally lack specific audience appeal (of the kind here mentioned) and move at a more leisurely pace.

Comparable problems are met in the terminology applied to other genres. It is often held that the word *tragedy* is appropriate only for dramas which culminate in a catastrophe and that the term *drame* or *Schauspiel* should be reserved for serious plays with nontragic conclusions. The question has particular reference for the interpretation of the tragedy of the second part of Goethe's *Faust*. It may be held with good reason that despite its conciliatory termination the work is a tragedy because the essential criterion is the display of suffering rather than the issue of the conflicts which produced the suffering. A similar problem is the definition of the term *tragicomedy* and its distinction from Schauspiel, on the one hand, and comedy proper, on the other. Another difficulty arises when one considers the ballad, a form affiliated with the lyric and the epic and even, through the use of dialogue and a climactic structure, with the dramatic mode. Goethe called the ballad a "mysterious" literary form which could expound "die ganze Poetik gar wohl . . . weil hier die Elemente noch nicht getrennt, sondern wie in einem lebendigen Ur-Ei zusammen sind," and he also pointed to it as an example of the conjunction of the "drei echten Naturformen der Poesie."[16]

These biological references take us back to the beginning of our account and to Viëtor's presentation of the genre problem. He offers illuminating remarks on the difference between the concepts of the biological and the literary genres: "Which animal species belong to the genus 'mammal' can be easily and objectively determined by one criterion . . . namely, that they bear and nurse living young. But where is there such a criterion in the case of literary works? Possibly, at best, for the literary natural forms." He goes on to discuss the hermeneutic problem involved in dealing with the history of literary genres by quoting the words of Günther Müller: "A dilemma of all writing on the history of genres is that we apparently cannot decide what belongs to a certain genre without first knowing what is characteristic of that genre; yet we cannot know what is characteristic of that genre without recognizing this or that as belonging to that genre."[17]

This dilemma of course applies to other fields of inquiry as well. But taking the epistemological problem for granted, there also remains the difference between genres and kinds, Gattungen and Arten. One can normally tell more or less at a glance from the printed page whether a volume of literature contains what purports to be a novel, a drama, or a collection of poems, just as one can tell, usually instantly, whether one is looking at an animal, a plant, or a mineral. It is only when one has to decide what kind of drama (tragedy or comedy, etc.), what kind of novel (historical, psychological, etc.), or what kind of poem (song, ode, elegy, etc.) one is dealing with that closer examination of the text becomes necessary, quite apart from the careful reading required for the understanding or the appreciation of the text as an individual piece of writing.

The dilemma faced by the historiographer of literary genres according to Günther Müller is a difficulty scientists do not have to confront to quite the same extent. Literary works belonging to all genres are artifacts, as well as being organisms subject to definable, though highly variable processes of genesis and evolution. Unlike the products of nature they have a history as well as manifesting the laws of evolution. The contrast stated by Goethe in his poem "Die Metamorphose der Pflanzen" applies even more aptly to the creative writer than to man in general:

> Kriechend zaudre die Raupe, der Schmetterling eile geschäftig,
> Bildsam ändre der Mensch selbst die bestimmte Gestalt.

The change a creeping caterpillar undergoes when it turns into a butterfly is a process it cannot alter or arrest by its own volition. For better or worse man can change himself: he can be the agent as well as being the subject of his own transformation, and he can experience *Bildung* as well as *Metamorphose*.

In even greater measure this freedom of choice rests with the creator of a literary work in whatever genre, a choice not open to the member of any biological genus. The lore of the literary genres has long since ceased to be prescriptive and normative. Its essence today is hermeneutic. Full recognition is now granted to the independent, if often willful, variations writers have introduced into established literary genres.

Notes

1. The example quoted from Goethe is not stringent: "beide (*roman* und *drama*) könnten in ihrer art vortrefflich sein, nur müssten sie sich in den gränzen ihrer gattung halten." [Goethe 19, 180 (*Wilhelm Meister* 5, 7).] It is conceivable that Goethe meant that individual works belonging to the categories "novel" and "drama" can excel only if they adhere to the superior rules governing their respective genres, but it is more likely that in this statement the word *Art* signifies "manner" rather than "species" or "kind."
2. *Deutsche Vierteljahrsschrift für Literaturwissenschaft und Geistesgeschichte*, eds. P. Kluckhohn and E. Rothacker (1931), 9:425f.
3. Friedrich Schiller, *Naive and Sentimental Poetry and On the Sublime*, trans. Julius A. Elias (New York, 1967), pp. 145–47.

4. Ibid., p. 126.
5. Ibid., p. 158.
6. Ibid., p. 115. Cf. also the note at the beginning of "Elegische Dichtung."
7. An indication of the procedure that might be followed in such an inquiry can be found in Victor Lange's "The Reader in the Strategy of Fiction," *Proceedings of the XI Congress of the International Federation of Modern Languages and Literatures* (1973). He examines "the issue of a writer's purpose of building into his work a system of directions that will set the perspectives and presuppositions of the text," and states that among these directions "the most comprehensive and variable are the literary genres" (p. 89).
8. Goethe, *Sämtliche Werke, Jubiläumsausgabe,* 5:223.
9. Viëtor, *Deutsche Vierteljahrsschrift,* p. 426.
10. "Genre Theory, the Lyric and *Erlebnis,*" in *Discriminations* (New Haven, 1971), p. 235.
11. Ibid., pp. 240ff., particularly the critique of *Erlebnislyrik,* poetry as the expression of feeling and experience, culminating in the statement: "One must abandon attempts to define the general nature of the lyric or the lyrical" in favor of the "study of the variety of poetry and . . . the description of genres which can be grasped in their concrete conventions and traditions" (p. 252).
12. The term *Darstellung* has an interesting history when related to *Vorstellung.* See my article on the subject in *Gestaltprobleme der Dichtung, Festschrift für Günther Müller* (Bonn, 1957), pp. 283–98. Parallel developments may be seen in the increasing use of the word "presentation" in England in the late eighteenth century. *Darstellung* can also be profitably distinguished from *Darlegung,* which is normally used for the presentation of a scientific or a philosophical argument. The difference may be shown by reference to two of Goethe's works. The poem "Die Metamorphose der Pflanzen" is a *Darstellung* of the *Darlegung* contained in the earlier scientific treatise.
13. José Ortega y Gasset trenchantly asserts that the epic and the novel are complete opposites. For a German version of his treatise on the literary genres see *Merkur* 13 (1959): 602.
14. This is perhaps the reason why it has been generally found easier to dramatize Novellen than plots from novels or ordinary short stories.
15. Cf. Victor Lange, "Strategy of Fiction," p. 88.
16. *Werke, Hamburger* Ausgabe, 1:400; 2:187.
17. *Deutsche Vierteljahrsschrift,* pp. 438; 441.

SPECIAL ASPECTS OF GENRE THEORY

Robert Champigny

SEMANTIC MODES AND LITERARY GENRES

In *Le Genre romanesque* (1963), *Le Genre poétique* (1963), *Le Genre dramatique* (1965), I started to develop a taxonomy of semantic modes. In *Ontology of the Narrative* (1972), the following distribution is proposed:

	Cognitive-practical	Ludic-aesthetic
Designative (universals)	Nomic (cognitive variables, genera)	Conceptual (philosophical)
Designative (individuals)	Historical predictions and retrodictions	Descriptive and narrative fiction
Gestural (performative, conative)	Magic; social performance of practical roles	Dramatic (performance of ludic roles)
Poetic (meaning as felt quality)		Poetic

Some of the labels in this classification suggest a tie with a theory of literary genres. But my approach is philosophical, while theories of literary genres are likely to be historically oriented. Another difference is that my perspective is broader: the schema is not limited to ludic-aesthetic modes. The word *genre* in the titles of the first three essays mentioned above might be misleading. It is preferable to speak of "modes," or "functions," or "dimensions."

The schema is concerned with modes of meaning which uses of a "natural" language like English can develop. Semantics, in this sense, encroaches upon phonology: meter and harmony incite the reader, or rather the reciter, to adopt a poetic perspective of interpretation. It should also be noted that no gulf is to be assumed between linguistic and nonlinguistic meaning. Purely visual and tactile signals may signify the same object as a statement about a door. This is a condition for linguistic meaning to have cognitive value. Furthermore, nonlinguistic media may signify in the same *way* as the linguistic medium. The labels "gestural" and "dramatic" postulate such a semantic homogeneity. The visual enjoyment of a landscape may be a "poetic" experience. We should not forget that a value may be apprehended negatively: one may sorely feel the lack of poetry in daily experience. This is a condition for poetry in words to be "significant," that is to say, to have a value of resonance, instead of cognitive reference.

A classification such as this shows that semantics has a finger in every philosophical pie. The definitions of "cognitive," "practical," "aesthetic" involve decisions in epistemology, ethics, aesthetics. The status to be granted to the various modes involves decisions in ontology and axiology. In order to orient a perspective of interpretation, a mode must be able to provide a linguistic piece as a whole with a basic organization. In this respect, the modes may be called "styles," or even "logics," though a formal logician would not recognize them as such.

A semantic approach to philosophical questions leads one to view all relations as semantic operations. According to the proposed schema, causality, for instance, is to be construed as an inductive operation, that is, as a conjunction between the nomic mode and the historical mode: phenomena interpreted as events belonging to class X signal subsequent events belonging to class Y. The difficulties attendant upon the theory of induction are accounted for (not solved) by the uneasy conjunction between two different modes (logics). Questions concerning space and time, individuals and persons, would be translated into questions relating to spatialization, temporalization, individuation, and personification. In this respect, the similarities and differences between the two versions of the descriptive-narrative mode (history and fiction) should be of interest.

On the other hand, a semantic approach must not turn into a linguistic, or semiotic, reductionism. Language is only one semiotic medium and semiotic media do not mean by themselves. The text proposes; the interpreter, more precisely the interpretative experience, disposes. The same text may be received as fiction or history, according to the interpreter and to his mood. Semantic modes are modes of comprehension.[1] Writers and speakers are held as responsible to the extent that they interpret what they write or say (contrast speaking machines, humans speaking in a trance or practicing automatic writing).

The modes may be viewed as modes of "intentionality," in the phenomenological sense. However, classical phenomenology is so taken with its basic category of being in the world that it tends, in my opinion, to underestimate the originality of ludic-aesthetic functions. I should not mind using the notion of world to designate what is ultimately intended in any attempt to comprehend. But the chosen term would have to name an ideal value: "cosmicity" might do. The sorely felt lack of this value in daily experience, the failure to constitute the practical field as a cosmos, would then appear as the *raison d'être* of the playful and aesthetic shifts of intentionality. If the field of our practical incarnation were a poetic cosmos, there would be no need, and no possibility, to write and recite poems. Furthermore, *Weltanschauungen* are differently oriented: though there may be alloys, poetic sense differs from dramatic sense. Equated with an appropriateness to be felt, comprehension may be recognized as the basic motive. This move would be in accord with the existentialist developments of phenomenology. But "being in the world" had better be replaced by "feeling the lack of cosmicity." After all, this is what is suggested by the stress which existentialists have laid on moods like *Angst* and nausea.

The need to comprehend testifies to a lack of meaning. The variety of semiotic media and the plurality of semantic modes show that meaning, existentially identified with value, cannot be the only fundamental category. An ontology in accord with the proposed schema should posit categories which would serve as nonlogical foundations for the various modes. The foundation of the temporalizing mode would not be time. It could be named instead "contingency" or "actuality."

The schema includes philosophy as one of the modes. It is itself an example of the philosophical mode. The schema ranges philosophy on the ludic-aesthetic side. Its own significance is a matter of resonance, rather than of cognitive reference. In some cases, behavioral evidence could be claimed. For instance, if during the performance of a play, an actor shouted "Fire!" and a spectator got up and fled, it would appear that this spectator had interpreted the verbal gesture of the actor as having to do with the practical field in which they both embody themselves, not with the fictional world of the play. But such evidence is not plentiful, and it may be ambiguous: the spectator might be pretending, he might be playing a game of his own. In order to be scientific, a framework of modes of comprehension would need an apparatus which, for instance, would translate what happens in the brain of a reader into curves showing the amount of the modes. Such an apparatus does not exist at present.

The schema tries to achieve a kind of cogency which it is possible to achieve with words. I assume it should have some significance for others as well as myself, in view of the fact that, to some extent, the distinctions I adopt agree with distinctions that others have deemed it proper to make. But, like any philosophical classification, the way in which I divide the conceptual whole cannot claim to be the best for everyone under any circumstances. Someone may accept some of the distinctions, reject others, add others. Someone else may prefer radically different categories. What is for me basic would be for him secondary, insignificant. His own semantic decoupage would correspond to a different ontology, to a different way of conceiving ontology. Or the same words might be used to name categories, but defined differently: for instance, if "cognitive" were taken in a broader sense than the positivistic sense I adopt, philosophy might become "cognitive." Or the same conceptualized names and the same definitions might be adopted, and yet their application to the same text lead to different results for two analysts, because they would interpret either the words in the definitions, or those in the text to be analyzed, differently. Semantic concepts cannot be applied like chemical reagents.

A language such as English offers many words to name semantic relations. Why not welcome them all in one's schema? Botany distinguishes between thousands and thousands of species. Lacking empirical checks, relying on words exclusively, a philosophical classification has to be much more modest: imagine an ontology which would enumerate 234 categories. In French prosody, normal feet have two, three, or four syllables. Likewise, I find that, beyond four divisions, conceptual schemas become unmanageable. Regarding semantic functions, many dichotomies—poetry and prose, extension and intension, reference and sense, denotation and connotation, cognitive and emotive, stative and performative, transitive and intransitive—strike me as insufficient, sometimes misleading. I have contrived to stretch the list of basic modes to seven by combining a binary division, a ternary division (on the cognitive-practical side), and a quaternary division (on the ludic-aesthetic side), with correspondences between the two sides. If someone proposed a schema of thirty-three basic modes, I should applaud and beg to be excused. I do not know whether the distribution I adopt would please a Pythagorean; Hegelians would not like it.[2]

"Literary criticism" often appears to be equivalent to "metaliterary analysis." The schema dispenses with the word "literary." It suggests that, whether philosophy is considered as part of literature or whether the label of literature is limited to the other three ludic-aesthetic modes, the stylistic study of basically philosophical texts should be developed. This does not mean that philosophy should be confused with, say, poetry; on the contrary. But it does mean that the differences between philosophy and the three other modes are not a priori assumed to be more radical than the differences between these three.

The basic mode of literary criticism itself would be philosophical. On the one hand, this orientation is opposed to the claim, or pretence, that literary criticism is a science. On the other, it militates against the rift which is still noticeable between *purs littéraires* and *purs philosophes*. Literary critics should do their own philosophizing. When one is content to snatch lables, a Burgundy wine is liable to turn into a burgundy dress. The schema does not grant a privilege to its own mode. Philosophical understanding is not "higher" than others (in a Platonic way), nor is it a "synthesis" of the others. The tendency to reduce all modes of comprehension to one is particularly apparent in structural analyses *à la* Greimas, which erase such differences as those between cognitive and aesthetic, narrative and poetic.

A natural language such as English does not offer a specific syntax, morphology, or lexicon for each of the modes. According to circumstances and context, a sentence like "The door is not locked" may be interpreted as a poetic evocation, an indication of a fictional event, a true or false indication of a historical event, an invitation to get out, either in the practical field or in the fictional world of a drama, as an example of grammar (nomic mode), or as a philosophical illustration, which is the way it is used here (the other modes are only mentioned).

English does not provide a special verb form for nontemporalizing sentences: "John is on a bicycle"; "John is a man." This feature contributes to the communication between the historical and the nomic modes: an individual as process and an individual as subclass. But it also obscures the difference between permanence and nontemporality, between individuals and universals, also between philosophical concept and scientific genus or variable.

Meter helps set poetry apart; capitals and Christian names serve to designate some individuals; the suffixes *ity, ness, tion* are convenient to devise names of concepts. But conventional means of differentiation cannot determine the interpretation of a narrative piece, for instance, as true-or-false, rather than as neither true nor false. The imperative mood stresses the gestural dimension, yet instructions may be given in the indicative.

Basic artistic constraints arise from this situation. On the one hand, each ludic-aesthetic mode must preserve its lines of communication with other modes: if poetry cut itself away from prose, recitation would be reduced to humming (which is what happens with *lettrisme*); attempts to establish a pure philosophical diction result not in a calculus but in a jargon. On the other hand, stylization in the spirit of a mode must be able to provide the conditions of lucid estrangement and aesthetic enjoyment. In particular, it must allow the interpreter not to confuse resonance with reference. But it cannot mold the common linguistic material in such a way as to force the interpreter to adopt a certain modal perspective.

The development which follows explains the divisions proposed in the schema and the decisions which are involved. Remarks about literary genres will end the essay.

A linguistic piece is cognitive to the extent that it indicates historical individuals (events, states of affairs, processes). "Referential" may be used as equivalent to "cognitive": something is a referent to the extent that it is signified as historically situated. Historicizing statements are to be judged more or less true and false. They cannot be judged totally false, for this would eliminate all referentiality and the status of the *significatum* would veer to fiction. "It is false that this dress is blue" implies "It is true that this is a dress." What is held to be true (or false) remains subject to verification. The historical field is the field of what is to be verified and of operations of verification.

On the contrary, if it is interpreted as fictionalizing, a narrative is axiomatic (apodictic). Narrative fiction thus represents the inaccessible ideal of historical statements. But it cannot be said to achieve this ideal, since it drops referentiality. Interpreted aesthetically, a narrative can be neither true nor false; it may be more or less coherent and incoherent. Only the wording can be checked. If they are taken to belong to different stories, sentences interpreted aesthetically cannot contradict one another. There are many fictional worlds; there is, or rather there must be, only one historical field.

By itself, this conception of knowledge shows a positivistic bias. I should not claim that logical empiricism solves all epistemological difficulties. One does not solve problems in philosophy; one can only shift the burden, substitute a less bothersome for a more bothersome difficulty, according to one's taste and purpose. This is the advantage which I find in the positivistic concept of truth. But logical empiricists are chiefly interested in true or false statements. Originally, they even tended to confine meaning to this mode, a move which results in depriving of meaning the very language in which it is presented. As a whole, my semantic schema manifests an antipositivistic bent, in view of the deployment granted to ludic-aesthetic modes. It adopts a fairly restrictive concept of knowledge and truth, but militates against a reduction of ontology to epistemology. What is an object of knowledge is not, as such, what is ontologically basic. The significance of the ludic-aesthetic modes of meaning depends on this distinction. Comprehension is not to be confused with cognition. Cognition involves comprehension: in order to interpret a sentence as true or false, one has to adopt a cognitive perspective of understanding. But one can also adopt a noncognitive perspective.

The historical field is the field in which the interpreter objectifies himself as he interprets. This is the existential basis of historicity. An event is historical for me if I relate it spatiotemporally to my own practical incarnation here and now.[3] Historical statements may be predictions as well as retrodictions. A retrodiction implies a prediction, namely, that it will not be disconfirmed. No limit is set to the historical span: a statement about the origin of our solar system is historical if it is verifiable.

The nomic mode points to the imperfections of intuitive cognition (memory, clairvoyance). General rules are established to determine singular historical events. It is to this extent that combinations of universals can be cognitive (referential). Otherwise, they are philosophical.

The examples (sampling) on which a scientific generalization is based have to be interpreted as true reports. Philosophical examples may all be hypothetical: taken by themselves, they might all be interpreted as narrative fiction. For their purpose is not to offer proof for the theory, but to contribute imaginative help to the definition of concepts. Counterexamples would not show that the conceptual framework is false, but that it lacks coherence and comprehensiveness.

Classification is a feature common to the nomic and philosophical modes. But the scientific tendency to mathematize (quantified probability, for instance) is not philosophical; and the ontological and axiological aspirations characteristic of philosophy are absent from the nomic mode. An essay on the foundations of knowledge is metacognitive, not cognitive. The schema can thus be said to manifest an anti-Platonic bent: a universal can be indicated, stated; but only singular historical events and processes count as referents.

Either in its ludic or practical versions, the gestural mode of meaning does not designate, but performs, what is signified. A plaintive or angry tone will cover the designative meaning of "It hurts" with gestural meaning. "Perform" is preferred to "express," because we are dealing with a kind of meaning which can be carried by language. Rather than expressing pain, "Ouch!" helps to perform the role of an Anglophone in pain. The gestural mode can thus function in a ludic-aesthetic manner (an actor playing Hamlet) as well as in a practical way. In the latter case, the performance may be more or less sincere and insincere. To analyze the meaning of verbal gestures involves an explication of purposes. The analysis may have to *state* a purpose which the performance signifies by masking. Practical hypocrisy may be interpreted as deliberate ruse, Sartrean bad faith, or, according to some, psychoanalytical theory of unconscious motives.

Practical attempts to influence involve reference. More radically, practical prescriptions (to oneself, to others, to things) and cognitive predictions can be viewed as the two sides of the same coin. This is made possible by the imperfection of knowledge. If human cognition were certain and complete, there could be no *attempt* to influence. In view of the masking aspect of gestural meaning, the relation between prediction and prescription may not be a straightforward correspondence. A superstitious speaker may predict X in order for X not to happen. If we translate his prediction, we shall reveal a hidden prediction in contradiction with the overt statement.

Scientific laws and the historical predictions which are derived from them can themselves be viewed as orders given to nature, hence as belonging to the category of magic. The prescriptive side of the coin is more obvious in sociopolitical codes. A precept like "Act according to nature" shows the gap between the nomic and the historical, a gap which the gestural mode is somehow entrusted to fill. An actor-role relation is proposed to compensate for the insufficiency of an individual-class relation. Idols like "Real

Man" and "Real Woman" play upon a confusion between biological species and dramatic *personae*.

Passwords, vocatives, imperatives are characteristic of the gestural mode, which emphasizes speaking to rather than speaking of. In this respect, it should not be forgotten that, whomever one addresses, one addresses oneself: a missionary will covertly try to persuade himself while overtly trying to persuade others. And it should also be noted that a monologue or dialogue may be designatively incoherent and dramatically coherent. The commentators of "absurdist" dramas who spoke of a "lack of communication" and of "meaninglessness" failed to make this distinction.

A poetic recitation differs from a dramatic performance. Pronouncing is what matters: a poem as such is to be heard internally. Reciting a poem does not consist in performing the role of a character nicknamed "the Poet." Poetic meaning does not designate. Understood poetically, the pronoun "I" does not indicate an individual. Nor does it name a concept. Philosophy conceptualizes qualities. The way in which poetry means is itself qualitative. Meter and harmony help the meaning of words to be experienced as an aura enveloping the phonic *act* (not to be confused with a writing or speaking *event*, either historical or fictional). For instance, the substitution of poetic harmony for dramatic melody should help one to convert the prosaic distinction between question and statement into a difference between moods. Of course, this is not enough: the wording of the pseudo-question should block the road to an answer (thus: "Where are the snows of yesteryear?").

"Poetics," "Poetry," "poet" have often been used to cover the aesthetic uses of language. Instead of equating "poetic" with "aesthetic" and "prosaic" with "cognitive-practical," the terminology I adopt allows ludic-aesthetic, as well as cognitive-practical, versions for prosaic modes, while it offers no cognitive-practical version for poetry.

Ludic-aesthetic experiences are not mystical raptures. An aesthetic perspective needs a practical perspective as a frame. If I enjoy what a narrative means as fiction, I do not historicize the narrative as a writing event. But I still have to historicize my reading. In order to interpret a performed play aesthetically, I must interpret the performance of the play cognitively. These remarks would tend to grant a primacy to cognitive-practical modes of meaning. Most philosophers and linguists postulate this primacy, when they do not simply ignore playful and aesthetic functions. Witness the way in which linguists talk about shifters.

On the other hand, cognitive-practical modes are modes of comprehension; and as such they can be construed as rough attempts to aestheticize. If the field of human incarnation were a cosmos, there would be no need and no possibility of a logos, that is to say, of attempts to *make* sense. Historians are forced to stylize. Facts are selected, neatly arranged, and framed, so as to compose the spirit of a period or a cohesive process.

One could make a case for the primacy of the practical uses of language by noting that cognitive and ludic activities take practical time and are thus answerable to moral requirements. This would be the basis of a theory of literature as committed. On the other hand, practical activities are not autotelic. They derive their moral meaning from ludic experiences: the moral ideal would be achieved if all experiences, human and animal, were lived in an atmosphere of play. There would be no evil (no lack of moral value) if all suffering were played as an actor plays the "suffering" of a fictional character, though there could still be a lack of ludic-aesthetic value (poor play, ugliness). The strategy of the aesthete consists in pretending that the moral ideal is achieved by reducing (in words) evil to ugliness.

A text in which one of the ludic-aesthetic modes is clearly chosen makes it easy for an interpreter to orient his perspective. But the choice of a mode results in a subordination, rather than in an elimination, of other modes; thus, narrative examples in an essay. Furthermore, a text which, for instance, appears to push the poetic conversion of meaning further will not necessarily be judged aesthetically better. An interpreter with a strong dramatic bent will enjoy a text aesthetically to the extent that it includes dramatic elements, whether the text is basically dramatic or not. One may also particularly like alloys, or hybrids, which do not make clear which ludic-aesthetic mode is basic.

Any linguistic piece may be viewed as a historical document of some sort. But this perspective is clearly distinct from an aesthetic enjoyment. A satirical text may rely, for comic effects, on a discrepancy between elements to be construed as true and elements to be construed as fictional. An inability, or reluctance, to distinguish between ludic-aesthetic and cognitive-practical modes of meaning is another matter. A perspective which confuses the two sides I call mythical. A confusion between fictional character and historical individual produces a legendary figure. A confusion between ludic role and practical role produces an idol. Since the same syntax, the same morphology, and to a great extent the same vocabulary serve on both sides, it may be assumed that no interpretative experience is totally free of such confusions. If they were exceptional, the distinction between ludic-aesthetic and cognitive-practical would lose much of its point.

The tie between "ludic" and "aesthetic" manifests an opposition to the somewhat religious attitude which is still often adopted regarding literature, or at least "great" literature. On the other hand, the use of two labels instead of one suggests that some distinctions might be made. Mystery stories, for instance, are designed to enhance the ludic interest which predominates when a text is read for the first time and which can be summed up in the question: "What is the text up to?" This interest disappears on rereading (assuming that the rereader remembers the ending). A narrowly aesthetic experience is satisfactory to the extent that the interpreter identifies with the signifying text as a whole (not with what is signified, with a narrated character for instance, let alone the historical author). Consequently, it can occur only when the text is reread, or recited, a condition which critics often seem to forget, and which reduces the import of the distinction between "temporal" and "spatial" arts. In a broadly ludic perspective, on the other hand, the text has to function as playful adversary as well as teammate: on first reading, the stylistic clues in a mystery story are designed both to reveal and to conceal.

A broadly ludic perspective fits the philosophical appreciation of a text even on rereading. It is an appropriately philosophical attitude to keep considering a text as a playful adversary, even if one feels in deep agreement with it. Literary critics have generally been reluctant to welcome philosophy and mystery stories into the literary fold, an attitude which suggests the possibility of equating "literary" with "narrowly aesthetic."

There is some correspondence between the decoupage I adopted and the ways in which literary historians and critics generally distinguish between texts according to genre and subgenre. Forms like sonnets and pantoums are defined by features which belong to the phonological aspect of the poetic mode. A major genre, drama, points to the gestural mode. Labels like "poetic drama" and "dramatic poem" appear to rely on a distinction between the poetic and the dramatic dimensions of meaning.

But what about the English term "novel" and the French term *roman*? One might gather the impression that these labels apply to fairly long texts, which are basically and coherently narrative, and which are interpreted as fiction. Yet these labels have also been given to texts in which the predominance of dialogues tends to reduce narrative parts to stage directions. In Proust's main work, the essayistic (philosophical, analytical) aspect tends to reduce narrative elements to examples. Yet this text is generally called a *roman*, or a *roman d'analyse*, rather than an *essai romancé*. Some texts published in France in the 1950s consist mostly of narrative fragments which do not constitute one coherent narration. But most commentators remain hypnotized by the word *roman;* they do not say how they distinguish between a *roman* and a lengthy prose poem. In most texts called "novels," commentators are likely to recognize some sizable elements as historical, rather than fictional. The criteria which govern the application of the term "novel," as against "historical novel," are not made clear. Some texts, which are presented as histories of literature, deal with some authors presented as historians. Is history a literary genre? Or are there special conditions which allow a book of history to be considered as part of literature? Does the historian of literature consider that what he is writing fulfills these conditions? Does he make a distinction between the kind of book he is writing and a "historical novel"?

Some genre specifications may lack import from the standpoint of semantic modes. This may be the case with the distinction between short story and long narrative. However, if it is shown that a difference in length corresponds to differences in descriptive-narrative techniques, the distinction becomes significant from the standpoint of spatiotemporalizing stylization. Mystery stories belong to a technically significant category, since they concentrate the interest on some narrative axioms which are held in suspense until the end of the narrative: the establishment of the investigated events is the goal and result of the investigation sequence. Within this category, the stories which Poe called "tales of ratiocination" justify a distinction between short story and long narrative. For the analogy with the exposition of a problem and solution which they cultivate reduces to a minimum the *raison d'être* of narrative style.

Entwicklungsroman, Bildungsroman, Schicksalsroman may be explained in terms of content, but they also suggest different ways of composing a process, hence different ways of specifying the logic of space and time. Epic and courtly romance are versified narratives. The thematic distinction would be significant from my standpoint if it could be shown to correspond to differences in descriptive and narrative stylization.

Resorting to content as a principle of classification irreducible to form does not necessarily produce conceptual inconsistency. The label "novel of manners," for instance, suggests that differentiation according to content would intervene once the differentiation according to form has been settled. But does the term "novel" itself belong to a coherent classification of basic forms, literary and nonliterary?

It might be objected that such classifications, like the schema of modes which I adopted, would be nonhistorical, because they would not correspond to the ways in which the authors and their contemporary audience distinguished between linguistic pieces. But if this objection were taken seriously, it would ban, for instance, a history of ancient Greek literature, because there is no word synonymous with the historian's "literature" in ancient Greek. It should also be noted that the stress on ideological differences between periods and cultures leads one to underestimate differences between interpreters, or interpretative experiences, within the same period and culture. Nowadays, an American philosopher may feel intellectually closer to Hegel, Marx, or even Plato, than to a positivistic colleague.

Basically, what makes an outlook historical is the interpreter's self-inscription in the historical field. His conception of the past as such depends on his conception of the present and future. If he writes as a historian, his presentation of the past depends on an appraisal of the present linguistic situation. It is he who decides about the way in which to cut up the past into cultures, periods, ideologies. And it is in his own idiolect that he will have to characterize and explain the ways in which, for instance, other interpreters, past and present, distinguish between linguistic modes or genres. No doubt, a historian of philosophy will have to avoid making it appear that Descartes was influenced by Kant or Russell. But his interpretation of Descartes will not be independent from his interpretation of Kant, nor indeed from his interpretation of the philosophical present and his conception of what will be done, or should be done, philosophically in the future.

Regarding linguistic genres or modes, it appears that the most straightforward way of assuming one's historical responsibility is to make explicit the schema which one chooses in order to interpret other classifications, past or present, a schema whose divisions, since they have to be used to analyze any linguistic material, will not be chronologically ordered, and thus be nonhistorical. In the case of some forms, the choice may be said to be scientifically justified. A recognition of the sonnet form, for instance, involves only counting the number of lines and taking into account phonological features (meter, rhyme) which are amenable to measurement. But most genre labels are not of this kind. In whatever way a critic or historian tries to historicize these labels, his philosophical responsibility is involved.

To historicize an entity, one has to spatiotemporalize its manifestations. A material copy of a book is a *bona fide* individual (process). Its existence is regarded as spatiotemporally continuous like that of a ship, of a tree, of a snake, of a human individual. Its trajectory, its vicissitudes, from printing to destruction can, in theory at least, be tracked. But the perspective of a historian of literature differs from that of a bibliophile. He has to spatiotemporalize his material by way of interpretative experiences occurring somewhere at a certain time.

Genre labels may be historicized philologically. In this case, what counts as a historical occurrence is a use of the label itself, not the writing or reading of a text so labeled. For instance, a historian may collect dated occurrences of the use of the French word *roman* up to the present. But, if this word is to be recognized as a genre label, considerations regarding meaning, not just spelling and pronunciation, will have to be entertained. In a way, the historian will not be responsible for the discrepancies between the meanings which contexts reveal that the different users, or the same user, gave to the word. Yet, in another way, he will be responsible for them, since, in order to point out and define these discrepancies, he will have to choose a conceptually coherent language of his own. If, for instance, the historian writes in English, he will have to decide whether to use the term "novel" or not, and if he does use it, whether what he means by "novel" is equivalent to what someone else meant by *roman*. If several users of the word *roman* define it with the help of the French word *fiction*, he will have to decide whether these different users mean the same thing by *fiction*, on the basis of what he himself means by the English word "fiction," or by some other word or phrase.

The manifestations of a genre, not of genre labels, are to be historicized through records and testimonies of writing, reading, performing events. The historian may be interested in the ways in which a particular text was interpreted from the time it was produced to the present. His approach will then be similar to the philological approach already mentioned. He will have to explain differences between recorded interpretations in his own language and according to his own terminology. For instance, he will have to decide if Jones interpreted the text as an example of what he, the historian, means by "history," while Dupont interpreted it as an example of what he means by "fiction," if he chooses to use this opposition, and whether Jones and Dupont used these terms or not.

One may instead take into account only the production dates and places as historical manifestations of texts. One may then consider a genre as a universal, as a property or set of properties, which materializes itself historically through production events which are not necessarily clustered spatiotemporally. Since these events are accepted as discrete, gathering them obviously depends on a conceptually coherent and distinct notion of genre. It is to be noted in particular that, in this perspective, though the production events are assumed to involve interpretative experiences, the ways in which the original readers (including the writers) interpreted the texts are irrelevant, or simply a matter of curiosity.

Instead of shaping a genre as a universal which manifests itself through discrete production events, one may try to individuate a genre as a process. In this case, the production events have to be linked so as to provide the spatiotemporal continuity necessary to the identity of a changing individual. This strategy has the advantage of allowing the historian to use a more flexible notion of genre. Yet he still needs conceptual limits in order to distinguish the evolution of genre X from that of genre Y. The sky may be blue, then grey; it may even be partly blue and partly grey at the same time. Yet the changing sky is not the changing earth. For example, if a historian, or critic, wishes to view the narratively incoherent texts published in France in the 1950s as part of the evolution of a genre called "novel," the fact that narratively coherent texts continued to be published at the time and are still published now need not bother him too much. He may say either that the narratively incoherent texts are freaks, monsters, which do not announce a generalized mutation, or that the narratively coherent texts are residues, remnants from the past (such decisions show how the interpretation of past and present is linked to a conception of the future). But why should these narratively incoherent texts be part of the evolution of the novel rather than, say, of the prose poem? The historian may refuse to consider so-called prose poems as a genre, or as part of the evolution of poetry. He may instead prefer to say that some "prose poems" at least are part of the evolution of what he is pleased to call "novel." Or he may admit the possibility of hybridation. These decisions again show the necessity of conceptual limits.

The identity of a genre as a historical process depends on continuity. To insure this continuity, the historian will have to rely on fairly close production events and link them through assumptions of influences. He may recognize similarities between Homeric epics and *chansons de geste*. Yet, from his standpoint, the *Iliad* and the *Roland* would not be part of the same process, hence of the same genre. The influence of the *Odyssey* on Joyce's *Ulysses* would be, *from his standpoint,* irrelevant. The unity of the historical field as total process is based at present on the Einstein-Minkowsky model, according to which any event is linked to any other event within the speed of light. Within this limit, any event may be assumed to influence, or be influenced by, any other event. The model leaves the historian free to trace world-lines, that is to say, to compose partial processes, in any way he pleases. The decoupage of the field into partial processes may be dictated by practical reasons: for instance, the identity of a human body through change. It may also be decided for aesthetic reasons: this would have to be the case if someone wanted to constitute a genre as a process. The writer would have to stay within conceptual limits, as regards not only the selection of production events, but also the selection of assumed influences. He would have to select the influences which are pertinent to the evolution of the chosen genre X, as against those which would be pertinent to the evolution of genre Y. If one author contributes to the manifestation of genres X and Y, then only his acquaintance with contemporary works recognized as part of the evolution of genre X can be assumed as a direct link in the evolution of this genre through him. Other influences are irrelevant, since they could be said to have contributed to the evolution of genre Y as well as X through this writer. Apart from these constraints, the plotting of links would be quite easy, since it would simply have to obey a dialectic of similarity and contrast. Yet the contrasts would have to remain within conceptual limits, in order to be interpreted as variations within one process, rather than as a shift from one process to another, or as a confluence of two processes.

When we say that the personality of a human individual has changed, the question does not usually arise whether we mean a change within one personality, or a change from one personality to another, because these changes do not clash with our notion of the individual as one living organism. The question of identification regarding personality becomes logically bothersome only in cases of sudden and radical metamorphosis (split personality, mediumnic behavior). A historian who wants to constitute a genre as a process cannot rely on rules such as those which govern the evolution of chemical bodies or living organisms. If his only justification for maintaining the same name in spite of metamorphic manifestations is that the same label continued to be used, one may grant more logic to the discourse of an individual with a split personality who uses two names for his two *personae*.[4]

Historians of grand genres must envy Victor Hugo. Among his worthy visitors during the spiritualistic seances at Marine Terrace, there were not only Jesus, Shakespeare, the Ocean, Russia, but also the Novel, Tragedy, Comedy, *le Drame,* and Criticism. All of them communicated by means of raps directly translatable into French. Some of them were even so considerate as to show a preference for Hugolian alexandrines.

Notes

1. In *Validity in Interpretation* (New Haven: Yale University Press, 1967), E.D. Hirsch, Jr., presents a similar view: "Understanding is itself genre-bound" (p. 78). But he insists that the attempt to understand a text is simply the attempt to understand it as the writer had intended, more or less consciously or unconsciously. I have two objections to make:

    a. The attempt to understand a text as a whole differs from the attempt to understand the idiolect of a writer, that is to say, to establish a correspondence between the idiolect of the interpreter (*definiens*) and the idiolect of the writer (*definiendum*). This psycholinguistic enterprise could be equated with the attempt to make sense of a text *as a whole* only if one adopted the postulate that the writer's interpretation of his own text necessarily produces the most coherent result. I reject this postulate.

    b. Strictly speaking, the writer of a text is the writer of this text as long as he has not finished writing it. It follows that the assimilation of the meaning of a text as a whole to the writer's intention is self-contradictory.

2. The list of six functions (referential, emotive, conative, poetic, phatic, metalinguistic) proposed by the linguist Roman Jakobson shows only partial

agreement with my own schema. Furthermore, it might be misleading to assume that the same labels ("referential," "poetic") name the same concepts. Jakobson's philosophical choices are not clear to me.

3. When a play is performed, the characters are not cognitively perceived because they are not practically perceived. The projection of past or future events veers to the imagination of fiction if the interpreter feels no practical ties with his present (an unpleasant feeling of powerlessness may still be counted as a practical tie). Distant places and times have been used by dramatists as a means of aesthetic estrangement. The phrase "once upon a time" may function as a fiction operator. The tie between cognitive and practical is implicit in the positivistic conception of knowledge which makes factuality depend on verification. Fatalism echoes the postulate that the historical field is one, a logical condition of the possibility of coherent knowledge (checking and cross-checking). But, since human knowledge is uncertain and incomplete, a fatalistic attitude also tends to turn history into fiction. The shift from a practical to an aesthetic perspective may be considered as a goal (as a gestural meaning) of this attitude.

4. The gestural mode is the personifying mode *par excellence*. The impression of addressing, and being addressed by, the same spirit (*persona*, will) may correspond neither to the recognition of an atmosphere, nor to that of a physical body, nor to the definition of a universal. Kierkegaard's Abraham needs no theology. Marcel bestows on God a purely gestural status when he limits God's existence to that of a *thou*: in other words, "God," or rather *Dieu*, should be used only in the vocative case. But, even if a literary critic or historian has the impression that a genre is "speaking" to him, the logic of his discourse, if he speaks *of* this genre, will be designative, and the genre will have to be conceptually delimited.

Horst S. Daemmrich

THE AESTHETIC FUNCTION OF DETAIL AND SILHOUETTE IN LITERARY GENRES

In a recent study I pointed to a series of relational patterns and fields which characterize the internal dynamics of prose fiction.[1] The question arises whether the analysis of two concepts, detail and sihouette, can contribute to a more precise definition of genres. *Fabel*, plot, and action, narrative perspective and stance, uniqueness and interrelation of compositional elements form the basis of every literary work. The structure of texts also depends on elements which are clustered in fields and crystallized around clearly recognizable poles. The correlation of the poles, the specific arrangement of compositional elements, and thematic interrelationships determine a textual field. As a result of the various internal relations within spheres and their external links to each other, textual fields are expansive. They acquire a new dimension which is characterized by a kinetic structure, familiar to us from such natural phenomena as the V-formation of flying geese or the changing shapes of windswept dunes. These formations, determined by air currents, are part of an always changing, yet self-fulfilling order. Similarly, the dynamics of textual patterns originate in the relations of variable dimensions which differ in individual works. Since these relations can be shown to exist in all literature, they point to an inner logic of this art form. Their dialectic dependence characterizes texts; they determine aesthetic perception and give texts their dynamic potential.

In order to succeed, the fictional field of narrative genres requires an appropriate narrative voice, perspective, and presentation. Because the narrator's voice adapts itself to a given subject matter, it varies. Georg Lukács sees in narration and description two important rhetorical categories in fiction.[2] He argues that description begins to dominate fiction in a period in which authors have lost perception of the most significant element in prose writing, the characterization of a notable human destiny. By reducing persons to objects this technique aims at vivid but "meaningless representation" and projects static portraits without depth, vitality, and tension. Lukács doubts that descriptive details can convey an authentic picture of life. The narrator achieves a monotony of single scenes, in which the details lack meaningful connections to the fictional reality. The reader sees pictures but cannot grasp their relationship to a broad design.

In contrast to static description, the rhetoric of narration organizes events, establishes a dynamic relationship between present and past, and involves protagonists in actions that capture the reader's attention and enhance his comprehension of social, political, and historical forces. Furthermore, narration incorporates basically dramatic elements that shape the action and consequently heightens the reader's interest in the success or failure of literary figures. The sharp delineation of Lukács shows clearly why he prefers the narrative form of representation. Description presents man and social conditions as unchangeable and permanently fixed. Details are no longer meaningful because they fail to support either action or structural configurations. In presenting a dynamic portrait of man in conflict with social or historical conditions, narration concentrates on the essential elements of a story. Every detail is related to a significant human fate and affects readers as noteworthy.

This differentiation demonstrates possible weaknesses in texts, which may result from stressing one stylistic tendency. The complete independence of details or scenic units which lack interrelations with others limits textual dynamics. The detail becomes a still life in a series without beginning or end. The reader reacts to individual elements without perceiving their position in the total design. If one studies the examples cited by Lukács, it becomes evident that his criticism is leveled against texts in which description seems the dominant stylistic device. In order to succeed, however, every literary text requires a successful fusion of all stylistic elements. Texts exhibit an inner logic which demands that descriptive, informative, reflective, narrative, compositional elements, and other stylistic devices are appropriate to the overall perspective of the textual field. The relationship of descriptive and narrative elements to the composition as well as links established between concrete circumstances, extended perspective, and universal significance endow texts with their unique rhythm. The two structural poles of literary representation demarcating this rhythm are detail and silhouette. Their specific interplay makes literary composition possible and gives each text a dynamic movement. Furthermore, detail and silhouette guide the reader's aesthetic response, demand his active participation, and shape, broaden, and remodel his experience after the process of aesthetic perception has been completed.

Any detail referring to a familiar world makes texts, whether narrative, lyrical, or dramatic, accessible to readers. Yet, as part of the textual field, it is never visually perceptive in a strict sense. A detail gains its immediacy through relations, and it can capture the inner substance of an object through the extended perspective of the narrative which transforms the object into a subject. A few examples from poetry will demonstrate the nature and function of such details.

> Horloge! dieu sinistre, effrayant, impassible,
> Dont le doigt nous menace et nous dit:
> "Souviens-toi!"
>
> (Baudelaire, "L'Horloge")

> The sleek head emerges
> From the gold-yellow frock
> As Anadyomene in the opening
> Pages of Reinach.
>
> (Ezra Pound, "Medallion")

> Und der Himmel ist ein blaues
> Auge, das sich nicht mehr schliesst
> Über Herzen: ein genaues
> Wunder, schwankend unter Blättern.
>
> (Krolow, "Drei Orangen, Zwei Zitronen")

The effect of these lines springs from the immediate conception of the images, the relations they establish with each other, and the extended perspective inherent in their nexus. The concrete nature of the detail is retained even after its compositional significance has been recognized. Details also provide an important aesthetic function when their concreteness, historical accuracy, or precision captures and sustains the reader's attention or conveys to him the illusion of immediacy. In stage plays and narratives they form the basis of descriptive presentation. Details are fundamental building stones of scenes or dramatic tableaux that contain the social, economical, and historical background necessary to an understanding of the action, a fact demonstrated by Goethe's *Egmont*, Schiller's *Wallenstein*, many of Brecht's plays, and particularly by naturalistic dramas. As part of the textual design, a detail can also illuminate the motives of a literary figure or in a flash clarify the otherwise hidden sources of forces propelling the characters. Consequently the boundary between compositional and absolute (independent) value of details is fluid. Employed in characterization or as the primary basis for motifs and symbols, the effect of details depends on their internal relationships in texts. A reader does not respond to a succession of concrete details but concentrates on their relation and therefore on an added dimension that is not inherent in the relationship only. Thus while a detail stands out, almost isolated at times from surrounding textual elements, it also organizes a textual field through its relationship with other details.

Details can, but do not have to, agree with reality. Their most important function in texts is first to establish associations with other compositional elements, especially the action, and second, by revealing the interrelationships of ideas and ideational processes, to further an interpretation of the text. For example, the detail of the woodcut in Goethe's *Egmont* portraying how Egmont's horse is killed under him in battle has a twofold function. Clare's reaction to the woodcut reveals her deep love for him. Variations of the image of the horse which becomes identified with Egmont establishes a symbolic dimension. Egmont is portrayed as cheerfully galloping on his prancing horse through life. Since in a major scene of the play Egmont's antagonist Alba reacts almost instinctively to the vision of exuberant life, namely, Egmont on his horse, the detail further illuminates Alba's character and emotions.

In contrast, a perfectly concrete, almost photographic detail may be arbitrary if it remains isolated without a discernible relationship to the action, characters, or other structural components of a text. The isolated detail does not reveal, but rather veils, meaning. Still, such details can have an aesthetic value if they are ornamental or contribute to the purposeful ambiguity of texts. These "blind" details, such as the yellow-red carriage in Mörike's *Mozart auf der Reise nach Prag* or the bottle of foaming liquid in Hauptmann's *Bahnwärter Thiel,* present a riddle and stimulate the reader's response. Seeking an answer, he reads the text with greater attention; his perception is enhanced, even though his curiosity may never be satisfied.

The increasing use of details which apparently lack all structural interrelations with other stylistic elements, as in naturalistic fiction, in the *nouveau roman,* or in concrete and surrealist poetry, alters their traditional function. Once the detail no longer establishes any relationships, it becomes monotonous and devoid of meaning even when it incorporates minute observations. Such details lose their dynamic potential and expansive quality, an effect desired by some modern authors, though the manner in which it is achieved contradicts their professed aesthetic views. Exponents of concrete poetry, especially in Finland and Sweden, believe that a precise detail captures the essential qualities of an object. In revealing its essence, the object stands for itself. But once all meaning is extricated from a detail and all possible associations are negated, the fictional realm is reduced to a series of unrelated elements. Rather than expand, the reader's horizon of expectation contracts.

The structural character of the silhouette may be compared to the stylistic function of the pause in poetry. The difficulty, then, is to describe an element whose nature is fleeting and therefore usually escapes critical attention. The silhouette is an open section with one set of boundaries sharply drawn by characteristic details which predispose the reader through a series of specific signals, messages, and features to fill the space with his own imaginative details. We know that every literary work contains sufficient details to portray the textual field and characterize the figures. Yet texts, even those considered as standard examples of realism or naturalism, cannot delineate all possible integral parts of a scene or characteristics of a figure. In describing only a limited number of significant aspects, literary works stimulate the reader's creative imagination and demand that he contribute to the textual field. Consequently the second set of a silhouette's boundaries fluctuates. It is reshaped by each reader's sphere of experience and expectation. This essentially expansive and dynamic process differs not only from reader to reader but also from text to text. In the course of aesthetic perception, the silhouette assumes a distinct form which greatly enhances each reader's experience and provides the potential for a continuous process of reflection and interpretation.

As a result, readers, even expert critics, tend to attribute to texts numerous elements which can only be inferred. In his novella

Bergkristall Adalbert Stifter characterizes the children who are the focal point of the action only sparingly but presents a detailed description of the village, nature, and the mountain which are the setting for the action. The narrative shapes the reader's specific feeling for nature. Still he must add many elements from his own experience, fill in images of trees, grasp the contour of the path, envision spring, fall, or winter, and imagine the absolute loneliness of the children lost in the vast expanse of ice and snow. In contrast, a reader will be hard put to recollect a precise picture of the mountain in Thomas Mann's *Der Zauberberg*. Gerhart Hauptmann seems to adhere to the stylistic tendency of naturalism by rendering detailed descriptions of figures in *Bahnwärter Thiel*. A careful reading shows, however, that he too presents the characteristic elements of a silhouette. Thus Thiel is identified only as tanned by wind and weather, with neatly parted, oiled hair, a heavy, hairy neck, and halting speech.

Similarly, Joseph Conrad characterizes Captain Beard in *Youth* as a man who "had a nut-cracker face—chin and nose trying to come together over a sunken mouth—and it was framed in iron-gray fluffy hair, that looked like a chin-strap of cotton-wool sprinkled with coal-dust. And he had blue eyes in that old face of his, which were amazingly like a boy's, with that candid expression some quite common men preserve to the end of their days by a rare internal gift of simplicity of heart and rectitude of soul." The skipper's wife is identified as "an old woman, with a face all wrinkled and ruddy like a winter apple, and the figure of a young girl." Every reader will fill in other features and develop an integrated perception of these persons on the basis of a composite picture. The narrator's technique guides the process of perception; readers develop, however, an attitude toward fictional figures which may or may not be based on a specifically mentioned quality in their personalities. Mrs. Beard's deep concern for her husband and her motherly gesture in mending young Marlow's socks reveal a warm, friendly personality. As Conrad's narrative unfolds and presents Captain Beard's gentle yet inflexible stance toward the world, his stubborn, heroic battle with the all-consuming fire on board the ship, and his naive, simplistic attempts to save whatever possible for the underwriters, be it an old barometer or a piece of rope, readers recognize that "simplicity of heart and rectitude of soul" are indeed distinctive traits of his character. Thus specific details provide a point of departure and also guide the perception; the silhouette expands the imagination.

This process demonstrates the difficulty in analyzing the substance of a silhouette. Since every reader will round out a silhouette with elements from his own sphere of experience and expectation, its aesthetic effect resides in the unique interrelationship between text and reader. The structure of the scene in *Youth* in which an explosion rips the deck apart illustrates this observation: toward ten o'clock, Marlow leaves the watch to step down to the main deck for a moment.

> The carpenter's bench stood abaft the mainmast: I leaned against it sucking at my pipe, and the carpenter, a young chap, came to talk to me. He remarked, "I think we have done very well, haven't we?" and then I perceived with annoyance the fool was trying to tilt the bench. I said curtly, "Don't, Chips," and immediately became aware of a queer sensation, of an absurd delusion,—I seemed somehow to be in the air. I heard all round me like a pent-up breath released—as if a thousand giants simultaneously had said Phoo!—and felt a dull concussion which made my ribs ache suddenly. No doubt about it—I was in the air, and my body was describing a short parabola. But short as it was, I had the time to think several thoughts in, as far as I can remember, the following order: "This can't be the carpenter—What is it?—Some accident—Submarine volcano?—Coals, gas! By Jove! we are being blown up—Everybody's dead—I am falling into the afterhatch—I see fire in it."

The scene clearly shows the relationship between detail and silhouette. The narrator tries to convey a situation which few, if any, readers will have experienced personally. A precise, detailed description of the explosion's entire configuration would expand the narrative beyond recognition. The narrator concentrates on one revealing moment, a pinpoint of eternity, in presenting Marlow's sudden impressions and fleeting thoughts. Though the description is restricted to a series of sensations, the whole scene opens a range of possibilities for the reader's imagination. Basing his experience on prior reading knowledge, newspaper accounts of explosions, photographs of volcanoes, or impressions of falling and tilting, each reader will add to the silhouette. At the same time, the observation, "I see fire in it," establishes the transition in the flow of narration to the ensuing battle with the fire in the cargo rooms.

Literary texts require silhouettes for two reasons. The silhouette assures utmost terseness in texts, since the description of all possible elements would inflate texts to proportions which could not be handled by any fictional technique. Furthermore, the silhouette rouses the reader's imagination. Since narratives of literary realism are often cited for their precise details and realistic descriptions, a text from this period is exemplary for the relationship of detail and silhouette to description and composition. At first glance, Stifter's *Bergkristall* almost seems to confirm Lukács's observation.

> In den hohen Gebirgen unseres Vaterlandes steht ein Dörfchen mit einem kleinen, aber sehr spitzigen Kirchturm, der mit seiner roten Farbe, mit welcher die Schindeln bemalt sind, aus dem Grün vieler Obstbäume hervorragt und wegen derselben roten Farbe in dem duftigen und blauen Dämmern der Berge weithin ersichtlich ist. Das Dörfchen liegt gerade mitten in einem ziemlich weiten Tale, das fast wie ein länglicher Kreis gestaltet ist. Es enthält ausser der Kirche eine Schule, ein Gemeindehaus und noch mehrere stattliche Häuser, die einen Platz gestalten, auf welchem vier Linden stehen, die ein steinernes Kreuz in ihrer Mitte haben. Diese Häuser sind nicht blosse Landwirtschaftshäuser, sondern sie bergen auch noch diejenigen Handwerke in ihrem Schosse, die dem menschlichen Geschlechte unentbehrlich sind und die bestimmt sind, den Gebirgsbewohnern ihren einzigen Bedarf an Kunsterzeugnissen zu decken. Im Tale und an den Bergen herum sind noch sehr viele zerstreute Hütten.

Detailed descriptions of Christmas, the valley, the road, the mountain, and the snowfall lead the reader to suspect that description as such is the ultimate goal of the story. Textual analysis shows, however, a perfect integration of detail and silhouette, of description, narration, and composition. The novella follows a circular movement. It opens with a discussion of religious holidays and immediately establishes a meaningful relation between the individual and society and the possibility of human self-realization in the world (expanded perspective). Originating from this wide circle the narration moves concentrically along a path comprising a description of the village, the shoemaker's house, and the two little children, thus encompassing the smallest unit. From this point the narration sweeps into a large circle by relating the children's experience of complete isolation in the icy mountain wilderness to man's encounter with God. After the children have been saved the narrative perspective contracts by returning to the village.

This village is the center of a self-contained world of order, stability, permanence, and relative peace. The people love their village. Their stories center on the mountain which has become a symbol of permanence in nature. They live without facing great upheavals, grow, mature, and die, almost unconsciously patterning their existence after the seasonal changes they observe in the mountain. Human relationships are characterized by quiet respect and helpfulness. The shoemaker accepts this life after a brief period of youthful protest as poacher. Nevertheless, his wife and children are treated with great reservation because his wife comes from a different village and the children frequently visit their grandparents in the other village. Thus the community contains a potential conflict in the children as strangers. While the relationship between the shoemaker, his family, and the villagers is portrayed in detail, their appearance is scarcely characterized and thus open to the reader's imagination.

The presentation of the eternal rhythm of life almost necessitates a focus on the small world. The detailed description of the immediate moment is translated into a concrete universal as a result of the reference of village life to a cosmic order. At the same time the action achieves universal significance in the adventure of the children during the holy Christmas Eve. While the people in the village celebrate the holiday of human hope, the children miss the road and lose their way in the endlessly falling snow. Their search becomes symbolic for man's search for a home, for ties to others, and inclusion into a community. They are exposed to an incredible threat, experienced by the reader, though the children cannot voice it. Completely thrown back upon themselves, they stand before an unknown, inscrutable nature. They are lost in a vast expanse of ice without beginning or end. They see no valley, no house, cannot see the countless lighted trees nor hear the waves of sound rolling across the land.

The calm voice of the narrator and the detached perspective become fully noticeable in the section which describes the children's absolute loneliness. At this point the narrator makes an observation which momentarily threatens to destroy the narrative stance established at the beginning of the novella. "Nur zu den Kindern herauf kam kein Laut, hier wurde nichts vernommen; denn hier war nichts zu verkündigen." Beyond the range of the voice of hope, man is confronted by absolute nothingness. The hint of this possibility, which momentarily voids the message of hope, gives the narrative an enormous tension.[3] The plot is reintegrated through the answer contained in the simple, human gesture of a child. The young boy Conrad extends his help to his sister: he cares for her, gives her his jacket, his portion of the bread and comforts her. His love and his faith keep the children alive. The path that man's self-realization must take in the world is indicated in these actions, even if the children find their way back to their community only through the common efforts of the villagers. Because all the people in the village join in searching for the children, they bind them to the community. The rescue of the children clarifies the meaning of the story. The little world of the narrative becomes symbolic for a human order founded on love and worthy of being sustained. Detail and silhouette, concrete elements and universal significance are balanced. The concentric movement of the story closes harmoniously; the old order has been expanded to a new order which after it has gone through doubt permits man's self-realization in the world.

Detail and silhouette affect the reader throughout the various phases of perception in a constant alternation of concentrated attention and almost limitless expansion. This rhythm stimulates his creative participation and shapes the imagination by giving it a specific contour. For purposes of analysis we ought to distinguish between a primary and secondary factor in the creative imagination. The primary factor comprises the reader's reaction and intellectual struggle with the complex structure of a text. Consciously or unconsciously the reader enters into an agreement with the text; he listens to the author's voice and is guided by it. But the text also activates the imagination. Even when a reader cannot grasp the total structure or the full significance of a text, his reception expands his sphere of experience. Thus the secondary factor comprises a dialogue with the text and a productive assimilation. Associations prompted by the sphere of experience lead to a reflective attitude toward the text. The reader becomes conscious of textual details and their relationship; he elaborates upon the text by filling in the silhouette, transforms, and finally recreates the text in his mind. Only after the act of the reader's mental reconstitution is the text actualized. Without this creative act which functions in the perception of all literary genres the text would be a lifeless object. Walt Whitman characterized this phenomenon succinctly when he wrote: "The message of great poetry to mankind is: Come to us as equals, only then can you understand us. We are no better than you, whatever is in us is in you." The newly perceived elements elicit emotions and thoughts and lead to new associations which, by transforming the sphere of experience, restructure the reader's perceptual field. The receptivity is expanded; the conceptual ability is enhanced and enriched in a series of increasingly complex associations. Every link of the chain carries the seed for renewed interest and complementation. This continuous exchange with a text enables us to have experiences in reading which are otherwise impossible in life.

The relationship between detail and silhouette constitutes a basic structural unit in prose fiction. They also shape the dynamic process of contraction and expansion in the aesthetic perception of other genres, especially poetry and drama. However, since the specific structural configuration of detail and silhouette may differ markedly in individual genres, the definition of a genre would gain in precision if a textual field and its poles were clearly delineated. Instead of stressing contrasting elements, the traditional approach in studies of the novella and the novel, we should look for common elements and focus attention on their characteristic manifestation in each genre.

Notes

1. Horst S. Daemmrich, "Literaturkritik in Theorie und Praxis," *Uni-Taschenbuch* 311 (Munich, 1974).
2. Georg Lukács, *Probleme des Realismus* (Berlin, 1955), pp. 103–45.
3. This section of Stifter's text is part of a grand design of a silhouette, that is, man's relationship to numina. In itself it constitutes a *Leerstelle* or *Unbestimmtheitsstelle* in Iser's sense. See Wolfgang Iser, *Die Appellstruktur der Texte. Unbestimmtheit als Wirkungsbedingung literarischer Prosa* (Konstanzer Universitätsrede 28, 1970). While I agree with Iser and Hans Robert Jauss that readers elaborate upon such sections by adding material from their own experience, I disagree with the application of this insight to literary criticism. To be sure, critics are readers, but as critics they are usually aware of their sphere of experience and also realize the relativity of possible interpretations. This consciousness enables a critic to analyze the reader's sphere of experience and expectation and judge other interpretations.

Johannes A. Huisman

GENERATIVE CLASSIFICATIONS IN MEDIEVAL LITERATURE

The study of genres has seldom been given the respect due it within the framework of literary theory. We are still nowhere near possessing a practicable general scheme; we still lack any theoretical basis that goes significantly beyond Aristotle and Horace. From the standpoint of interpretation and evaluation, Karl Langosch signaled this defect: "In order to interpret and evaluate a literary work as a work of art, it is important to determine its place within its genre, also called literary form. This field is far too little cultivated; almost everywhere the documents must still be collected and examined; the genres must be sorted out according to formal, contextual, moral, and other traits; their story must be written and their inner structure must be worked out."[1] This claim holds true not only for literature in medieval Latin, but equally for the literature in the vernaculars that developed from and alongside it. The situation is no more favorable for the second component—the older Germanic literatures; Morton Bloomfield correctly speaks of "our ignorance of Germanic literary genres."[2] This statement loses little of its validity if the word "Germanic" is eliminated. The causes of this regrettable delay lie both in the difficulties presented by the object itself and in the multiplicity of the questions involved in the increasing number of directions pursued by scholars.

If we look more closely at the relevant entries in bibliographies, handbooks, and editions arranged according to categories, it becomes clear that necessity has largely been turned into a virtue and that the material has been arranged in genres based on a wide variety of criteria. M.S. Batts, for example, distinguishes seven types in late courtly literature: courtly poetry, lyric and *Spruch*, heroic literature, minor epic, didactic literature, religious literature, and history.[3] The term "courtly literature" has a sociological basis; "lyrics" are named for the musical accompaniment that was obligatory until the eighteenth century; "heroic poetry" takes its name from the content; "minor epic" from its length, and "didactic verse" from the poet's intention. This is not to fault Batts's method; practice cannot wait for theory to establish a definitive system of genres, if such is even possible. We cannot attempt here to pursue the causes of the comparatively mild interest in genre theory. Let us only point to the fact that literary genres do not exist in clearly delineated areas but form a widely overlapping continuum; that the applied criteria belong to so many different, variously intersecting categories that any system of genres requires a multidimensional model, quite unimaginable as a whole. As for the lack of interest shown by recent scholarship, we must note that neither the method of history of ideas nor that of hermeneutic interpretation has much need for genre theory; most especially is this the case for New Criticism, which fundamentally "turns against any overly strong systematization and classification of literary works."[4] Croce's extreme stance, which denied any significance to genres, did not evoke much response, however.[5] Genre theory was more or less pushed aside into its own subdiscipline—*systematic literary theory*. In this ambiance, however, it increasingly flourished. At the present time it is fertilized by the structuralist method. Generative poetics, which has gained ground in recent years, secures an important place in the total activity of literary scholarship for typology; several publications dedicated to this topic appear simultaneously or are announced, the present yearbook among them. This "boom" did not grow out of a vacuum. The historical-positivist method, the oldest of the directions taken by the discipline's investigations in the modern sense, has attempted from the outset, on the Aristotelian pattern, to categorize the mass of traditional and contemporary literature into *genera, genres, types,* or *forms*. This terminology from classical antiquity, it is well known, grew out of the system of the biological sciences.[6] It is, in the same way, arranged along historical-genetic lines; positivist scholarship is concerned with the tradition of the classical genera and their further development.

The positivists' claim of establishing an all-encompassing genealogy of species and superspecies on the basis of the total corpus of national literatures—even to construct a pattern that would apply to the entire medieval culture area by means of the comparative method—has foundered on the sheer magnitude of the work required. This method nevertheless remains useful for the Middle Ages, because the theory and practices of classical antiquity remain alive and effective in the medium of the common cultural language, Latin. Or, according to the formulation used by Baldwin in the foreword to his masterly book on medieval rhetoric and poetics, "Medieval theory, on the other hand, best being grasped as development from an inheritance, the plan of the volume is historical."[7] But that is not to say that genre scholarship in the Middle Ages could get along without modern theoretical systematics. F.C. Maatje correctly points out that the categories established by theoretical literary criticism lay claim to the widest possible universality and are also valid for research into medieval and classical literature.[8] Nevertheless, scholarship concerned with the literature of the Middle Ages and with its systems must deal with a special set of problems, which we will be dealing with in more detail. I will begin with a brief overview of the most recent developments and the state of the art, with special consideration of the accomplishments in medieval verbal art, understanding further that all the important findings cannot be cited.[9]

It is evident that new tendencies in philology are eventually adopted into literary theory.[10] Thus, after World War II, the structural view of literature won a prominent place in scholarship. Structuralism is not concerned with content or form from a historical point of view; it addresses itself to the structure of the work of art. Describing the system of the external and internal forms is its first and most crucial concern. Similar or related structures are thus able to furnish genre criteria. The relationship between *narrative time* and *narrated time* proved to be a useful differentiating trait among the three chief genres applied since classical times—lyric, epic, and drama—as well as the specific manner in which the spatial structure is concretized.[11]

In the Middle Ages, numerological composition turns out to have been a widespread structural principle. Many investigations were carried out in this field; the stimulus probably begins with E.R. Curtius.[12] After medieval lyrics were tested for this element, major epics underwent the same scrutiny.[13] The symbolic referential nature of the constituent numbers opened a viable approach to interpretation of the literature in question.[14]

But other formal criteria—such as the relationship to architectonic and musical forms—also led to valuable insights.[15] In this respect we think particularly of the extensive and fruitful work of Hugo Kuhn. The titles of his pertinent works appear to reflect a development from the genetic terminology of the "genre problem" to a "typology of literature" free of genealogy.[16] Kuhn was a structuralist from the first, when "neopositivism and interpretation [still] held the stage."[17] The structure of content, aside from its relation to the numerological arrangement of the material, remains an independent principle. Thus Kuhn pointed to *addition* as a new structural element of late-courtly literature and factual literature and to the "double way" of the hero in the courtly romance.[18] Koch observed in the plot of the romance a "steady alteration of movement and rest, forward-urging impulses and satisfying results" and ascribes to this rhythm the function of "diviso."[19] Beyschlag, Wachinger, Reiffenstein, and others have studied epic prognostication as a structural tool in Middle High German epics.[20]

The way from quantitative structuralism to a statistical theory of literary language is short; it was particularly smoothed by electronic preparation of the necessary masses of data.[21] This scholarly direction promises much for genre theory after having been utilized as a first step in determining authorship. L. Doležel was able to establish an extremely low median value for the length of sentences in modern drama.[22] On the basis of specific variations in the adjective-verb quotient, Bode distinguishes among "modern plays, drama, legal statutes, ... fiction, and scientific material."[23]

Even in the period when scholars focused most intently on the pure text of the work of art, interest remained alive for extratextual relations and functions; it was strongly promoted by the rise of the sociological method. From the point of view of information theory, Doležel formulated the necessity of this methodical enlargement of the research object: "The inadequate, often seemingly 'secret,' aesthetic component is revealed in the explication of the complex objective-subjective activity of three elements of the communication process: the originator of the communication, the structure of the communication, and the recipient (or interpreter) of the communication."[24] The "Critique of Pure Interpretation" was not long in emerging: "Interpretation, which today prevails in many monographs, pays for its appealing harmony with a renunciation of complex social interrelations and with the waiver of those categories that can be practically tested."[25] Speaking of medieval literature, Kuhn notes: "As a further criterion of type formation it is particularly in this period [the fourteenth century] that sociology of author, work, and audience comes to the fore."[26] The dual concept of production/reception, which gathers together all relevant pretextual and posttextual data, goes even further. The concept of *situation* also preponderantly depends on sociology; literature is created and acts within a particular (small or large) group or society. One can even speak of a "rehabilitation of the author's intention."[27] The author wants to affect his audience; the audience expects something of him or charges him with a task. Creation and effect are conditioned by the situation. Medieval animal literature, such as *Ecbasis Captivi* or *Ysengrinus*, are "sociologically centered on the home, the sect, the monastic family, and comparable secular and clerical societies."[28] When it comes to reception, we must distinguish between audience and critic; affect and function are the most important categories for the former, while the latter relies on value judgment, in which case, depending on the critic's attitude, a wide variety of standards is applied.[29] The critic can, for example, make his judgment according to the work's function—perhaps as aesthetic instance, as "pure" entertainment, as identification model, or as a social-change agent (social relevance in the narrower sense). Legitimate as this last criterion may be, it brings us dangerously close to an ideological total claim, as the Middle Ages knew it in the demand for transcendence (*Jenseitsrelevanz*) of literary works.[30] Along with production and reception, the structural connection with other art forms is used as an extratextual trait of literary genres. As early as Aristotle "spectacle and music" were seen to be essential constituents of tragedy.[31]

In the midst of the peak activity of structural literary criticism, a new method arose, also deriving from linguistics.[32] The transformational-generative grammar (TGG) of Noam Chomsky and his co-workers had raised the demand for a system of rules by which all sentences possible in human languages could be generated. Special systems are to be constructed for the individual languages. In principle a computer that had been fed all the rules and all the lexicons of every language should be able to produce all possible grammatically proper sentences. This grammar of generative sentences now leads to a generative textual grammar; it became possible only when the sentence limit in TGG is broken through. Of all existing and potential texts, literary ones form a special area; a *generative poetic* must be established for them.[33] We view the aesthetic function as a trait that distinguishes poetic texts as a subgroup of texts from all others: "Poetic communication is verbal communication with aesthetic functions."[34] This does not lead to the conclusion that poetics is to be only a special area of aesthetics; it belongs most properly to generative grammar. (This generative grammar must include the semantic elements in order to fulfill the demands of the poetics.) As so often, we are also dealing here with the average of two powers; any attempt at inclusion on one side or the other distorts the facts. We can only deal with the inclusion of individual groups of traits. At the beginning of the second part of his dissertation, T.A. van Dijk announced, "We want to describe explicitly, for example how literary texts such as poems show very special ways of concatenating sentences (or semi-sentences) and how literary narrative like any narrative on the one hand has macro-structures or text in general and on the other hand operations defining its literariness."[35] This statement contains the beginning of a system of literary types on the basis of a characteristic segment out of the totality of the rules. I. Levy speaks of the *code* of each literary type—that is, "the sum of the obligatory regulations which the chosen versions must follow for verbal or rhythmic reasons or in order to correspond to the literary conventions of each literary type (for example, the sonnet, the drama)."[36] As a consequence, generative poetic must encompass a general "set of features," a different set for each genre.

Because of the overpowering position of narrative literature, J. Ihwe suggests a special term—narrativics—for the generative subpoetics of this genre.[37] In his "Foundations for Typologies of Texts" van Dijk expresses the claim that of necessity results from this posture: "We claim, in fact, that no explicit typology can be established without having recourse to the theory of texts (a T-grammar)." And as for literary genre theory, "We want to argue that satisfactory typologies of literary texts have to be based on generative text grammars, and more specifically on literary text grammars." Such a typology is also a prerequisite for the study of the development of genres: "Diachronic change can only be described when the precise rules of the system underlying a given type are known."[38] We believe that these claims indicate the correct course. True, it is a very long and tedious road, but it is the only one there is.

Before tackling the specific prerequisites of medieval literature in reference to generative poetics, a few preliminary theses are called for. First we must decide whether genres are bound to epochs. If they are seen as different combinations of "features," they could in principle arise during very varied cultural periods. For the systematics of medieval literature, however, it does not matter whether particular genres do or do not appear in another period. Naming alone might be affected by a possible multiple presence. Further, we must decide whether or not to adopt a hierarchic order of genres. Wellek suggests that the term "genre" be reserved for " 'subdivisions' of groups of the second order."[39] Maatje distinguishes a pyramid of "het literaire werk," genres, subgenres, and types. But he does not assign any great importance to Lämmert's distinction between genre theory and typology.[40] We believe that we must start in principle from a nonhierarchic accumulation of types; the same is true for the constituting features. Not even the three classical prime genres are obvious realities in the Middle Ages. The Norse ballad, which dominated Scandinavian literature for centuries, is "epic, lyric, and dramatic (dialogical) all at the same time."[41] In this way it differs significantly from the Old French ballad, which had probably reached the north as early as the late twelfth century.[42] Only in the case of inclusion would the structuring of a hierarchic order be possible. However, the growing number of classes of criteria that are made the basis of the characterization of texts leads to the danger of far-reaching atomization. Thus T. Todorov points out that form and function, for example, as primary criterion classes lead to completely different genre divisions. "A contemporary novel should, for example, be related to the old epic trend in terms of its *function;* instead we relate it to the Greek romance on the basis of their common *prose* form.[43] As van Dijk notes, however, "it is impossible in principle to describe all aspects of an object, so that the researcher is forced to make a selection of the relevant phenomena. Such a selection will be in part determined by his personal views or the views held by his discipline at that moment."[44] Every period therefore develops its own typology. This circumstance dictates a primary limitation in the number of categories of features to be taken into account. It also limits their possible combinations and increases the number of examples in existing literary works to illustrate theoretical types. For the Middle Ages, bound as they were to tradition, there is little danger that no distinct and relatively heavily populated types will appear.

Let us now turn to the particular situation of medieval literature as the object of a generative poetics. We must note at the outset that such a poetics is only conditionally possible. Dead languages have no competence; the same holds true for dead literatures. If a competence does appear in special cases, it is secondarily derived from the literary performance. Therefore rules can only be abstracted from a corpus. This corpus, however, has been incompletely preserved for the early and high Middle Ages.[45] Though an abundance of texts from the late Middle Ages has survived, they have been only partially edited at present.

The scarcity of the extant texts shows up particularly in the fact that we have no autographs or authorized scripts of most texts. Many copyists showed little respect for their originals; in the late Middle Ages some conscious ridicule of serious texts can even be found.[46] But the minimal access to the extensive special and general literature does not prevent the construction of a generative grammar, since it does not belong here but to the corpus of the generative texts of the Middle Ages. That it was in part still composed in verse does not alter the situation.[47]

The tendency—useful for linguistic purposes—to a diplomatic technique for editing certain manuscripts instead of providing a critical text does hamper the literary critics' study of poetic works. Good critical editions, provided with a serviceable English translation, should not be dismissed as "unscientific" but are to be welcomed. They make possible the study, if not of all, at least of many genre-constituting characteristics; in addition, they have the eminent social function of making accessible the cultural treasures from the common past of many nations. Medieval Latin philology has until now been secondary to critical texts on the pattern of classical literary studies; the number of *en face* translations increases steadily. A rehabilitation of normalized text editions in the vernacular is urgently needed. Without them literary studies devoted to the Middle Ages will not participate fully in the development of generative poetics. For the late Middle Ages normative languages must be defined, just as they have been established for the medieval heyday, such as standard Middle High German by Karl Lachmann or classical Old Norse used in most of the older editions of the eddas and sagas.[48] These normalized historical languages are valuable not only for literary criticism; they are also of great significance for comparative linguistics and the establishment of partial generative grammars with the relevant glossaries; an example is the positive evaluation of normalized Middle High German by K.B. Lindgren.[49] A complication is introduced by the actual dialectic variation of the vernacular languages, since a generally applicable linguistic norm was not sought after until the increasing influence of a predominant region (France) impelled the others.[50] Over, alongside, and sometimes under these vernaculars, Latin remained active throughout the Middle Ages in the

European cultural area. Many authors are bilingual, and it is not a matter of alternating exclusivity, but of an oscillating, continuous concurrence.[51] This situation gives rise to the type of the macaronic, consisting of alternating verses or entire stanzas in Latin and the vernacular. Verses in two or more vernaculars also occurred. It must be noted that such mixed poems are entirely serious, without any comic intention.

In discussing the duality of prose/poetry, it must be noted that the transitions are to be seen as prose without qualification. The beginning is represented by the rhythmic *cursus* at the end of the sentence; rhyming prose followed; and in discussing Mechtild von Magdeburg, Kuhn speaks of "an—admittedly very free—'prosimetrum.' "[52] The modern transitional forms are rather to be seen as "emprosed" verse forms and belong to the category of poetry. This has to do with the "triumphal march" of prose; "the omnipotence of verse in the Middle Ages corresponds today to an omnipotence of prose."[53] This image reflects the fact that the verse inserts, so beloved from the Old Irish cycles and the Icelandic sagas to Goethe's Mignon, have disappeared from the prose novel.

The style—to use the word in its narrow sense—of medieval authors is recognizable by the choice of words, grammatical figures, tropes, and *loci communes;* it is strongly determined by the classical tradition. It remains to be researched to what extent these stylistic figures and common plans are bound to genres. (The choice of words is typical for court literature.) Throughout the Middle Ages they determine an important function—which, however, was quite different in, say, the *Chanson de Roland* from what it was at the end of the twelfth century.[54] A strong tie between stylistic level and genre, as was common in classical Greek literature, probably never came about in the Middle Ages. According to K. Langosch, the Middle Ages recognized, not the classical three, but only two stylistic types: the *ornatus facilis* and the *ornatus difficilis*.[55] This criterion disappeared during the later Middle Ages; speaking of the Old Norse *rímur* (strophic ballads), R. Meissner notes, "While the classical period had a refined sense of style that distinguished among poetic language, elevated prosaic language, and everyday speech, the language of the *rímur* is composed of elements of all three."[56] The "ornatus facilis" could descend to the "ton trivial," which O. Jodogne included as a trait of the fabliaux in his definition of the type.[57] The same holds true for a number of German farces and carnival plays.

Concerning the surface structure of medieval literature, it is further to be noted that it would be quite feasible to carry out statistical researches concerning word frequency, verb-noun quotients, word length, sentence length, alliteration, end rhyme, or number of syllables. Such studies are generally decreasingly affected by the use of normalized texts, to the extent that the amount of the investigated works increases; potential corrections undertaken by scribes or editors will hardly affect the percentages in the great fullness of materials. When he suspects "inauthentic" passages, the editor should not simply delete the words in question but leave the passage open. It is not always necessary to find an interpolation; the "inauthentic" verses may have displaced the original lines in the tradition. For the metrical form, the decline of the classical quantitative system is of crucial significance.[58] In the Romance languages, syllable counts can still be seen in part as a continuation of classical meters, which also entered skaldic verse. For the rest, however, the suspension of metric unity holds true for the entire Germanic area. The second thoroughgoing innovation is the introduction of end rhymes. In the Germanic and Celtic north, these displaced alliteration, but they had to be content with sharing in the skaldic strophe. The verse type can be a trait of the genre; the fabliaux, for example, were all composed in a decasyllabic measure.[59] As in the classical period, more than one verse form can occur within the same poem. The high point of such prosodic plurality is represented by Snorri Sturluson's prize song for King Hakon of Norway; in this song he uses one hundred verse forms, some of them invented for the occasion.

The stanza holds special significance for the form of medieval poetry. The term should not be rendered useless by extending it to contextual structural units. In the Germanic area the stanza is younger than the arrangement of verses; in the Romance world the two are separated by the *laisse*.[60] The stanza made up of four long lines became the principal form for the German and Scandinavian poets working with Germanic materials. Sequences of double and triple stanzas are typical for the lai; so is the canzone stanza for minnesong in its early stages, but thereafter it is transferred to *Spruch* verse.[61] Around 1300 the rhymed couplet, the continuation of the long line, came to dominate fictional, pseudo-historic, and religious narratives, didactic large works, all short forms, and the vernacular clerical drama in Germany.[62] It is characteristic of the Old Norse ballad that several stanza forms (and melodies) are used sequentially within the same work.[63]

We have already mentioned numerological composition, which

was of supreme importance in the Middle Ages. It cannot be studied without regard to its referential nature. For the medieval person what is essential is not the phenomenon we are aware of but the immanent divine order based on measure and number. The widely read Vincent de Beauvais expressed it plainly: "Ratio numerorum contemnenda non est. . . . Non enim frustra in laudibus Dei dictum est: Omnia in mensura et numero et pondere fecisti. . . . Tolle numerum in rebus omnibus et omnia pereunt."[64] Only the study of the referential function of numbers can break through the closed circle between "beautiful" numbers and hypothetical medieval metrics. This vicious circle led Wolfgang Mohr to give up investigating metrical number structures.[65] The elaboration of medieval statements to numerological interpretation is one of the tasks of the Münstersche Arbeitsstelle für Bedeutungsforschung.[66] Additionally, the direct or obvious clues in undamaged preserved poetic texts remain to be collected systematically.[67]

The structural analysis of numerical compositions in general encounters strong resistance, especially in England.[68] Only a few scholars have successfully studied this structural principle in the earliest English literature. The reasons for this reluctance lie on the one hand in the previously mentioned uncertainty in relation to the textual shape and the metrics, on the other in the rash assumption of structure-shaping numbers. We have previously called for the difficult but important closer determination of the probability of a fluke and in particular for the minimal conclusiveness of the sum of the digits of a number and the inclusion of imprecise symmetries.[69]

As far as the sum of the digits is concerned, we can now go into greater detail. If a particular verse in a poem of one hundred verses occurs, for example, in sixty-fifth place, then, other considerations aside, the chance ratio is 1:100; it could appear in the ninety-ninth place just as easily. But the chance ratio for the sum of the digits as to placement is 1:18 because there are only eighteen possible sums of all the digits of all the numbers from one to one hundred. If we reduce these sums to one-place digits, we see that the chance of coincidence is even greater (1:9). Our claim for precise proportional requirements must therefore be modified to state that medieval poets may, from a sense of piety, consciously have built in minor irregularities. A similar situation obtains in the architecture of surviving gothic cathedrals. Oriental rugs often show an obviously intentional deviation from the regular pattern, which are explained as humility in the face of Allah's works; only these should be perfect in every regard.⁷⁰ A law of "imprecise regularity," though it fits beautifully into the analogical cast of mind of the time, requires more precise definition before it can be operable.⁷¹ Nevertheless, this assumption considerably increases the chance rate, even if we recognize only minor deviations.

We now turn to the work's content. Major writers—such as Chretiens de Troyes—tend to arrange the material according to the impact of the separate episodes on the total narrative.⁷² The result of this expansion and contraction need not coincide with the numerological formal structure according to verse and stanza number.⁷³ The material itself is strongly bound to tradition. It originates in the classical, Germanic, and Celtic components of the medieval world; this trinity corresponds to the three genres of the classical novel (Alexander, Aeneis), the heroic epic (Chanson de geste, Nibelungen), and the Arthurian romances (along with the Tristan material). Within this division of materials, concatenations gradually occur, culminating in the cycles built on historical personalities, such as Siegfried (= Arminius, the oldest historical figure surviving in legend), Etzel (= Attila), Arthur (Artorius), Dietrich von Bern (= Theodoric the Great), the Merovingian Hugdietrich, and Charlemagne, all of whom lived within the first thousand years of our era. The heritage of the classical age included Oriental literature as well, among it the Bible. As the foundation of Christianity, it formed the most important source for religious literature, earlier than the lives of the saints. The Crusades represent especially important direct source material, forming the bridge between Eastern and Western culture. The correct term is "Crusade literature" to include both lyric and epic works. In the fourteenth century an "omnipresence of all and every material in every combination" existed.⁷⁴ Even the Bible was no longer safe; Jehan Malkaraume not only included stylistic borrowings from Ovid, but also absorbed the entire story of Pyramus and Thisbe into his Bible.⁷⁵ We must, however, remember that the divine was so unalterably held to prevail and was so far beyond discussion that without arousing indignation it could be made the basis of satirical texts, such as the *Passio Francorum secundum Flemingos*.⁷⁶ Latin collections of exemplary short stories and anecdotal events, the *Promptuaria Exemplorum*, were universally used as the source for sermons and novels.⁷⁷ The *Gesta Romanorum*, a huge collection of materials in Latin, also furnished sources for the most diverse genres. The medieval sermon—the formal but functionally adapted sequel to the classical *oratio*—was distinguished, depending on content, into "sermones de tempore" and "sermones de sanctis."

Alongside the historically traditional material, the medieval poet preferred to use stereotypical motifs. Thus the marriage motif, most particularly the search for a bride, with a happy ending, is the structurally predominant element in the minstrel epic.[78] The theme of courtly love characterizes both the minnesong and the later minne speech. The theme of the Crusades determines crusade lyrics.

Along with the theme, the "controlling idea," on a deeper level, is important for the structure of the genre. In Vergil's *Aeneid*, it is "the idea of Roman destiny." Dante's *Divine Comedy* is "a vision of the progressive freeing of the will." The idea of the minnesong lies in the conviction that courtly love for the noble lady spiritually elevates and ennobles the knight; the Crusade lyric implicitly or explicitly states that the love of God is to be preferred to worldly love of women. For the Germanic people Baldwin correctly noted, "Their epic conception is typically not of a progressive story, but of a *situation*. The hero is imagined in a crisis."[79] The heroic poem can grow into the heroic epic only when the monastic culture becomes familiar with the thought of a major epic through the academic author, Vergil.

The duality of the religious and the secular is very important for the Middle Ages. The unity of church and state, the actual spiritual and political predominance of the church, led to an extensive specialized theological and religious literature. For literature in the narrower sense, we must point out the sermon, the *vitae sanctorum*, the legends and visions, as well as mystical writings. The transcendent meaning of literary activity is such a matter-of-course presupposition that it sounds almost like a formulaic expression when a poet disavows his earlier secular poetry in the prologue to his legend. The direct reference to the beyond characterizes *vita* and legend, vision and sermon. The ethical *Spruch* literature is created in the name of the Christian life, which focuses on the blessed beyond. The *Merigarto*, which at first glance looks like special geographical literature, aims at glorifying God in His works; the physiologue does not care about knowledge of the animal kingdom but about the allegorical or analogical interpretation of the gospels. Feudal man did not consider political powers competent to declare war; a higher cause, manifested in cosmic occurrences (swarms of shooting stars, solar eclipses, comets), orders and controls events.[80] Lords receive their power from God, the

Pope is the delegate of Christ. From a modern point of view, almost all of medieval epic would have to be called religious, with the exception of Gottfried's *Tristan,* the *Roman de la Rose,* and a few others. The active characters in modern literature are usually carefully delineated as individuals. In medieval works they appear rather as types, with the exception of the Old Icelandic saga figures and in Chaucer, whose character delineation foreshadows the modern novel. In courtly poetry not only are the peasant, the fisherman, and the shepherd typical figures, but so are the knight and the noble lady.[81] The historical Alexander appears as the paragon of knightly virtues. The de-individualization of a historical hero can go so far that the poet hardly finds it important whether particular laudatory deeds in fact belong to some other hero. This is especially the case in the lives of saints.[82] This schematization simplifies systematics insofar as it is based on a classification of the active characters. To differentiate such modal operators as negative fact, negative possibility, and negative probability, it must be noted that particularly Celtic literature is characterized by unbounded fantasy.[83] Germanic poetry is more reserved in this regard; only in such popular genres as the minstrel epic or later Nordic *lygisögur* does rational control notably diminish. The lying song, still well known in folklore, which goes back to the classical period by way of the *Modus Florum* (eleventh century), however, recognizes the *ratio* in that its surrealism sets itself against it. We must remember, by the way, that for the medieval person the saying "Everything is possible to God" still had absolute validity. Here we encounter the unavoidable time-limitation of many criteria; after positivism had rejected everything that could not be explained by calling it impossible, modern science tends to tolerate many inexplicable phenomena as possibly *not yet* explicable.

Having briefly searched out the time-bound features of some immanent aspects of medieval literary texts, we wish to include in our considerations several nontextual features. While in our age the producer of a literary work only seldom keeps his name secret, and in such cases at least formally follows the general custom of signing a pseudonym, in the Middle Ages the anonymity of the poet is a generic trait for the minstrel epic, the heroic epic, and the Old Norse sagas, quite in contrast to the courtly epic. This fits in with the sort of reference to sources which is equally anonymous in the former genres but in the latter names authors (Wolfram von Eschenbach's Kyot, Gottfried von Strassburg's Thomas von Britanje). This has to do with the individual's withdrawal in favor of the society. Autobiography is possible only when it is exemplary and encourages the Christian life, on the pattern of Augustine's *Confessions*. Even when the name is known, for the most part we know very little about the poet. This is caused by their usual median social standing. "It was not the nobles who wrote romances, but more frequently their clerks or other minor figures, as in the case of Chrétien."[84] The great Middle High German epic writers around 1200 all belonged to the minor nobility or the bourgeoisie, the poets of the heroic epics to the clerical estate (probably on the lower level). The great Heidelberg song manuscript, arranged according to the poets' standing, leads from the emperor Henry VI to the bourgeois Hadloub. Kuhn rejects the popular sociology according to which the minstrel epic and *Spruch* literature were composed by wandering poets; nevertheless, many questions remain unanswered. The term coined by Kuhn, "literary profession" [Literatenberuf], probably best suits the period after about 1220.[85] The title became common only in the early Renaissance; Dante, Boccaccio, and Chaucer were barely concerned with this problem. The class to which the poets belonged is sometimes used by scholars as a genre criterion. Thus Hermann Schneider distinguishes among "heroic poetry, clerical poetry, knightly poetry" [Heldendichtung, Geistlichendichtung, Ritterdichtung]. In the meantime, however, it has become clear that heroic literature was composed in the main by clerics.

The poet's intention during the classical period was, according to Horace, "aut prodesse volunt aut delectare poetae." And the best poets were able to combine both aims—"omne punctum tulit qui miscuit utile dulci." For the Middle Ages, too, we may take our point of departure from this widely read author of the *Ars Poetica*. But what is meant by *prodesse*? Our first thought must be the spiritual welfare of the reader or listener. A mirror is held up to the knight wherein he is meant to see the exemplary ideal image of the Christian knight. But a further kind of *prodesse* must be kept in mind: the medieval writer is convinced that his works can serve as a remedy for the "accidentia seu motus animi," that they have a psychotherapeutic effect.[86] The struggle against pain and boredom, which might easily damage the animal and human psyche, appears in this context as an absolutely respectable poetic motivation. Along with this claim of the general weal, a narrowing of vision occurs in the political *sirventes* and *Spruch* literature; the welfare of the bread-giver takes the place of the ethical and physical improvements of mankind.

It is questionable whether the medieval poet was usually able to determine his own goals.

This question brings us to the social situation in which the literature is created. Sometimes a school assignment came out so well that it could claim a place in literature.[87] The literary feuds between contemporary poets are often fought under the banner of the struggle for existence.[88] The transformation of generally moralizing forms, such as *Spruch* literature and beast epics, into the political, often satirical debates can only take place by commission, or at least under the protection, of a powerful lord. In the German struggle for the Reich, Walther von der Vogelweide must of necessity place his genius in the service of whoever happened to be his employer. The author of the famous Middle Dutch epic *Van den Vos Reinaerde,* Willem van Baudeloo (a Flemish monk commissioned by the count to conduct some realty business), stands in a dependent position at the center of the political battle for Flanders. Major epics may, probably with consideration of the patron, show a political bent; Lohengrin is one example.[89] Kuhn has pointed out that additions to the core of Middle High German epics were partly made by poets working in the service of great courts.[90] The employer often determines not only the matter and the attitude but also the form. French writers make their noble patrons responsible for the selection of prose.[91] During the waning Middle Ages "urban literature" is "actually carried on by the educated middle class (communal officials, academic professions, occasionally also artisans) and the monastic establishments socially compatible with this stratum in fifteenth-century cities."[92] Only then can we legitimately speak of real independence for most literati. Modern authors, it may be noted, have hardly more freedom in the face of their patrons, whose demands are dictated not by personal taste but by marketing considerations. "The typical contemporary author is no longer the individualist writer, creating for himself, but the media supplier, whose job it is to furnish precisely defined commissioned work for press, radio, and television."[93] The market is not the only reason the writer takes the public into consideration. An author needs his public as well. Creation from an inner impulse, Goethe's "writing something out of one's soul," presupposes communication in order to be effective. Thus, consciously or unconsciously, the writer counts on the expectations of his listeners or readers. If he sets himself against the peasants who have grown rich but are not civilized, he can count on approval from the impoverished aristocracy. This satiric theme becomes widespread in France and Germany in the thirteenth century as a direct reflection of the social developments of the day.[94]

The countertendency is not long in coming. In the Neidhart plays (fourteenth and fifteenth centuries) the Neidhart figure becomes the target of scorn on the part of the peasants. In the Künzelsau Corpus Christi play the provincial listeners are urged "opfer und zehent reht zu geben"—this clearly in the interest of the clerical patron. Conversely, in the Frankfurt play there is evidence of open aggression against the Jews, who held an important position in the financial commerce of that market city. Völker correctly explains this difference by the historically provable difference of the intended audience in each case.[95]

Not everything in the medieval work of art, however, relates to the audience. Though the often extensive and encoded number symbolism, for example, could not be grasped by the listener, that fact does not negate its deliberate use. A. Wolf properly points out that "medieval cathedrals were also built to be looked at; nevertheless many aspects of them were in no case visible to the visitor of the day."[96] The poet's intention encompasses sometimes more, sometimes less than the actual function of his work in society. His work can have unintended effects; the intended effects can get lost or they can be much stronger than the poet foresaw. Thomasîn von Zirclaere accuses Walther von der Vogelweide of having seduced thousands into ignoring God's and the Pope's laws; the "wîse man" should cultivate the virtue of *mâze*.[97] The effect is directly dependent on the reception; the position within the tradition of the individual work and the oeuvre of any author therefore generally furnish a good indication of the effect produced. But here too intention and effect cannot be equated. The writer can compose a work out of his political motivation which contains great qualities as entertainment and especially from that aspect can find wide distribution and gain a large audience. The powerful expansive pressure of French courtly culture is the cause of a great demand for translations of romances into the other Romance and into the Germanic languages. The translators, however, take such liberties with their originals that we are usually justified in calling the results new creations.[98] The writer's omissions and interpolations throw a bright light on his central idea and his aesthetic attitudes. Sometimes he selects a new form; thus the *Roman de la Rose,* originally written in rhyming couplets, when translated into Italian was made up of 232 sonnets. The authors of the heroic sagas may derive from older, lost versions the flowing oral tradition in Bowra's sense.[99]

Between the author and his public stands the performance as the channel of communication. Oral delivery within the group is the rule for lyrics; even epics were not read privately until the late Middle Ages. The connection with other arts, such as music and dance, played a much larger role than it does today. Lyrics without music did not exist; the heroic epic was sung—that is, recited according to a simply structured, constantly repeated melody. We must not be led astray by the term "reading"; the *lectiones* during Mass are to this day not read out in a speaking voice but recited in prescribed tones, depending on the nature of the feast. The division of epics into cantos is not a metaphor but a reminder of their melodic performance. The accents in Otfrid's gospel harmony were established not to make the *quadrata equalitas sancta* of the verse conspicuous but to facilitate recitation.[100] That many lays are transmitted without music does not deny their melodic recitation; music manuscripts were very expensive, which is also why many minnesongs were handed down without musical notation.[101] Only in the later period do we find references to the reading of lays, though they were also sung.[102] Many lyrical genres—such as rondeaux, virelais, and ballads—were songs for round dances, to which the dancing community sang the refrain.[103] The connection between text and music is particularly close because as a rule the poet himself created the melody to his words (or the other way around), although this is not the case with the *Ezzolied*.

Pilgrims' songs and Crusade songs are, as far as we know, the principal forms of religious communal singing. This relationship with other arts sharply distinguishes the presentation of medieval literature from modern presentation; today lyrics and narratives are normally read only individually. In the religious dramas the Latin texts were also sung; stage directions clearly point to this form of recitation.[104] There were no closet dramas in the Middle Ages—just as this art form never achieved more than minor significance. (It is difficult to decide whether text or melody dominated in the medieval dance-song.)

The time used for recitation is often crucial in determining the length of a medieval epic. At the end of the *Skídaríma* the poet promises another ballad for the following Sunday. The *Skídaríma* contains two hundred ballad stanzas of four verses each.[105] A young Icelander tells the saga of King Harald at his Norwegian court in twelve evenings.[106] Beowulf "could easily have been delivered in three sittings."[107] Practical necessity can lead to the formation of cycles; the three mid-Cornish *Ordinalia* (mystery plays) were intended for performance on three consecutive evenings. In the Middle Ages the referential dichotomy of fiction-nonfiction did not depend on the content but on the form. While today we consider all historical and autobiographical literature as nonfiction, in the Middle Ages a work was considered fiction or nonfiction depending on form.[108] Prose is considered true, while verse indicates invention, as both author and audience agree. Hieronymus was among the first to equate the art of poetry with lying.[109] Truth is handed down in unrhymed form, lies in verse.[110] Nicolas de Senlis puts it bluntly: "Nus contes rimes n'est verais."[111] Around 1190 Henry the Lion ordered his *capellan* to write the *Luzidarius* in prose, for the sake of "truth."[112] The Icelandic prose sagas pretend to relate actual events; the fiction of the ballad, on the other hand, is immediately apparent to every listener. This formal assignment of the nature of fiction—so peculiar to modern readers—is explained by the excessive significance given to form in all medieval poetics and philosophy, as has become clear from other criteria as well.

It is questionable, however, whether the modern distinction between fiction and nonfiction is adequate here. The poet is always free to alter historical data according to need. In the *Kaiserchronik* the Roman emperors and the German emperors since Charlemagne are each said to rule for 409 years, to establish a parallel to the assumed equilibrium between the Old and the New Testament. The number of Roman emperors is reduced to thirty-two because of the eighteen German emperors.[113] But it is by no means the poet's intention to produce "fiction." He sacrifices historical truth, which to him is nothing but appearance, to penetrate to a deeper truth—the divine arrangement of the world. The lives of emperors must be exemplary, which is why good emperors die a peaceful death, while evil ones come to a terrible end, varying according to their degree of badness.[114] What matters is not the individual, but the function of his status or type within the society. For the same reason the lives of the saints were largely schematized. This, too, is probably connected with the peculiar monologue structure of conversation in clerical drama and the so-called debates.[115] Here the characters barely address each other; rather, they take turns declaring the point of view of their station in life. Celtic and Old Norse narrative, conversely, are marked by rich and lively dialogue.[116] The role typology of the fourteenth century at times degenerated into grotesquely hyperbolical, surrealist representation, for example, in the depiction of the peasant in Wittenwiler's "Ring."[117]

As a final criterion we will briefly discuss the evaluation of literary texts. Not until the New Criticism has this aspect been openly included in literary scholarship. Maatje differentiates between evaluation according to the personal value system of the reader or critic and judgment from the theoretical model. The latter is constant and transferable, can be formulated precisely, and is conscious, simple, predictive, and logical.[118] The concept of constancy stands in opposition to the individual value system, which is differentiated according to the person and the situation. It is impossible to have constancy across times and places; therefore D.W. Fokkema demands "various 'literature tests' based on the various literary value systems that prevail or coexist in different places and at different times."[119] In principle, for the Middle Ages the degree of conformity with the prevailing norms could also result in a value criterion; a negative judgment from the Marxist sociocritical standpoint, however, was given a positive evaluation in the contemporary value system. The evaluation of feudal ideology is therefore seen by Kuhn as "dogmatic falsification."[120] But as a value-free trait, the degree of progressivity could serve very well as a genre trait. In the course of scholarship a fairly generally accepted evaluation of medieval works has formed. Kuhn attempts, not very convincingly, to honorably salvage the minnesong after Walther.[121] It is not by accident that the "rediscovery" of Heinrich Wittenwiler and Oswald von Wolkenstein singles out two poets who were always considered very significant, if until now in the framework of their time.[122] Expressions of personal feelings did not count for much in classical times and during the Middle Ages; Catullus's *Lesbia* songs are only *nugae,* and Plutarch did not ascribe much significance to his own *rime.* The temporal and cultural distance is especially significant for those genres that have since died out, such as the biblical epic and didactic verse. The latter is "far removed from our understanding, it may appear even stranger to us than biblical epic, so that we are unsure of ourselves in judging and evaluating works of this genre."[123]

In conclusion, let us add a few remarks on genre terminology. Fixed names for the genres, defined as masses of abstracted features, are necessary and possible from the point of view of modern scholarship. "The notion of 'features' and in logic the notion of property are defined precisely in set theory as the *name* of a class, viz. the class of the objects sharing that property."[124] It is desirable to use the traditional designations as genre names as far as possible; to do so, the tradition of manuscripts is important, as are the research practices that have accumulated over more than 150 years.[125] Anyone deviating from these must generally be able to prove the advantages of his proposal.[126] The Middle Ages, as is well known, do not recognize an unequivocal genre terminology.[127] Such names as *maere, rede, spel,* and *bispel* lack precision.[128] Only a few appear distinctly limited in the corpus of the handed-down texts, such as *tageliet, (vasnaht)spil, leich.*[129] There are genres, such as the transitional form between fable and *maere,* for which no names have been preserved; for some others all we have is the name, without a single text that appertains to it, such as the *winiliet.*[130] In dealing with medieval book titles, we gain an indication of form and content; there are others that are formed only by the content, and the author, and no longer allow us to recognize form and genre from the outset.[131] The vernacular genre designations are only rarely the etymological outgrowths of the Middle Latin ones, and when they are, a strange displacement of meaning occurs. Corresponding to the half-historical, half-literary Latin *gesta* are the "chansons de geste" as heroic epics and Maerlant's "Alexander's Gheesten" as Middle Dutch courtly romance.[132] Many genres, such as the *fabula,* lose their individual designation and are absorbed in a more encompassing genre, in this case the *bispel.*[133] Besides genre references used in the works themselves, the classifying criteria of manuscript tradition are important for a knowledge of contemporary terminology. Within author and type works, for example, an apparently closed group, such as minne speeches or *schwankmaeren,* can point to a more differentiating genre awareness of the time.[134] In this process unexpected limits may come to light: "The [Neidhart] plays are never listed with lieder and farces but always separately."[135] From the headings we sometimes learn a generic name familiar, if not to the author, at least to the scribe; for example, "aber ein nithart; aber ein ander nithart; ein ander nithart."[136] This generic name is interesting for genre history because it is derived from the name of a poet and thus furnishes us with a *terminus a quo;* equally "ein teichner."[137] A third source is Middle High German special literature; in this group we find tabulations and other writings by the meistersingers, rhetoriqueurs, and rederijkers. However, we must beware of conclusions from these about the "good old days" of the twelfth and thirteenth centuries.

This brings our reflections to a close. A great deal, of course, had to be omitted that is significant for structuring a generative poetics of the Middle Ages. We hope, however, that these considerations have stimulated thinking about the possibilities and modalities of such a specialized genre theory; medieval studies must not wait for generative poetics to dispose over a mature and accepted scheme of features, or even until it has established its general type system. In today's situation of scholarship, collaboration has become more important than innovation.

(Translated by Ruth Hein)

Notes

1. *Lateinisches Mittelalter,* p. 77.
2. *Generative Grammatik und Literaturtheorie,* p. 212.
3. *Numbers and Number Symbolism in Medieval German poetry,* pp. 111–12. Cf. his statement on p. 6; similar examples can be found elsewhere. Cf. Tilo Brandis, *Mittelhochdeutsche, mittelniederdeutsche und mittelniederlaendische Minnereden,* p. 19.
4. W. Erzgraeber, *Moderne englische und amerikanische Literaturkritik,* p. ix.
5. Cf. R. Wellek and A. Warren, *Theory of Literature,* p. 235; W.V. Ruttkowski, *Die literarischen Gattungen,* p. 7.
6. R. Grimminger, *Zu einer Poetik der Typen,* pp. 375–76.
7. C.S. Baldwin, *Medieval Rhetoric and Poetic,* p. vii. Baldwin had earlier written an excellent book on rhetoric, *Ancient Rhetoric and Poetic.*
8. *Literatuurwetenschap* (1970), p. 35. Like Maatje I regret the progressive isolation of medieval and "modern" literary studies. Generative grammar and generative poetics could bridge this separation.
9. Cf. Ruttkowski, *Gattungen,* pp. 137–49.
10. In literary studies as well as in history of music, sociological methods influenced the theory of genres. Cf. W. Arlt, ed., *Gattungen der Musik in Einaeldarstellungen, Gedenkschrift Leo Schrade, Erste Folge,* p. 12.
11. G. Mueller, *Erzaehlzeit und erzaehlte Zeit;* Maatje, *Literatuurwetenschap,* (1974) pp. 133–64, 165–82.
12. *Europaeische Literatur und Lateinisches Mittelalter,* pp. 493–500. Cf. H. Fischer, *Deutsche Literatur und lateinisches Mittelalter,* pp. 1–2.
13. J.A. Huisman, *Neue Wege zur dichterischen und musikalischen Technik Walthers von der Vogelweide;* A.T. Hatto, *On Beauty of Numbers in Wolfram's Dawn Song;* K.H. Schirmer, *Die Strophik Walthers von der Vogel-*

weide; Batts, *Numbers and Number Symbolism in Medieval German Poetry;* H. Eggers, *Symmetrie und Proportion epischen Erzaehlens;* H. Rupp, *Deutsche religioese Dichtungen des 11. und 12. Jahrhunderts;* J. Rathofer, *Der Heliand. Theologischer Sinn als tektonische Form;* W. Haubrichs, *Ordo als Form;* H. de Vries, *Materia mirable.*

14. M. Ittenbach, *Deutsche Dichtungen der salischen Kaiserzeit;* V.G. Hopper, *Medieval Number Symbolism;* F. Tschirch, *Schluesselzahlen;* F. Brunner, *Creatio numerorum, rerum est creatio.*
15. B. Mergell, *Tristan und Isolde;* H. Kuhn, *Minnesangs Wende,* pp. 109–42, distinguishes three types of the German *Leich* parallel to the musical forms: *Estampie, Sequenz,* and *Lai.* Cf. F. Gennrich, *Die musikalischen Formen des mittelalterlichen Liedes,* p. 61.
16. *Gattungsproblem der mittelhochdeutschen Literatur; Zur Typologie muendlicher Sprachdenkmaeler; Versuch einer Literaturtypologie des deutschen 14. Jahrhunderts.*
17. H. Fromm, *Doppelweg,* p. 64.
18. Kuhn, *Minnesangs Wende,* p. 192; *Dichtung und Welt im Mittelalter,* p. 170. Cf. Fromm, *Doppelweg,* p. 65.
19. Koch, op. cit., pp. 16–17.
20. I. Reiffenstein, *Die Erzaehlervorausdeutung in der fruehmittelhochdeutschen Dichtung,* with extensive bibliography.
21. Kreuzer, *Mathematik und Dichtung: Versuche zur Frage einer exakten Literaturwissenschaft;* R. Wisbey, "Ein computerlesbares Textarchiv zur Frage einer exakten Litteraturwissenschaft," *Jahrbuch fuer Internationale Germanstik* 1, no. 2 (1969): 37–46; E. Oksaar, *Stilstatistik und Textanalyse,* p. 632 (cf. n. 9). About the historical development of statistical style analysis cf. R.W. Bailey, *Statistics and Style: A Historical Survey;* the first computer-assisted study on medieval stanzas written by A.H. Touber, *Formschulen und Formtraditionen in der mittelhochdeutschen Lyrik.*
22. *Zur statistischen Theorie der Dichtersprache,* pp. 56–57.
23. Cf. Oksaar, *Stilstatistik,* pp. 645–46.
24. Doležel, *Theorie der Dichtersprache,* pp. 43–44.
25. K. Baumgaertner, *Interpretation und Analyse,* p. 180.
26. *Versuch einer Literaturtypologie des deutschen 14. Jahrhunderts,* p. 267.
27. R. Posner, *Strukturalismus in der Gedichtinterpretation,* p. 225.
28. K. Hauck, *Haus- und Sippengebundene Literatur mittelalterlicher Adelsgeschlechter von Adelssatyren des 11. und 12. Jahrhunderts her erlaeutert,* p. 167.
29. In a publisher's advertisement of the series *Werk und Wirkung* [edited by Henning (1974)] one reads: "The work and its reception is the coordination in a documentary form of the text of the first edition of a literary work with the first-hand signs of its reception by the readers and critics."
30. It can happen that the leading social class becomes degraded in terms of literature. Cf. K. Bertau, *Deutsche Literatur im europaeischen Mittelalter,* 1: 758.
31. Baldwin, *Ancient Rhetoric and Poetic,* p. 145.
32. The meaning of the title of Zolkovskij's article "Die strukturelle Poetik ist eine generative Poetik" (p. 239) mistakes the new stand of generative poetics. One could say in a reversed way, however, that each generative poetics is necessarily structuralistic.

33. Bierwisch, *Poetik und Linguistik;* K. Baumgaertner, *Der methodische Stand einer linguistischen Poetik und Interpretation und Analyse;* M.W. Bloomfield, *Generative Grammatik und Literaturtheorie;* J. Levy, *Generative Poetik;* T.A. van Dijk, *Taal, Tekst, Teken.*
34. R. Posner, *Linguistische Poetik,* p. 513.
35. *Some Aspects of Text Grammars,* p. 165.
36. J. Levy, *Generative Poetik,* p. 559.
37. J. Ihwe, "On the foundation of a general theory of narrative structure," *Poetics* 3 (1972): 6.
38. *Foundations for Typologies of Texts,* pp. 307, 311, 312.
39. Wellek and Warren, *Theory of Literature,* p. 239.
40. *Literatuurwetenschap,* pp. 108–9.
41. H. Borelius, *Die nordischen Literaturen,* p. 4.
42. H.M. Heinrichs, *Satirisch-parodische Zuege in der Prymskvida,* p. 504.
43. *Das methodologische Erbe des Formalismus,* p. 20.
44. *Taal, Tekst, Teken,* p. 18.
45. Cf. G. Eis, *Vom Werden altdeutscher Dichtung,* pp. 7–27. Eis proved that the most important documents were preserved. The situation is much less fortunate as far as earlier times (for example, the Carolingian era) are concerned.
46. Cf. Gabriel Sattler in the second half of the fifteenth century. Cf. J.A. Asher, *Der ueble Gerhart,* p. 421. I should like to express my gratitude to Dr. Lambertus Okken for this reference as well as other advice.
47. The point in question is especially the *Reimpaarform.* Cf. Kuhn, *Versuch einer Literaturtypologie des deutschen 14. Jahrhunderts,* p. 267. Eis criticized the history of German literature (as discussed in *Geschichte der deutschen Literatur,* edited by H. de Boor) because its title speaks about "literature" in general but the book contains nothing about nonfictional literature. This criticism is totally unfounded: nonfictional literature might be the subject matter of textual or linguistic studies; it is definitely not the subject matter of literary studies. (Eis, *Vom Werden altdeutscher Dichtung,* p. 38, n. 10.)
48. About tendencies toward a Middle High German Koine cf. M.M. Guchmann, *Der Weg zur deutschen Nationalsprache,* Part 1, pp. 45–125; for Old Norse, for example, the *Altnordische Sage-Bibliothek,* eds. G. Cederschiöld, H. Gering, and E. Mogk.
49. *Mittelhochdeutsch,* p. 415.
50. About the importance of Old French as court language in the twelfth century and its role as language model cf. K. Voretzsch, *Einfuehrung in das Studium der altfranzoesischen Sprache,* p. 2. About Veldeke's language cf. K. Ruh, *Hoefische Epik des deutschen Mittelalters,* pp. 70–71.
51. Hanns Fischer considers the Ottonic and early Salic literature rather complementary than contrary to the Carolingian literature.
52. *Minnesangs Wende,* p. 174. About rhyme-prose and the "cursus" cf. Langosch, *Lateinisches Mittelalter,* pp. 63–65.
53. W. Besch, *Vers oder Prosa?,* p. 766.
54. E. Vance, *Notes on the Development of Fomulaic Language in Romanesque Poetry,* p. 431.
55. *Lateinisches Mittelalter,* p. 73. Walther von der Vogelweide, however, speaks of "drier slahte sanc, den hôhen niederen und den mittelswane." In case of sermon Augustinus distinguishes three kinds of style, the *genus submissus* (or tenue), the *genus temperatum* (or medium), and the *genus grande.*

(Baldwin, *Medieval Rhetoric and Poetic*, p. 68.) For the Middle Ages in general, it can be said that it was rather distinguished between three parts according to subject matter. Galfredus de Vinosalvo once stated about it: "Quando enim de grandis personis vel rebus tractatur, tunc est stylus grandiloquus; quando de humilibus, humilis; quando de mediocribus, mediocris." (H. Sparnaay, "Zu Walthers 'drîer slahte sanc,'" in *Zur Sprache und Literatur des Mittelalters*, p. 264.

56. Trad., *Skidis Traumfahrt*, p. 53.
57. *Considérations sur le fabliau*, p. 1053.
58. The movement to the West took place via church poetry (Syrian hymns). Cf. R. Wisniewsky, *Significatio des Verses*, p. 694.
59. Jodogne, *Considérations*, p. 1053.
60. W.P. Lehmann, *The Old Germanic Verse Form*, p. 24. In England the ballad became popular in the "Barren Age" (fifteenth century).
61. S. Beyschlag, *Walther von der Vogelweide*, p. 744.
62. Kuhn, *Versuch einer Literaturtypologie des deutschen 14. Jahrhunderts*, p. 266.
63. Meissner, *Skidis Traumfahrt*, p. 52.
64. T. Zagrodzki, *Plans des villes créés au moyen âge*, p. 459.
65. *Vorstudien zum Aufbau von Priester Arnold "Lodlied auf den heiligen Geist" ("Siebenzahl")*, p. 322.
66. H. Meyer, *Die allegorische Deutung der Zahlenkomposition des Psalters*, p. 212.
67. For example, Spenser's hint in stanza 340 of his *Faerie Queene:* "Right in the middest of that Paradise." (M.P. Baybak, *Placement "In the Middest" in the Faerie Queene*, p. 228.)
68. "Yet among students of English literature there seems to be a definite 'set' against such investigations, a set, incidentally, that is visible, but much less so, on the Continent." (A.K. Hieatt, *"The bird with four feathers": Numerical Analysis of the Fourteenth-Century Poem*, p. 18.)
69. J.A. Huisman, "Gewollte und gewachsene Struktur in der mittelhochdeutschen Dichtung," *Zeitschrift fuer duetsche Philologie* (Sonderheft) 90 (1971): 68, 75–80.
70. Reference of Mr. D.W. Kinebanian in Amsterdam.
71. Cf. Fromm, *Doppelweg*, p. 64.
72. Baldwin, *Medieval Rhetoric and Poetic*, p. 265. The same technique can be found in Vergil. "He reduces the mating of Aeneas with Dido to a grave summary, in order to give salience to those other emotions which for the *Aeneid* as a whole were leading." (Baldwin, *Ancient Rhetoric and Poetic*, pp. 200–201.)
73. For example, in *"The bird with four feathers"* (A.K. Hieatt, p. 27).
74. Kuhn, *Versuch einer Literaturtypologie des deutschen 14. Jahrhunderts*, p. 266.
75. J.R. Smeets, *La "Bible" de Jehan et Ovide le Grant*.
76. Cf. J.A. Goris, *Passio Francorum secundum Flemingos*. Dietse Warande en Belfort 26 (1926), pp. 681–88.
77. H. Fischer, *Deutsche Literatur und lateinisches Mittelalter*, p. 17.
78. W.J. Schroeder, *Spielmannsepik*, p. 13.
79. Baldwin, *Ancient Rhetoric and Poetic*, pp. 199–200; *Medieval Rhetoric and Poetic*, p. 278, 147.

80. P. Rousset, *Un problème de méthodologie: l'événement et sa perception*, p. 315.
81. The most extreme typology of characters can be found in primitive forms of comedy in the Middle Ages. Cf. Baldwin, *Ancient Rhetoric and Poetic*, p. 188.
82. R.S. Farrar, "Structure and Function in Representative Old English Saints' Lives," *Neophilologus* 57 (1973): 89.
83. Van Dijk, "Foundations for Typologies of Texts," *Semiotica* 6 (1972): 318.
84. E. Vance, "Notes on the Development of Formulaic Language in Romanesque Poetry," in Pierre Gallais and Yves-Jean Riou, eds., *Mélanges offerts à René Crozet a l'occasion de son soixante-dixième anniversaire*, 1: 431.
85. *Minnesangs Wende*, pp. 187, 179.
86. Eis, *Vom Werden altdeutscher Dichtung*, pp. 76–93.
87. For example the *Waltharius*. Quintilian lists under preliminary studies in composition retelling of fables and paraphrase of poetry. (Baldwin, *Ancient Rhetoric and Poetic*, p. 63.)
88. The cause of the literary argument between Walther von der Vogelweide and Reinmar von Hagenau was the position of a court poet at the Viennese court.
89. H. Thomas, "Der Lohengrin, eine politische Dichtung zur Zeit Ludwigs des Bayern," *Rheinische Vierteljahrsblaetter* 37 (1973).
90. Cyclical court epics seems to be the literature at the courts of sovereigns. Cf. Kuhn, *Minnesangs Wende*, p. 176.
91. H. Herkommer, *Ueberlieferungsgeschichte der Saechsischen Weltchronik*, p. 221.
92. P.G. Voelker, *Ueberlegungen zur Geschichte des geistlichen Spiels im Mittelalter*, p. 256.
93. Kulturbrief Inter Nationaes, D. 6.
94. "Le thème du villain enrichi, qui reste puant et sans manières ... se repand dans la litterature chevaleresque au XIIIe siècle." (E. Vance, *Notes on the Development of Formulaic Language in Romanesque Poetry*, p. 433.) At the same time the so-called Neidhart-literature originated in Germany, first in poetry and later in dialogue and in plays. In the Fabliaux not only is the farmer the laughingstock but sometimes also the citizen.
95. *Uberlegungen*, p. 273.
96. *Strophisches, abschnitthaftes und fortlaufendes Erzaehlen in frueher deutscher Epik des Mittelalters*, p. 520.
97. Cf. K.K. Klein, *Zum dichterischen Spaetwerk Walthers von der Vogelweide*, p. 549.
98. "Translation" is defined here as its own special literary genre and not just as linguistic transformation from one language into another one. (J. Levy, *Die literarische Uebersetzung. Theorie einer Kunstgattung.*) This "free" approach of the medieval translators of novels has had some impact on the writers of the time. The interest in literature of "originals," however, led to the neglect for example of the extensive body of Scandinavian *riddarasögur*.
99. M. Bowra, *Heroic Poetry*.
100. R. Wisniewski, "Significatio des Verses," in *Backes* (1972), p. 700.
101. I. Glier, *Der Minneleich im spaeten 13. Jahrhundert*, p. 162.
102. Ulrich von Lichtenstein: "der leich vil guot ze singen was, manc schoeniu vrouwe in gerne las." (Ibid., p. 164.)
103. F. Gennrich, *Die musikalischen Formen des mittelalterlichen Liedes*, p. 69.

104. R. Bergmann, *Studien zu Entstehung und Geschichte der deutschen Passionsspiele des 13. und 14. Jahrhunderts*, p. 25.
105. Meissner, *Skidis Traumfahrt*, 1922.
106. F. Ranke, *Altnordisches Elementarbuch*, pp. 80–83.
107. M. Deanesly, *The Pre-Conquest Church in England*, p. 264.
108. Cf. the scheme of Van Dijk, *Foundations for Typologies of Texts*, p. 319.
109. Herkommer, *Saechsischen Weltchronik*, p. 216.
110. W. Besch, *Vers oder Prosa?*, p. 753.
111. Herkommer, *Saechsischen Weltchronik*, p. 221.
112. Kuhn, *Versuch einer Literaturtypologie*, p. 276.
113. F. Urbanek, "Herrscherzahl und Regierungszeiten in der Kaiserchronik," *Euphorion* 66 (1972): 220.
114. E.F. Ohly, *Sage und Legende in der Kaiserchronik*, p. 19.
115. Voelker, *Uberlegungen*, p. 253.
116. There exists a striking correspondence between the dialogue in the sagas and in the Mabinogion. (Buber, *Die vier Zweige des Mabinogi*.)
117. Kuhn, *Versuch einer Literaturtypologie*, p. 268; P.B. Wessels, "Wittenwilers 'Ring' als Groteske," *Wirkendes Wort* 10 (1961).
118. *Literatuurwetenschap*, pp. 6–9.
119. "The problem of generalization and the procedure of literary evaluation," *Neophilologus* 58 (1974): 269.
120. Kuhn, *Versuch einer Literaturtypologie*, p. 268.
121. *Minnesangs Wende*, pp. 194–96.
122. Jones, (1971), p. 8.
123. H. Rupp, *Zum "Renner" Hugos von Trinberg*, p. 233.
124. Van Dijk, *Some Aspects of Text Grammars*, pp. 95–96.
125. Cf. K. Düwel, "Werkbezeichnungen der mittelhochdeutschen Erzaehlliteratur" (Ph.D. diss., Goettingen, 1965).
126. Though the genres of *Spruch* and *Lied* are getting closer to each other over the centuries there is no question about basic differences. Cf. S. Beyschlag, *Formverwandlung in Walthers Spruchdichtung*, p. 744.
127. Kuhn, *Versuch einer Literaturtypologie*, p. 263.
128. K. Grubmueller, *Deutsche Tierschwaenke im 13. Jahrhundert*, p. 100.
129. Glier, *Der Minneleich im spaeten 13. Jahrhundert*, p. 161.
130. Grubmueller, *Deutsche Tierschwaenke*, p. 101; cf. H. Mayer, "Ein unbekannter Beleg fuer 'Winilieth,'" *Neophilologus* 58 (1974).
131. P. Lehmann, *Mittelalterliche Buechertitel*, p. 5.
132. H. Grundmann, *Geschichtsschreibung im Mittelalter*, p. 39.
133. About the "bispel" cf. U. Schwab, *Inedita aus dem Leonebuch*, p. 278, n. 26.
134. Kuhn, *Versuch einer Literaturtypologie*, p. 265.
135. D. Boueke, *Materialien zur Neidhart-Ueberlieferung*, p. 2.
136. Ibid., p. 30.
137. E. Laemmert, *Reimsprecherkunst im Spaetmittelalter. Eine Untersuchung der Teichnerreden*.

Bruce A. Rosenberg

THE GENRES OF ORAL NARRATIVE

The shift in emphasis in the way we value and study man probably made inevitable the new attitude of many American folklorists toward their subject. This shift has in some instances been gradual, in others dramatic; in nearly all cases it has involved an appreciation of the unique and the distinctive in human existence, and a concern with the individual. We are currently less interested in laws, rules, and precepts than we are with each singular being, less now with *langue* than with *parole*.

In each of several disciplines this shifted perspective has assumed a varied form. Philosophy has felt the incursions of Existential thought, which William Barrett claims "seeks to bring the whole man—the concrete individual in the whole context of his everyday life, and in his total mystery and questionableness—into philosophy." In the writings of the so-called Existential theologians, philosophers, and writers—Kierkegaard, Unamuno, Marcel, Jaspers, Buber, and Tillich, amongst others—religious faith has been "recast in relation to the individual. Each has put religion itself radically in question." The center of this new faith "is the unique experience of the single one, the individual...."[1]

Existentialism's concern for the uniqueness of experience has led to an analogous movement in psychology, of which Rollo May is the most famous partisan. Sympathetic orientations are also to be found in "Client-Centered Therapy," and in those neo-Freudians who allow the patient to define his problem, regardless of the therapist's preconceptions and diagnoses. In anthropology this emphasis has been described by Clifford Geertz in *The Interpretation of Cultures*:

> Becoming human is becoming individual, and we become individual under the guidance of cultural patterns, historically created systems of meaning in terms of which we give form, order, point, and direction to our lives. And the cultural patterns involved are not general but specific—not just "marriage" but a particular set of notions about what men and women are like, how spouses should treat one another, or who should properly marry whom; not just "religion" but belief in the wheel of karma, the observance of a month of fasting, or the practice of cattle sacrifice. Man is to be defined neither by his innate capacities alone, as the Enlightenment sought to do, nor by his actual behaviors alone, as much of contemporary social science seeks to do, but rather by the link between them . . . , his generic potentialities focused into his specific performances.[2]

This attitude is also reflected in the law of our land which, by ruling that former privileges are inalienable rights, protects the status of the individual within the society to which he contributes nothing and who may actually be seditious.[3]

The work on the Serbo-Croatian heroic singers by Milman Parry and Albert Lord in the 1930s moved the focus of our attention from the psychology of the audience to the dynamics of the performer, hence reducing our interest in the singer's tradition by heightening our consciousness of the individual's talent. Parry and Lord tried thereby to reconstruct the compositional process of the Homeric epics, and however successful they were in that ambition, they did more successfully examine that unique communication between the performer and his audience in the folklorist event.

During the past several years nearly all humanists have shown an intense fascination in the unusual man and have exalted the nonconformist; folklorists, caught in this broad and swiftly moving current, have become deeply involved in performance-centered dynamics. Genre, given this bias, is no longer conceived as a preexistent frame to which the performer seeks to shape his communication; rather, it is a creation of the moment, culturally learned to some extent, but strongly influenced by such occasional phenomena as time, location, the composite personalities of the audience and their mood, and the social reasons for the occasion. These conditions, always in flux, bring about genre during the folklore transaction, and will obtain as long as the participants, in relatively stable circumstances, continue to find them meaningful.

Seen in this way, tradition is merely one of many shaping forces, more stable than many of the others, but nevertheless swayed by them. The process is no stranger to students of literature: they know how Sidney imitated Petrarch's sonnet form, how Shakespeare modified its structure for his own purpose, how Milton—and following him Wordsworth—further altered it to fit newer expressions, and how it has now all but disappeared as a current communicative mode. Though the form of octet (stating the conditional clause) and the sestet (stating the conclusion or response) had value for Shakespeare, he did not feel inviolably bound by it, nor was he constrained from experimenting with three quatrains and an Alexandrine. And the creator of *Paradise Lost* chose to break down the sonnet's internal modules in seeking directness and cogency in a form which he still called sonnet. In each of these instances the traditional form of the genre was a "given," but only one of several givens in the composition of the sonnet. Anthropologist Gregory Bateson sees traditions in culture the same way, as part of the given facts of a society, as premises which influence but do not determine cultural structures.[4]

History, then, is not all bunk, but only as much as we want it to be.

A little more than a decade ago Alan Dundes complained that folklore, nearly alone among academic disciplines, lacked a theoretical base and even a definition: "The problem ... of defining folklore boils down to the task of defining exhaustively all the forms of folklore."[5] But that was in another time; under the new dispensation such a statement could hardly be made, at least not in that form and for such ends. Just four years later Roger Abrahams had reversed this strategy by making genre a means rather than an end: "Perceptions of genre are of greatest importance in understanding the ceremonial communicative interactions of small groups."[6] So genres are with us still, though they are now seen as more amenable to occasion, and as one of several means to be examined in our exploration of the traditional communicative process.

The communicative process has become as important as the transmission. We may take E.D. Hirsch's observation on genre theory to have validity in an interpretation of oral genres as well as written: the type (intrinsic genre) is that sense of the whole by which we may understand all of the parts.[7] Such an understanding must be shared by the performer as well as his audience before the "sense of the whole" can materialize. Genre, revealed through language, gesture, circumstances, and so on, properly evokes certain assumptions in the audience and the performer: their receptive capacity prepares them for the medium and the message, his creative potential guides his performance.

Let me take for an example that most inelegant of oral genres, the "traveling salesman's joke." When we hear just the first few words, "let me tell you the one about the traveling salesman . . . ," or even the first six words of that formulaic entrance, we already know, if we are actually going to hear what Hirsch has termed an "intrinsic genre," much of what is to come. We anticipate, for instance, the number of the dramatis personae: three. We know who they are: the salesman, a farmer, and his daughter. We know a little about their characters, at least as much as is relevant to the story: the salesman is a clever, relatively sophisticated urbanite who is contemptuous of the old farmer and who lusts after his voluptuous daughter; the old man is very conservative of his daughter's putative chastity and mistrustful of the stranger's intentions, while she is equally intent on sharing the attractive stranger's bed. We know the situation, too: it is near dusk in the remote countryside, the salesman is out of gas or for other reasons is forced to spend the night where he is, and the farmer offers—or is asked for—hospitality. The story, the joke, is realized because the salesman's slyness and craft overcome the farmer's obstacles to his girl's seduction, while she, often a naive though seldom innocent Jezebel of the backwoods, is a lustfully willing partner in the stranger's plans.

This genre of joke well demonstrates our expectations about certain indigenous "types," but it is not so well suited to our understanding of other, and more complex, oral genres. For one thing, "salesmen" jokes cross nearly all American social and economic boundaries, and are part of the tradition of us all. A problem would arise as soon as we tried to apply our understanding of particularly American genres to the oral types of other cultures. Certainly one of the major difficulties in defining folk genres has been the folklorist's preconceptions about types. Dan Ben-Amos has termed these types, which are the categorizations of anthropologists, "analytical."[8] But the people themselves from whom lore is collected, he notes, often do not classify their own traditions as do academics, making generalizations and theorizing about such taxonomies worthless. As long ago as 1943 William Bascom found, in his work among the Yorubas, that the essential taxonomic criterion was whether the accounts were believed or not. And the same persistence of natives to select their own generic categories—usually at odds with those of the folklorists—has been found right to the present.[9]

Ben-Amos, in establishing principles which few American folklorists have challenged, would classify genres according to the category of the folk: "ethnic genres." The argument for doing so is persuasive. Since the form of the types depends on the exigencies of cultural expression, they can be usefully understood only from the perspective of the culture which created them. To understand genre, then, we must know why they came about and under what conditions they were perpetrated. Native, or ethnic, categories have qualitative and subjective principles of organization.[10] They reflect the situation of the performance, social propriety, form, the speaker, and his audience.

To come to terms with ethnic genres, Ben-Amos proposes three new categories by which to define a native taxonomy. "Prosody" concerns the language of the performance, what literary critics would call "style," what Ben-Amos thinks of as "sounds uttered in time." Theme, or thematic considerations, encompass those of the actors, their actions, and the metaphors of performance. "Behavioral attributes" concern the social circumstances and "composition" of the communicative event.

Oral genres, as we said, are being seen less as preexistent forms which guide the shape of each subsequent performance than as means which are useful in the expression of the performance's message. Abrahams has argued for a generic taxonomy in terms of the audience's (or listener's) involvement, a spectrum ranging from "Total Interpersonal Involvement" to "Total Removal."[11] James Joyce articulated a similar conception in the later chapters of *Portrait of the Artist as a Young Man*. But for Abrahams as for Ben-Amos, the genre is determined by setting, time, place, and purpose. Context is most important; it determines how the participants in the traditional performance will interpret the performer's actions, whether, that is, they will understand the genre intrinsically or extrinsically. And they will consequently know how to respond.

On the basis of these clues, one can begin to formulate "notes toward a definition" of those two popular (analytical) genres, the legend and the folktale. The latter has more fixed conventions, perhaps beginning with "once upon a time," and concluding with some such formula as "they all lived happily ever after." Intermediary conventions include most, if not all, of those "Epic Laws" described by Axel Olrik: the law of two to a scene, the law of contrast, that of twins, of beginnings and endings, and so on. The legend will not have these conventions necessarily—in fact it may have few prosodic conventions at all, which may be the cause for its relative shapelessness as "narrative."

Max Lüthi has recently written on the psychology of the *Märchen* (the folktale), pointing out its course of the hero's maturation and growth, the repeated theme of parental struggle, and in general the restraining bonds of childhood and adolescence, and the search for the "core of the true personality."[12] We might add that the villainy or lack with which Märchen begin, the central quest to the outer world and the struggle with hostile forces, and the eventual successful and safe return of the hero, often with the establishment of a new family, argue for the recapitulation of common Western life cycles: the search for a family and dynasty of one's own, the quest to make one's way in the world outside of one's immediate family, even for the daily cycle of leaving home to forge one's way in a hostile world, thence to return at night.

The legend has no such thematic pretensions. It is often little more than a belief about a piece of landscape, an event, or an episode in a life. It may not have a beginning, middle, or end. As a belief item the legend may be transmitted informally, as through a chance or offhand remark, which could be possible in the most informal and unstructured of circumstances. One could imagine a legend being transmitted with some such opening as "once upon a time," though that would hardly be necessary and we would not be disappointed if it did not. Probably the very wide variety of contexts in which the transmission of a legend could occur is directly related to its formal looseness. Related also to generic formulations are the contexts in which each, legend and folktale, would be recited: the one very casual and occasional, the other more ceremonial.

The epic illustrates several of the problems we face in classifying genres analytically. Our sense of the form comes from Aristotle; but he meant by it something like "the uttered word" and then went on to define the genre with the *Odyssey* and the *Iliad* in mind. Most of the heroic poems which have been recorded in native traditions and which we commonly call "epic" bear little resemblance to Aristotle's description.[13] The Serbo-Croatian songs, closest in space and mood to Homer's narratives, are nevertheless not epics in any valid literary sense. Furthermore, Albert Lord implied that the flexibility with which the Jugoslav *guslars* could alter the story—or even abruptly end it—made generic distinctions difficult.[14] In attempts to classify these heroic songs of the Balkan peninsula, one encounters several of the barriers— quite beyond any of Lord's strictures—on which attempts to classify folklore genres have foundered.

Lord's conclusions in *The Singer of Tales* therefore imply a disappointment: we had hoped to learn about the genre of these fascinating songs of the *guslars*, but we were told instead that their nature was almost necessarily amorphous; that consequently they had no form; and that (with like consequence) they could not be defined generically. In reaching this conclusion, Lord reminded us of several features of the songs' performance which he and Parry had observed in Yugoslavia. All concern the relative freedom of the *guslar:* he does not, as some of the men themselves say, "memorize" the narratives. Nearly all aspects—language, the verbal composition of episodes, even the selection of them—are to some degree improvised. Certainly this is true of those verbal components, Parry's "formulas" (defined as "a group of words regularly employed under the same metrical conditions to express a given essential idea").

But to some extent it was true of episodes as well. The *guslar* is much like the stage performer in that he has immediate contact with his audience, and his dramatic relation to them is symbiotic. If they are bored or restless—either because his singing is ineffective on that occasion or they have had a hard day in the fields—the *guslar* has several options. He can insert episodes ("themes") or certain passages ("runs") which are proven crowd-pleasers, and he can thereby gain his listener's attention. Or he can truncate his performance, either by deleting certain episodes and descriptions, or—in despair—he can bring his narrative to an immediate and abrupt end.

Under these circumstances, when the very form of the narrative is "subject to change without notice," a generic definition—almost necessarily based upon structural considerations—would be impossible.

Or would it? What do we actually find when we abjure this oral theorizing and go to the texts themselves?

All of the songs had been in oral circulation for a number of years. It would have been surprising—indeed astonishing—if they were not subject to many of the same laws which affect, and influence, and even shape other oral narratives. We should be surprised if the observations of Anderson, Olrik, Thompson, and recently of David Fowler, were operative in nearly every part of the world outside the Balkans, but not there.[15] And we should have been surprised if the Serbo-Croatian heroic tradition had not gathered unto itself over the flow of years many of the materials (motifs and tales) which have been recorded in the indexes, as well as the very shape of folktales. Here would be a demonstration of the ability of geography, context, time, and circumstance to mold form.

A look at the text shows that there are no surprises. As a demonstration we should analyze song number 17 in the Parry collection, "The Ragged Border Warrior Wins the Horses," acquired from Salih Ugljanin:

> Bojicic Alija, thirty of his comrades, and thirty maidens, are captured by the Ban of Zadar while harvesting wheat. With the aid of the ragged border warrior, Mujo and Halil rescue them all and punish their Turkish captors. The ragged one then tells them: "I shall find good horses for you . . . such as are not to be found elsewhere in the whole world." All three begin the quest for these superb horses, and at Korman they encounter Nastasija, daughter of the king, who is playing with a golden apple. She helps them get the horses, and with them escapes back to their homeland, where Halil marries the Princess.[16]

Even in this brief summary the core of the folktale—or perhaps of two—emerges quite clearly. Particularly, but without attempting a positive identification at this point, some form of quest seems to be involved, such as found in the Thompson Types of the 465 series (quests to the otherworld for various magical objects) or in Type 530, "The Princes on the Glass Mountain," a story in which the princess is offered to the hero who can take three golden apples from her while she sits atop her glass mountain.[17] The sequence numbered from 460 to 499 is concerned with "Supernatural Tasks." Both salient motifs from these folktales— which are among the most popular, as it happens—the quest for some unusual object in the otherworld, and the maiden who is in some way associated with it, are present in "The Ragged Border Warrior." That this song begins with the rescue of Bojicic, his friends, and the thirty maidens does not alter the pattern or the fact: this episode, which consumes fewer than 250 lines out of 750, may be seen either as preliminary action (in the terms of

Propp's morphology), or as the first Move (the self-contained module) of a two-Move tale. It may even be a motif which the core Tale Type acquired, since we know that the beginning and the end are the most likely places for variations to occur.

However one analyzes this song, it is not formless: the heroes set out to rescue Alija, and end their mission successfully. In the tale's major portion, they set out to capture the wonderful horses of Korman, and in the end they do so. The story has beginning, middle, and end, not only in the Aristotelian sense but in the Proppian. Such a tale is the antithesis of formlessness; and a generic taxonomy cannot be a controversial matter.

A similar pattern informs "The Wedding of Haiduk Gol Alija," Parry's song 11:

> The Sultan desires to marry a princess (Nastasija) who dwells in far-away Korman, and sends a hero to obtain her: Haiduk Gol Alija. With the aid of his sister Fatima, the princess' lady-in-waiting, Alija makes good the abduction, and returns with her to Bosnia. Once there, however, he marries her himself, and as a final insult has his bride-to-be greet the aged Sultan as her father.

This adventure seems to be based on some version of Type 516B, "The Abducted Princess," though there may well be some influence from that more famous sequence of quest-for-a-bride stories in the 301 series (quest for the Princess, or simply the strong man who journeys to the otherworld). As in "The Ragged Border Warrior" the symmetry and balance of "The Wedding" is clear. It is also curiously like the Tristan story: his lord, too, had sent him to secure a bride, and he too takes her for himself—though not so decisively as does Alija. In this view one suspects influence from Type 855, "The Substitute Bridegroom," present in the Serbo-Croatian song as well.

"The Song of Bagdad" appears to be founded on a folktale outside the range of Thompson numbers 300–749, namely "The Disguise of a Woman as a Man to Go as a Soldier," Aarne-Thompson Type 884 (A or B). The core of this heroic song is the ride of Fatima, Alija's betrothed, to Bagdad, where she abducts the Queen. The return to Bosnia is successful and there, after several complications, the lovers are married.

The marriage is gratuitous. The story is "about" war with Bagdad and its successful conclusion because of the daring of the

Bosnian woman disguised as a soldier. Propp's morphological parameters may not apply, but the story is a variant of a known folk narrative nevertheless. Thus, it has a discernible structure, just as does "The Ragged Border Warrior"; and like that sung folktale, it can, consequently, be defined.

Other heroic songs seem to be little more than sung legends, or other single motifs. Such a one is "Marko Kraljevic and Musa the Highwayman" (Parry song 7), one of the minor adventures of the great warrior-prince of the Slavs. To insure free passage on the district's roads, the Sultan frees Marko from prison to fight Musa. Like many another hero, Marko has a special sword forged for his personal use, then with it sets out on his own search-and-destroy mission. Hero and villain fight; but although Musa is slain, Marko is not exultant; rather, he departs for an "icy cave" from which he has not since reappeared. Too short to be a folktale derivative, it is nevertheless of the stuff of oral tradition—probably a legend or *Sage*.

These four narratives are somewhat different in form, and consequently in genre. The folktales—those traditional narratives whose type numbers fall between Aarne-Thompson numbers 300 and 749—begin with a crime or lack, and end when the crime is avenged or the lack is liquidated. This is the traditional pattern of the folktale, as indexed by Aarne and as described later by Vladimir Propp. It is the very antithesis of amorphous structure. Its purpose, its direction, what Kenneth Burke has called its curve, is clear and precise. Propp has shown us how accurately we may define the genre of the folktale: those narratives, whether sung or not, which are morphologically compatible, may be similarly defined.

A similar observation must be made about such heroic songs as "The Song of Bagdad," though it falls outside the formal parameters of the Märchen. The song begins with the familiar counsel of war which resolves to ask Alija to attack the Sultan. Instead it is Fatima who (in disguise) wins the day. Nevertheless, the problem posed at the beginning of the song is resolved at the end—by one hero or another. All the intermediary events conspire toward the tale's conclusion, and with the economy we have come to expect of oral narrative.

So too, finally, with the legend of Marko and his struggles with the highwayman, Musa. The narrative begins with a problem: the roads are blocked. And it ends with a resolution: they are cleared. At least as important is the fate of Marko. He begins in the Sultan's prison, and ends in the "icy cave." His task has been to rid his people of the oppressor; upon killing Musa he finds that his three hearts are entwined with serpents, and recognizing his better, departs. Surely the blending of these three themes, so beautifully balanced and contrasted in their presentation, is anything but formless.

How are these observations to be squared with Parry's and Lord's experience with truncated or abruptly terminated performances? Could we make the same observations about these songs if our *guslar*, seeing his audience hopelessly bored, for instance, had decided abruptly to call it a night? Of course we couldn't, but neither would the resultant performance change our conclusions by so much as a micron.

We have to consider that the *guslar* has a specific story in his mind which in the beginning he is prepared to sing. He will not have memorized the rhetoric, as we know, but he will have prepared the "plot outline" of his song. If he departs from that narrative scheme, surely we have to consider the departure as deviant. We are entitled to make this judgment because if we ask whether subsequent performances would be similarly deviant we are forced to answer "no," or at the very least to say that such deviation would not be the *guslar's* original intention. An analogy is to be found in the oral reading of a written poem: if the poet abridges or in some other way modifies his work at any particular reading, do we not have the "real" poem still in the printed text? And isn't the modification of major narrative functions in a single performance simply the distinctive, atypical, unrepresentative aberration of a basic story? What is the version of "The Song of Bagdad" which Salih Ugljanin would wish to sing to us? Surely it is the version collected by Parry in *Heroic Songs*, and not some stunted version which had been abbreviated to mollify a bored audience.

We are just now able to inquire about the ways in which these songs are altered. Does the *guslar* merely cut down on the length of his descriptive themes or does he eliminate them entirely—either of which would alter the narrative's structure? Or does he delete certain intermediary episodes, but retain the initial and terminal actions so as—again—to keep the story's "curve" intact? Lord was not very detailed in his descriptions of such variants, and only close and detailed examinations will give us a clear idea of what happens when the *guslar* decides that he has had enough for one night.

Rather than writing the final page on the matter of the genre of the oral epic, Lord has only begun the first. His great achievement has put us in a position to ask these first questions. That some of the heroic songs are Thompson-type folktales, that others conform to yet other kinds of known oral narratives, that yet further heroic songs are sung legends should suggest to us that, first of all, when we speak of these songs we are not confronting a single genre at all but a mixed collection; Bynum is right when he insists that epic is a genre of the Balkans before the age of literature, and beyond that understanding it is not safe to trespass. And, second, there is more than enough evidence and incentive to investigate these songs anew in terms of their genres and to understand them in relation to the folk narratives from which they derive.

Are the songs of the *guslars* "autobiographical" in the same very special sense—that of recapitulating several concurrent life cycles—as the folktales from which they derive? We have touched upon the implications of the folktale which Propp's morphology enabled us to see with great clarity. But morphology has other implications as well, namely that man's mind, or at least his imagination as concerns the folktale, is fixed. If Propp has adequately described the folktale, in much the same way that transformational grammarians have described systems of grammar, then man's story-telling capability is in this important respect finite. What does this say about the limits of man's imagination?

Less restricting are the insights of Kenneth Burke, for whom literary form is the psychology of the audience.[18] Form is no more finite than man's capacity to interpret aesthetic information. Few literary critics lend themselves so readily to an understanding of oral genres as well:

> Form is the creation of an appetite in the mind of the auditor, and the adequate satisfying of that appetite. This satisfaction—so complicated is the human mechanism—at times involves a temporary set of frustrations, but in the end these frustrations prove to be simply a more involved kind of satisfaction, and furthermore serve to make the satisfaction of fulfillment more intense.

These observations were formulated to apply to literary narrative genres, so when they are transferred to oral genres some selectivity must be exercised. But the general principles enunciated by

Abrahams and Ben-Amos are implicit in Burke, if we consider that "the psychology of the audience" is another of such "givens" as situation, time, place, and context. In the literary performance it almost goes without saying that time, place, situation, and often even context will vary slightly, certainly less so than in the performance of most oral genres. And few, if any, have cited literature as a demonstration of man's finite capabilities.

In order to explain the evolution and form of oral genres many critics have sought to elucidate their ideas in terms of literary genres and modes. The advantages of comparing the unfamiliar with the known are obvious; one of the most sophisticated and articulate of these is Robert Kellogg's:

> If we grant that a work of written literature really exists only when, through the agency of the inked shapes on the page, a connection is made between the mind of an author and the mind of a reader, and that the work is the reader's experience during those minutes or hours of "intersubjectivity," there is still a constant authorial state of mind behind each such reading "performance." In oral literature such is not the case. As a constant behind each performance is not the mind of an author but an ideal performance, an aspect of the tradition that is shared by performer and audience alike. For this reason the performer in an oral tradition is analogous not to an author but to a skillful reader of written literature. As written work remains in a kind of limbo until a reader picks it up and "performs" it, so an oral work exists as an abstract body of rules and ideas until a performer embodies some of them in a performance.[19]

Yet the comparison between the unread text and the unrecited "ideal performance" is not precise enough. The written text is fixed, it is unvarying, the inked shapes upon a page will never change. Even my own analogy, used above, between an oral reading of a printed text in which the reciter is free to improvise, is imprecise, again because nothing in oral narrative is unvarying. If an "ideal" exists in such performances, it is in the singer's mind (though different members of the audience will have different ideals), from which ideal any number of circumstances may force him to vary.

But what is this "abstract body of rules and ideas" like? Certainly it could not be as precise, specific, and particular as the printed opus, however assiduously unread. Perhaps a more fruitful comparison would be between Kellogg's oral abstractions and

Aristotle's *Poetics*—or some other body of rules and ideas which lies behind each literary genre. And then, how much like the written performance is the oral? How much like the reader of a text—subtle and changing as successive readings may be—is the transmitter of oral lore? Surely the more useful comparison is with an actor in a very intimate theater-in-the-round. The oral performer gestures, uses facial expressions, varies the tone and timbre of his voice, moves his body expressively, and changes the syntax and lexicon of his utterance, probably each time he "performs" a folklore item of a certain length.[20] This is not what happens when one successively reads printed pages.

Kellogg recognized this himself when he wrote that "the appropriate way to read and to judge such works is for the reader to recreate not the state of mind of an author but an ideal oral telling or singing."[21] The oral performer is in large measure an actor for his audience, be it only of one, and that a child. But he is also a creator of sorts—or more accurately a recreator—and while in that sense his role does resemble an author's, the degree of novelty in his creation is much less than that of the literary artist. Jan de Vries said it well when, in a discussion of medieval epic, he contended that "it is an epic of the people in the sense that the subject-matter, the legend, is actually the property of a popular tradition." But the men who have given us the literary versions of these legends—Wolfram, Chrétien, Gottfried, Turoldus, Thomas, and Béroul—"these men had the feeling, even if they had models in front of them, of creating an entirely new work."[22] Turoldus—to use just one example—did not have to be an actor: he did not have to sing well, to be "photogenic," to have a "stage presence"; but the countless mute, inglorious Turolduses who developed the *Chanson de Roland,* who were probably not literary talents of any note, might well have had to sing, and play, for their suppers. It is with this comparison that oral performance and literary experience, oral genres and written, can best be understood.

As I have shown elsewhere, certain kinds of stories demand certain characters and certain kinds of actions.[23] When Beowulf arrives in Hrothgar's court to declare his intention to accomplish what all of Hrothgar's men could not, it is necessary—almost essential—that he be challenged by a resident courtier who evokes from him a statement certifying his heroism. In popular legend it is crucial that our heroes die at the hand of a traitor: like Siegfried, like Roland, like John F. Kennedy at the hands of a C.I.A. plot. It is important that the hero's death be questioned: like Charlemagne, like Christ, like Che Guevara (like Hitler, alive in Argentina!), again, like Kennedy, alive but not so well, on Onassis's island across the seas, like Arthur in Avalon, awaiting the hour of his country's great despair, when he will come again.

Such necessities would describe in part the content of narratives. The configuration of those narrative elements comprises its genre; and that will be determined by the interaction of performer, audience, situation and context, and so on, which have been discussed previously. Behind the oral genre there is a tradition, a community of understandings about the performance which it encompasses. The genre of an oral performance may be said to be this abstraction. It may never be realized; it may not be realizable. It exists not in fixed form, as does the genre of a sonnet, hymn, or elegy, but as a rather fluid ideal because it is dependent on fluid forces which are continually reshaping it: the mood of the audience, that of the performer, and all the accidents, misunderstandings, mistakes, and flaws that human communication is heir to.

When Kellogg tells us that "the primary contribution a study of oral literature can make to the study of literature in general is the breadth of possibility it opens in the consideration of such concepts as authorship, tradition, originality, authorial voice, or persona," we feel that he does not go far enough.[24] We know that the best writing comes out of cultures with thriving oral traditions: Homeric Greece, medieval Iceland, the American South. If we study oral traditions—and I speak here only of oral narratives—we learn something about narrative. The distinction may seem like one so fine that it is hardly worth making. Perhaps; but I make it to remove that condescending suggestion that oral genres are valuable only in the ways in which they help us understand the written. On the contrary, they are valuable in themselves. They are, in fact, primary in that they precede writing. People told stories before they wrote them, and as folklorists can testify, they tell them well. We should not assume that the spoken word is inferior; it too is worth every bit as much of our attention and our appreciation as is the written counterfeit of it.

Notes

1. *Irrational Man* (New York: Doubleday, 1962), pp. 275; 17; 13.
2. New York: Basic Books, 1973, p. 52.
3. See Charles A. Reich, "The New Property," *Yale Law Journal* 73 (1964): 733–87.
4. *Naven* (Berkeley: University of California Press, 1958), p. 24.
5. "Texture, Text and Criticism," *SFQ* 28 (1964): 252.
6. "The Complex Relations of Simple Forms," *Genre* 2 (1968): 104–8.
7. *Validity in Interpretation* (New Haven: Yale University Press, 1967), pp. 68–126.
8. "Analytical Categories and Ethnic Genres," *Genre* 2 (1969): 275–301.
9. "The Relationship of Yoruba Folklore to Divining," *JAF* 56 (1943): 129–30; for a recent example, see Ruth Finnegan, *Limba Stories and Story-Telling* (Oxford: Oxford University Press, 1967), p. 28.
10. Ben-Amos, "Analytical Categories," p. 285.
11. "Complex Relations," pp. 110–19.
12. "Aspects of the Märchen and the Legend," *Genre* 2 (1968): 162–78.
13. See David Bynum, "The Generic Nature of Oral Epic Poetry," *Genre* 2 (1969): 236–58.
14. *The Singer of Tales* (New York: Atheneum, 1965), pp. 99–123.
15. Walter Anderson's so-called Law of Self-Correction, Olrik's "Epik Laws of the *Sage*," Stith Thompson's observations which range over four decades, and Fowler's *A Literary History of the Popular Ballad* (Durham: University of North Carolina Press, 1967) all argue for an inevitable shaping of oral narratives.
16. Milman Parry and Albert B. Lord, eds. and trans., *Serbocroatian Heroic Songs* (Cambridge: Harvard University Press, 1954).
17. I intentionally avoid a specific designation lest the major argument be discredited by attacks on moot particulars.
18. *Counter-Statement* (Berkeley: University of California Press, 1968), p. 31.
19. "Oral Literature," *NLH* 5 (1973): 58.
20. Short genres—the riddle, short songs, superstitions, etc.—are usually memorized, thus reducing "textual" variations.
21. "Oral Literature," p. 63.
22. *Heroic Song and Heroic Legend*, trans. B.J. Timmer (London: Oxford University Press, 1963), pp. 166; 165.
23. "The Necessity of Unferth," *JFI* 6 (1969): 50–60; and in *Custer and the Epic of Defeat* (University Park: Pennsylvania State University Press, 1974).
24. "Oral Literature," p. 66.

Rolf Tarot

STRUCTURE AND RECEPTION

The following reflections are a sequel to some views on literary theory which I published a few years ago under the title "Mimesis and Imitatio."[1] At that time I was concerned with critically discussing the conclusions about genre theory reached by Käte Hamburger's *The Logic of Literature* and with developing a self-validating genre theory on the same theoretical basis.[2] I must begin by outlining the different conclusions because I want to return to my first draft with more precise definitions. My primary topic, however, is not reflections on genre theory but an attempt to elucidate the relationship between the structure of a work and its reception.

Hamburger's *Logic* makes a break with the concept of three genres, the three "natural forms" of literature, which dominated the field of literary genre theory since Goethe. Instead of the trinity of lyric, epic, and dramatic, she postulates two basic categories or basic genres: the fictional or mimetic and the lyrical. They are joined by the "special forms" of the ballad and the first-person narrative. In spite of her insight that in the ballad "fictional narrative is taking place" and "that we do not have any lyric phenomenon" where "a narrative function is at work," Hamburger did not assign such verbal structures to the fictional genre; she treats them as a "special form." And although the first-person narrative is controlled by "conditions structurally similar to those of the lyric," which have their origin in the "logical structure which is common to both" and "by the locus of both in the statement system," Hamburger insists that the I-tale as "a mimesis of reality statement" remains a "special form" which, as a "feigned reality statement," is distinguished from the structure of autobiographical statement by "its character as narrative literature," having only "the *form* of reality statement," and, from the point of view of verbal logic, proving "an alien within the epic sphere."[3]

It seemed to me that the conclusions about genre were not logically derived from the linguistic-structural analysis, being in part overloaded with ideas more properly relating to the psychology of audiences and analysis of content. I especially missed the inclusion of the form of drama which Brecht called epic theater, and I was not satisfied by either the arguments presented in the chapter on the lyric or by the categorization of the "special forms."

Summarized, my argument was that the many possible forms of creative language may be reduced to two basic types, mimesis and imitatio. I used the term *mimesis* to mean the same thing as Hamburger's concept of fiction; like Hamburger, I understood it as a basic category of the use of literary language. In my view, it can be shown to exist in all three forms of presentation: in the third-person narrative, in drama, and in the figural poem.[4] Imitatio—the distinguishing trait of the second basic category of creative language—takes the place of the verbal structure of feigned reality statement, which Hamburger showed to be a structural characteristic of first-person narrative. I used the term *imitatio* because the feigned reality statement is not "a mimesis of the 'genuine' reality statement" but its structural imitation. In contrast to Hamburger, I see a possibility of using this structural form, like mimesis, in all three presentational forms—that is, imitatio in the epic, the lyric, and the dramatic forms.

At the time I used the epic theater as a valid example of imitation in the dramatic presentational form, and I was widely praised for this—improperly, as I subsequently realized.[5] My example took insufficient account of the different verbal structure—which I did not recognize at the time—between the "street scene," the "model of the epic theater," and the epic theater scene. I used the terminology of verbal theory and argumentation to follow Brecht's proofs and arguments; his analogy of the street scene and the scene of the epic theater reads so convincingly that I know of no Brecht scholar who has taken issue with it. The following analysis of verbal structure, however, is intended to correct my earlier reasoning. Further, I intend to use it as an example by which to analyze verbal structure and to lead to reflections on the relationship between structure and audience.

The "street scene" in Brecht's *Messingkauf Dialogues* analyzes "an incident at any street corner":

> An eye witness demonstrating to a collection of people how a traffic accident took place. The bystanders may not have observed what happened, or they may simply not agree with him, may "see things a different way"; the point is that the demonstrator acts out the behaviour of driver or victim or both in such a way that the bystanders are able to form an opinion about the accident.[6]

About the epic theater Brecht has said that "to be major theatre it need at bottom only contain the same elements as a street-corner demonstration of this sort."[7]

Let us examine the structural relationship once more. The essential element in the street scene is the repetition of something that actually happened—a traffic accident—by the demonstrator, who "acts out the behaviour of the driver or the victim or both." The entire performance as report, mimicry, and gesture depends on the "demonstrator." Since he does not conceal the reverberative nature of the performance and does not identify with the characters he presents, he functions not as a performer but as a reporter or narrator. From a structural point of view, the indicating demonstrator is a genuine statement-subject; his statements are genuine reality statements purely on the basis of this fact.[8] Structurally, his demonstration belongs to the statement system of language—in other words, what he produces belongs to the area of noncreative language. These facts, described in their structural traits, are the reason why the bystanders—of course also genuine statement-subjects—can be in touch with him.

Brecht was convinced that "the elements of natural and of artificial epic theatre are the same." "The epic theatre's choruses and documentary projections, the direct addressing of the audience by its actors, are at bottom just this."[9] But in fact the theater audience cannot turn to the actors to set them right, for example, as the bystanders in a street demonstration can and should. The cause is not in the difference between actual events (the traffic accident of the street scene) and fabricated story (as in *Mother Courage*). Brecht's real reason can be discovered by bringing theoretical and structural linguistic insights to the following passage.

> And true enough, the epic theatre is an extremely artistic affair, hardly thinkable without artists and virtuosity, imagination, humour and fellow-feeling; it cannot be practised without all these and much else too. It has got to be entertaining, it has got to be instructive. How then can art be developed

out of the elements of the street scene, without adding any or leaving any out? How does it evolve into the theatrical scene with its fabricated story, its trained actors, its lofty style of speaking, its make-up, its team performance by a number of players?[10]

The difference does not lie with the fabricated story, the trained actors, or the makeup; it lies with the "team performance by a number of players." What seems merely a quantitative expansion—instead of *one* street demonstrator, *several* actors—turns out, on a linguistic-structural level, to be a qualitative change. The interplay of several actors creates a dialogue structure that can no longer be considered the utterance of a single statement-subject. The epic theater scene does not have a narrator, as does the genuine reality statement of the street scene; it has several performers, and though their form of presentation is analogous to that of the street demonstrator, since each performer "tells"—or rather "shows"—his character, the totality of what is performed is not the product of *one* narrator. The reception of the epic theater scene is affected by the dialogue structure, which operates to further the illusion, allowing the spectator to experience the performance as reality. While the street scene can easily maintain the feature of repetition, the epic theater scene can attempt to create it only moment by moment, interrupting the illusion; and even this is possible only partially, if at all, since dialogue is one of the most powerful means of shaping fiction.

The linguistic-logical comparison of the street scene and the theater scene makes it clear that in spite of its avoidance of the habitual theatrical performance, epic theater is structured mimetically and therefore cannot furnish an example for imitatio in drama.

There is no fundamental obstacle to the logical-structural transformation of street scene into theater scene. (If Brecht had consistently transferred the structure of the street scene to the stage, there would have been no "Brecht ensemble.") The chief obstacle is not structural but the prevailing form of theater, which is the product of mankind's dramatic and theater history and no longer functions without a group of players. Nor does the structure of the familiar form of monodrama fulfill the requirements of imitatio because in monodrama the number of the fictional characters is simply reduced to one. The single performer *is* the performed character; he does not tell or show him.

Basically linguistic-structural analysis is not obliged to prove a congruence between its logical catalogue and the historical possibilities. If we nevertheless search for examples of imitatio in dramatic presentation, we find the most logical expression most easily in cabaret revues. This form often contains skits with a single actor who, for example, "pre-sents" one or more figures from political life, without consciously striving for transformation from demonstrator (cabaret artist) to person demonstrated (historical personality), because the behavior of the person being demonstrated is treated and judged with critical irony or satiric distance. The process frequently involves direct contact with the audience. A master of this form is the German cabaret artist Werner Finck, who frequently performs without stage or platform; if external circumstances permit, he moves among the audience as he talks, reacts to audience reaction (by a direct reply, for example), refers to a cabaret scene from the early 1930s which had political consequences for its performer, repeating this scene in part by telling and performing, and casually talking to relate it to new scenes.

What may appear to the audience as improvisation is in fact the result of a carefully planned program which in the totality of its performed texts and scenes is created neither spontaneously nor solely by the performer. When he performs, Werner Finck slips into the role of the telling-performing cabaretist. The degree of feint of the statement-subject is frequently indistinct in such performances; identity with the genuine statement-subject is not to be presumed as a matter of course, though in the case of particular sketches it cannot be completely dismissed. In such scenes the genuine statement-subject in general feigns itself as the telling-performing cabaretist, whose performance has the nature of a role. The question of the degree of feint and the difficulty of unequivocal determination on the graded scale of feint has become current for I-tales since Hamburger made her analysis.[11]

This objective difficulty, identical with the structure of the feigned reality statement, has from time immemorial made it seem natural in the reception process—as well as in literary theory—to identify the statement-subject with the autobiographical *I* of the writer; that is, it is common practice to assume a real, genuine statement-subject in the forms of literary language marked by the statement structure. Because the feint of the statement-subject does not emerge clearly in the reception process, texts of epic imitatio attain a strongly authentic character which is, in fact, a false authenticity. Thus we encounter a discrepancy phenomenon between structural form and form of reception; we will return to this crux in another context.

Genre theory as it has developed is able, thanks to the preceding analysis, to list epic theater in the basic category of mimesis. The conclusion that there are only two fundamental categories (mimesis and imitatio) remains unaltered.

The first advantage to be gained from this theory accrued to the lyric, which turns out to be no more of a basic genre than are epic and drama. The division into mimetic structures and forms of feigned reality statements also holds good for the lyric.[12] Thus the concept of the "lyrical I" has returned to its coinage by Margarete Susman: a designation for an I that is not identical with the individual I of the writer (genuine statement-subject).[13] Assuming a genuine statement-subject to underlie the lyrical form of presentation is to say that a poem is nothing more than a specially structured personal confession.[14] Hofmannsthal correctly rejected such a concept, which misunderstands literature as ornate avowal. The position of a genuine statement-subject in the lyrical poem would result in the recognition of a reality element in the work of art. This in turn would cast doubt on the essential status of literature, since the necessary difference between art and reality, the "distancing of the works from empirical reality," would be eliminated.[15] In the area of statement structure it is solely the unrecognizably modified form of the statement-subject which authenticates the autonomy of the work of art and the negation of empirical reality.[16] The contradiction between structural form and audience experience is perhaps nowhere as distinct as in the case of lyrical poems.

The example of the lyrical form of presentation demonstrates how we can derive contributions to the essential status of literary works of art—as well as questions of reception theory and practice—from a linguistic-structural analysis primarily directed to genre theory on the basis of a precise apparatus of concepts. We could just as easily use the same consideration for the form of feigned reality statement in an epic form of presentation. Taken to its logical conclusion, the postulation of a genuine statement-subject would result in a definition of epic poetry somewhat in the sense of "conscious fantasizing."[17] Speculations that claim to rescue the genuineness of the statement-subject for determining works of literature, however, lead to a dead end.

Regardless of the method used to develop nonaesthetic investigations of literature, they cannot evade the basic question, which

Wladimir Weidlé formulated as follows: "Art is always language, but language is not always art. It is therefore of concern to find out what, besides the aesthetic, distinguishes the language of art—good art as well as bad—from all other kinds of language."[18]

The linguistic-structural proof of difference is clearly more easily provided for the mimetic structures (mimesis) than for the form of feigned reality-statements (imitatio). Mimesis, however, is only more overtly distinguished from genuine reality statement than imitatio. Both, as presentational forms of creative language, are categorically separate from the noncreative language; they are further distinguished from each other by their varying conditions of presentation and reception.

The insights of a genre theory based on language structures are not limited to the area of genre theory but of necessity lead to questions concerning reception theory and practice. I intend to demonstrate this truth by the example of the ballad.

Hamburger assigned the ballad to the "special forms" because it, like the other special form (the I-tale), seems to deny its innate structure. Since Hamburger thinks "fictional narration is taking place" in the ballad, she can adduce arguments of audience psychology to claim "that we no longer construe the content of the ballad as statement of a lyric I, but as the fictive existence of fictive subjects. Where a narrative function is at work, we do not have any lyric phenomenon."[19] Since I believe that when linguistic-theoretical considerations are involved, the poetry form cannot "neutralize" the structural relations fixed in the text, it would be logical, once the narrative function has been proved, to speak of mimesis in the lyrical form of presentation. The use of audience psychology within a linguistic-logical investigation makes it urgent to pay closer attention to the aspects of audience psychology.

Maria Wagner, who also objected to including the ballad among the special forms, arrives at a different result in her attempt to categorize the ballad among the genres. Using the statement relationships analyzed by Hamburger, she proceeds "to clarify the statement relations in the ballad, which have seemed contradictory until now, to mark the limits of fiction and reality statement in the ballad from each other, and to find the 'leading intention' that directs the ballad to one of the literary genres." She rejects Hamburger's attempt to assign to the lyrical sphere "a statement structure explained as fictional," since the lyric is marked by the structure of (genuine) reality statement. Wagner finds an unresolved ambiguity in the discrepancy between Hamburger's definition of the lyrical "as a type of literature within the scope of the experience field of a genuine statement subject" and the claim (stated above) that the ballad takes up the fictive existence of fictive subjects. Wagner draws her conclusions from an interpretation of the concept of "figural poem": if the ballad is called a "fictional figural poem," we would be dealing, as in the case of picture poem and role poem, with a form of poetry "with persons in the object-pole." To her, the behavior of the statement subject seems unchanged by the concept of "figural poem," that is, even in the figural poem the object pole is not omitted from the experience field of the statement subject. Therefore, in contrast with Hamburger, she sees no difference between the two poems "Der stille Grund" and "Waldgespräch."[20]

Correctly (in my view) Hamburger called the I in "Waldgespräch" "the I of a fictive figure" and therefore assigned the trait of the ballad to this poem. Wagner argues: "In 'Waldgespräch' Lorelei is made the subject of a fictive I-statement, of an I that is not identical with the lyrical I of the poem." She considers it deceptive for Hamburger to conclude that in "Waldgespräch" we are no longer dealing with a lyrical I; this false conclusion results "from narrowing the statement to the speaker in the object pole ... so that the interpretation of the lyrical I as 'structural element of the statement'" is lost "and the decisive factor" is displaced "in favor of a 'speaker.'"[21]

The following argument forms the basis of Wagner's eventual assigning the ballad to the lyric form:

> It is, however, crucial for the statement structure, not who is speaking, but where the origin of the lyrical I-statement is to be found. The statement content of "Waldgespräch" is not the report about a conversation that took place but the feeling content of fear and temptation, guilt and punishment emerges during the conversation. The speaker-statement in the object pole does not become autonomous, it fulfills an ancillary function as a partial aspect of the total statement. Speech and counterspeech in the object pole do not obviate the lyrical I if the events in the object pole return a feeling or mood content to the subject pole, which is understood as a lyrical I statement. In spite of the altered grammatical situation, in spite of the second speaker, "Waldgespräch" is experienced just as lyrically as "Der stille Grund." In the reader's experience Lorelei's turning into an I has not produced a change. In spite

of the grammatical I in the object pole, Lorelei's statement remains in the experience field of the lyrical I. The reader does not experience an essential difference between the two poems.[22]

Continuing this argument, we note that the definition of the term "figural poem" contains a determination of the structural relations. For in dealing with poems "with persons in the object pole," these poems must be assigned to the structural formations marked by a subject-object relation—that is, they have the structure of statement. Since the structure of the statement inevitably includes a statement subject—which need not necessarily appear in the text—Wagner can postulate the presence of an I (statement subject) without having to show its presence in the text. She can then conclude from this evidentiary process that "the ballad [belongs] unequivocally to the lyrical genre."[23]

Wagner's context and her attempt at definition ignore the fact that Hamburger speaks of the "fictional figural poem" and a "narrative function," excluding the postulation of a subject-object relation. But Wagner's approach is symptomatic for still another reason. Since she cannot introduce the existence of a statement subject into a structural argument, she shifts her arguments to the level of audience by introducing *its* horizon of expectation (ballad—statement) and equating it with the horizon of expectation of the reader. "The reader does not feel any essential difference between the two poems."

Little would be gained by my objecting that as a reader I do feel an essential difference, since one can argue eternally about the two different horizons of expectation involved here; everyone would consider his own reaction as a reader to be valid. I consider it more important to use this example, in its obviousness, to show the shift in the level of the argument. The transition from a strictly structural approach to one of audience psychology is not accidental and can be found repeatedly in Hamburger's work itself. Using her example, I want to call attention to the fundamental problems raised here, then return to Wagner's example.

At the outset of her analysis of epic fiction, Hamburger quotes the opening section of C.F. Meyer's *Jürg Jenatsch:*

> The noonday sun stood over the barren height of the Julian Pass, jutted with rocky peaks, in the canton of Bünden. The stone walls burnt and shimmered under the piercing, vertical rays. At times, when a billowing storm cloud welled up and

passed over, the mountain walls seemed to draw nearer and the landscape, contracting, uncannily to compress.... In the middle of the extending height of the pass, to the left and right of the mule path, stood the ruins of two pillars which might well have been withstanding time for more than a century already.[24]

As Hamburger has shown, this passage from the novel exhibits none of the earmarks of fictional structure; the reprinted text could just as well be a section of a travel diary, given an equally talented author. Hamburger argues—correctly—by shifting to the various receiving selves: "Were we to be presented with this passage out of context, we would be able to view this barren height of the Julian Pass, lying there in the noonday sun in the canton of Bünden, as being the experience-field of the reporting subject."[25] It may be asked whether—given a corresponding horizon of expectation on the part of the reader—he is not anticipating the emergence of a narrator because he is reading this passage, out of context, as a section of an I-narrative—that is, one of the forms of creative language.

Even when we know—for example, because we are reading these sentences in an edition of the works of C.F. Meyer—that these opening sentences are bringing us a novel, the individual reader's reception remains an open question to the end of the cited passage. Structurally, we can imagine the following shift to continue from the opening sentences: "In the center of the extending pass, to the right and left of the mule track, stood two broken pillars which, it seemed to me, may have defied time for over a century." Increasingly the narrating I (statement subject) could assert itself, telling either its own story or that of other characters.[26] In that case we would be dealing with a structure subsumed under the linguistic-theoretical category of imitatio (feigned reality statement). Structural analysis of the original text, however, reveals a different structure—that of epic fiction. The first stringent traits of mimetic structure are so subtly introduced by Meyer that we need not be afraid that a modish effect of reader psychology will be aroused. It is quite different in the case of Stifter, who in my view in "Hochwald" was so awkward in his transition from the deliberately stressed form of reality statement to narrative in the fluctuating narrative function (mimesis) that readers—as is shown in practice—frequently have difficulty getting their bearings in the transitional passage.

The opening of *Jürg Jenatsch* and the example given by Wagner may alert us to a possible discrepancy—at least for a period of time—between the form of reception and the structure of the text. From this we may derive various consequences and considerations for the relationship of linguistic-structural form and reception; it may also clarify a sometimes criticized paradox in all its paradoxical significance.

Proof of the fictional narrative form allows us, in discussing *Jürg Jenatsch*, to speak of the nonreality of what is represented in the sense of a structural concept. If we refer the structural concept formation of nonreality to the reception-psychological aspect of the effect of such a text to the recipient, we can reproduce the reception experience, for example, through the concept of "as-reality." This nonthematizing shift of the observation levels is the basis for such sentences as the following by Hamburger: "The as-reality, however, is semblance, the illusion of reality, which is called nonreality or fiction."[27] The structural analysis thus transcends the realm of the formal structures revealed in the text to include the reading experience. The paradoxical relationship between the structural nature of a text—for example, mimesis or fiction and nonreality—and its reception (appearance as reality) for the reader can be stressed even more strongly: the structurally proven nonreality is reality in the process of reception; or, put another way, the structural nonreality produces the experience of reality.[28] This paradox is part of the essence of creative structural possibility and its effect.

The paradox touched upon here leads us to a wider point of view, which relates structure and reception to one another.

The effect of speech-theoretical structures in the reception process cannot be precisely defined without empirical information. It would be especially interesting to study texts which, like the opening of *Jürg Jenatsch*, face the recipient with a somewhat unstable structure, so that he can temporarily respond according to his horizon of expectation.[29] Since there are two fundamentally different novelistic structures, we cannot simply equate the horizon of expectation of "the readers" with the expectation of fictional realization. A novel is a work of epic narrative art, not only when fictional persons appear (that is, when there is fictional narrative—mimesis), but also when the narrator (feigned statement-subject) tells feigned events from the past—that is, when he narrates in the form of imitatio.

Speech-structural analysis is competent in each case to demonstrate the present textual structure and to precisely document the classifying traits. Nor does it transcend its limitations when it attempts to point out possible effects of the structural facts on the reception process. But it can make assumptions only about the actual *course* of the reception; at best it can define the reception experience of the analyzing I, which is at the same time also a recipient I.

The difference in the reception of one and the same text may be conditioned by still another circumstance. We may again choose the ballad as an example. As a point of departure, let us consider the folk ballad. The history of the folk ballad tells us that it is the product of anonymous troubadours and jongleurs. Folk ballads are short narrative songs about legendary or historic personalities or frequently about typical experiences of human life—partings, reunions, death. The singers needed the audience "for a hearing" and the people "spread the song" in oral tradition. We are thus dealing with a text that developed in nonliterary ways and was not originally intended for written literary distribution. In contrast to art ballads, the folk ballad is not primarily a literary composition. The recording of such a text, which occurred at some time or other, does not turn it into a written text "but only a written representation" of an originally unwritten text.[30] Speech-theorectical analysis nevertheless treats it as a written text and in the process may falsify its "innate structure."[31]

The difference between the reader's reception of the apparently written text and the original experience directed to an aural reception of this unwritten text seems worth considering. The listener is, as a matter of course, granted one element in the performance: the person of the singer. As a listener, he cannot receive the musically chanted events otherwise than through the agency of the visibly present singer—that is, as events within the singer's experience field. Even when the singer uses dialogue, he does not disappear from the performance; on the contrary, his presence stresses the quoted nature of the dialogue.

The chanted narrative remains closely tied to the experience field of the statement subject which, because of its real presence, need not become an element integral to the text. The real statement subject disposes over a wide field of realization possibilities. The singer can give the narration an air of something personally experienced and faithfully reproduced; in such a case the listener will perceive him—a statement subject on the scale between the unambiguously genuine statement subject and the equally unquestionable feigned statement subject—as standing close to the pole of the genuine statement subject, perhaps even becoming identical with it in the audience's consciousness. He can, conversely, stress the feint of the statement subject or, as a neutral voice, he can assume the character of an "objective" reporter who is himself unimportant. Alternately, he can arrange his performance "dramatically" and render the dialogue passages as well as the narrative sections with mimetic and gestic expression. However we may imagine the performance of the historical singer, he can at best "neutralize" himself; he can never disappear from the performance.

According to its tradition and innate structure, the folk ballad is imitatio (feigned reality statement) in a lyrical form of presentation. Its traditional terseness allows only a limited amount of imitation, which is structurally unimportant.

As far as the art ballad is concerned, the relationship between "innate structure" and reception may be reversed or may become ambivalent. In its origin the art ballad is a written text. As such it can be shaped by the narrative function (mimesis). Even when the characteristics of the fluctuating narrative function are used to a lesser extent or less frequently than in epic fiction, the text which is to be received by a reader contains the potential of reception in the sense of the experience of reality (as-structure of reality).

Since many German art ballads have been set to music, one or another recipient may already have become familiar with a particular ballad in the concert hall before he receives the text in silent reading. It would be surprising if the horizon of expectation of this recipient were not shaped by the experience in the concert hall, during which the statement was communicated to him through the statement-subject of the singer. Anyone with some practice in objectifying or consciously adjusting his horizon of expectation may receive one and the same ballad as both mimesis and imitatio.[32] This possibility disappears when the structural elements of mimesis which have the strongest effect on reception psychology—verbs of interior processes, "erlebte Rede," interior monologue—are employed. The influence on the reader of the linguistic structure is so strong that a reception "against the grain," as it were, is unlikely.

The speech-structural singularity of the text undoubtedly influences significantly the reception process; but one should not entirely overlook how much freedom of realization is left to the reader. We must not forget the "dialectic of 'freedom and dependence' of the readers' consciousness."[33]

The example of the folk and art ballads points to several aspects of the relationship between structure and reception which may stimulate far-reaching reflections. It seems to me worthwhile to assume an imitatio structure in texts that are not originally constituted in writing if the statement-subject cannot, as in written texts, be determined as a text-immanent, unequivocally fixable element. This reflection, offered here as a hypothesis, may be carried beyond the ballad as an example for the epic or the fairy tale. Käte Hamburger has an observation concerning the fairy tale which, in my opinion, touched on this topic *in nuce* but quite unthematically: "Even the fairy tale appears as reality as long as we, as we read it or watch it enacted, abide within it; but nevertheless it does not appear as if it were a reality."[34] But does the fairy tale retain the as-if structure of reality (mimesis) if we receive it, not by *reading* it or *seeing* it enacted in the theater, but by *hearing* it? Might it not be that under certain circumstances the childhood experience of the narrating (not reading from the book) mother or grandmother remains for a long time—perhaps forever—a crucial influence on the reading adult's horizon of expectation? May he not, as he reads, interpolate precisely the statement-subject immanent in the text? Who would not find it easy to read the famous fairy-tale beginning, "Once upon a time ... " as well as all that follows, as a statement of the past and not as epic preterit? If there is any truth to the hypothesis, there should be obvious connections between the emergence of originally written texts and the disappearance of texts conceived for oral recitation. As long as the reception of literary texts by listeners was the norm, or as long as individual reading naturally meant reading aloud, even for a person reading by himself (it was a custom well into the nineteenth century to read aloud to oneself), imitatio structures must prevail except in drama. This assumption could be supported historically by the gradual emergence of mimetic narrative forms beginning in the second quarter of the nineteenth century. It is no accident that this period discussed the "objectivity" of narrative that has for its subject an objectivity not of content but of structure.

My experiments with texts by realists—including Gottfried Keller, Wilhelm Raabe, and Theodor Fontane—show how weakly these authors stress the fictional narrative form. As an example, let us choose the beginning of Keller's "A Village Romeo and Juliet," which figures in the immediate reception process as feigned reality statement (imitatio):

> It would be but tedious mimicry to tell this story, were it not for the fact that it is based on a true happening, proof of the depth of the roots in real life of each of the tales on which the great works are founded. The number of such tales is small; but time and again they reappear in new garb and seem to compel the hand to hold fast to them.
> Near a beautiful stream half an hour from Seldwyl, a cultivated height rises and disappears into the fruitful plain. Far at its foot lies a village which contains many a large farmyard, and years ago three magnificent long fields lay across the gentle plain, running alongside each other like three gigantic ribbons.[35]

The reader seems to hear the (neutral) voice of a narrator (statement-subject) who refers to a "true happening" for his narrative. This is the traditional stance of authorial narration, which likes to shield itself under the cloak of the "dissimulation or disguise of the authorial narrator as editor of a manuscript, and reporter and chronicler of an event allegedly told him by an eyewitness or participant, and so forth."[36] This tone is immediately compromised.

> On a sunny September morning two farmers plowed two of these fields—that is, each of the outside ones; the middle one seemed to have lain fallow and deserted for years, for it was covered with stones and high weeds, and a world of winged and humming insects hovered steadily above it. But the farmers, walking behind their plows, were tall, lanky men about forty years old, and at first glance they could be seen to be secure, prosperous farmers. (pp. 85–86)

Evident though not problematic from the point of view of reception psychology is the change to the preterit in the transition between these two textual passages. At the beginning the narrator still seems present, but gradually many readers—as was shown by a limited and unsystematic inquiry and therefore not a representative one—are won over to a presented reality, which gains a kind of independence by emancipating itself from the narrator. Time and again the narrator's voice comes through, however:

> After many stops and starts, the carriage came to a halt on the rise in the shadow of a stand of young linden trees at the edge of the field, and now it was possible to observe the two passengers more closely. (p. 88)

Or:

> Only when the deed was almost accomplished did he get word of the magnificent monument Manz had erected. Filled with anger, he ran out, saw what had happened, ran back and fetched the constable to lodge a temporary injunction against the pile of stones and to have the place legally impounded, and from that day forward the two farmers were in litigation with each other and did not rest until both of them were ruined. (pp. 101–2)

Examples of the more or less clearly stated presence of the narrator could easily be expanded, but I am not here concerned with demonstrating Keller's narrative methods. A classic reflection by the omniscient author—in the typical form of the present tense, encapsulated in a preterit context—may serve as a last instance.

> For though they were among the village's best farmers and had done nothing that two-thirds of the others would not have done under the same circumstances, they were nevertheless the object of silent stares now, and no one wished to be caught between them on the reduced, abandoned field. Most people are willing and able to engage in a prevailing evil if they happen to encounter it; but as soon as one of them has done it, the others are relieved that after all it was not they, that temptation did not strike them, and now they make the chosen one into the measurement of evil of their own traits and treat him with delicate distance as a deflector of the evil, marked by the gods, even while their mouths still water after the advantages he gained thereby. Manz and Marti were thus the only ones who seriously bid for the field; after a fairly persistent contest, Manz acquired it, and the auctioneer granted it to him. (p. 97)

Keller continues to use dialogue extremely sparingly; the narrative is limited to what can be perceived by the senses, whatever is accessible to the reception horizon of the narrator (statement-subject). Internal occurrences are for the moment touched on cautiously, almost nervously:

> The farmer, however, did not waste time on removing it. He may have thought that there was plenty of time left for that, and he was content for the present to act sketchily. . . .
>
> Now each surely saw what the other was up to, but neither seemed to see, and they disappeared again, each constellation drawing silently past the other one and diving down behind this round globe. (p. 95)

Subsequent passages, however, using immediate representation of the subjectivity and internality of the characters, are freely able to exploit the possibilities of the fluctuation narrative function:

> His son had seen nothing because as he walked he was lost in happy reveries. He noticed neither rain nor storm, neither darkness nor misery; for him there was lightness, brightness, and warmth inside and out, and he felt as rich and protected as a prince. Without cease he gazed on the lingering smile of the beautiful face close by, and he returned the smile only now, a solid half-hour later, with love-filled laughter straight at the night and winds and at the beloved face which everywhere approached him from the darkness, so that he believed Vrenchen in her way must surely see his laugh and grow fond of him. . . . (p. 121)

> Finally each cowered in a corner and began to spend the day in weary, arid bickering and quarrelling with the other, falling asleep now and again, tortured by restless daydreams arising in their conscience that woke them again. Only Sali saw and heard nothing of all this, for he thought only of Vrenchen. He still felt, not only as if he were unspeakably rich, but also as if he had had proper schooling and knew an infinity of good and beautiful things, now that he knew so clearly and surely about what he had seen the day before. This knowledge had descended on him from on high, as it were, and his happy astonishment knew no bounds; and yet it was as if he had always and ever known it, filling him now with a wondrous sweetness. (p. 122)

This is immediately followed by the narrator, reflected in the present tense.

> For nothing compares to the wealth and permanence of the happiness that approaches a man in such a clear and distinct form, baptized by the minister and given its own name, which resounds like no other. (p. 122)

Given the narrative tradition, the horizon of expectation of Keller's contemporaries was much more clearly directed toward the expectation of an imitatio structure than are today's readers. Precisely when a narrative text deviates from the structural possibilities, mimesis or imitatio, as is typical in the evolutionary form of narration practiced by the realists, the personal horizon of expectation of the reader will significantly influence primary reception.

The realists' narrative method, fluctuating between the two structural forms, may prove to be a particularly interesting area for research about empiric reception. It would be equally interesting to learn if and how the reception of epic mimesis and epic imitatio differ. The experience of as-if reality may hold true not only for it-narrative (mimesis), but presumably also for I-narrative (imitatio), although we are confronting clearly differentiated structures.[37] In most I-narratives, however, the trait of authenticity created by the structural elements of the statement-subject will predominate.[38]

The foregoing reflections refer to the reception *process*—that is, to the time that passes while the recipient dwells in the representation as he reads or watches. This is the stage I call primary reception, which may be distinguished from a secondary form of reception. A structurally fictional text is absorbed as a living, current reality during primary reception; when the received text is no longer an experience (primary reception) but a possession, it becomes a piece of reality in the recipient's consciousness. The fact that this is a consequence of primary reception allows us to understand, for example, the disappointment of the schoolboy who learns that the encounter between the Queen of Scots and Elizabeth I in the third act of Schiller's *Mary Stuart*, which impressed him deeply, is not a historical event; in fact, the two queens never met, the depicted meeting is the product of Schiller's imagination. A person who never learns this truth will presumably incorporate the encounter in his consciousness as a piece of history.

To cite another example, there is the disappointed youthful reader of the novels of Karl May who is told by "initiates" one day that his favorite heroes were the creations of a criminal. Since Karl May makes structural use of feigned reality statements, and since these are received as genuine especially by naive readers, the author appears to the disappointed reader as a liar.

Both structures allow the probability that the given time and place indications are understood as concrete and concretizable indications. The author's efforts to let the structural nonreality appear as an image of reality, without their being de facto copies or reproductions, is precisely aimed at "deception" through illusion produced variously by the two basic forms.

The difference, shown in our examples, between the findings of structural textual analysis and the results of structural facts for primary and secondary reception once more raises the question of the function of the epic preterit. As much as can be determined by structural analysis was already noted by Hamburger and need not be detailed here. In the fictional context the preterit loses its grammatical function of designating the past.[39] For the primary reception, the question of whether the epic preterit in its apreterit character is received can be answered definitively only by empirical findings. The preterit as a temporal form probably cannot be held responsible when "the sequel seems to recognize 'true reality' ... in the fictional image."[40] The capability of the preterit to express concluded actions can surely not be crucial to the singular reception phenomenon of observing the fiction unreflected as empirical reality. Dramatic fiction, which cannot use the epic preterit, produces the same effect as epic fiction.[41] It seems to me more crucial to the possibility, opened up by literary language, of experiencing as existing what is nonexistent, never was, and never will be. Experienced Being, however, carries within itself the claim to be accepted as such. It enters into the recipient's consciousness as memory and imagination, just like genuine experience. The "timelessness" of literature thus becomes timebound and historical for the recipient.

These considerations are not sufficient to explain why the preterit is the usual narrative tense in fictional narrative structures, although it loses the temporal function of genuine reality statements to characterize past action. The feigned reality statement has the preterit thrust upon it as the "natural" narrative tense. It is the primordial tense of tales, since genuine reality statements are also told in the preterit (or perfect) tense, though this does not exclude the use of the reflecting present, which in the reception process stresses the time point of the narration and the narrator, and the occasional use of the historical present through the narrator in genuine and feigned reality statements. Ott's assumption that a novel "can be told only in the preterit" is not correct. It does not even hold true for the narrative in imitatio form, which may be told in the present throughout—though, in the form the historical present, it admittedly functions like the preterit.

Epic fiction can also use the present.[42] Though it rarely employs the device, that may be because the preterit already functions as the "natural" narrative tense in extraliterary narration and is used by extension even where its original function of designating completed action, and therefore facticity, is lost. Today we can only speculate in this regard. Current theories of literature are limited by their present means and methods.

In the context of our reflections on the relationship between structure and reception, we must also touch on the question of autonomy, which is concretized in a particular way in the aspect of structural studies. In closing, I would like to investigate at least a few basic traits in order to acquire a definitive point of view for the problems concerning reception theory.

Structural analysis proves the autonomy of works of literature by demonstrating the categorical difference between the two structural forms of literary language and the structural form of nonliterary language (genuine reality statement). The manner in which an author employs autonomy in order to design realities within the structural opportunities cannot be determined by any norm. It is in no way limited by a reproduction regulation which necessarily turns its reality design into a copy of an original.[43] The age-old demand for imitation was never identical with reproduction. Production can never mean reproduction—unless a normative-poetic claim exists, as for the *pictura* of the emblem, or an extra-artistic reproduction verdict to which the author must bow. The structural study must stress the fact that reality, as a design of reality, is a "world of its own," categorically divorced from our empirical experiential reality.[44] This is one aspect of the question of autonomy.

The production horizon thus acquires incalculable and indefinite possibilities of representation, beginning with the historical-documentary intention of representation, which bows to every minute fact, up to the design of utopian worlds, which have no counterpart in real life. We should not attempt to discredit this freedom with the pejorative "arbitrariness," as Pracht does. The artistic freedom "of determining artistic production as a free activity" and the autonomy of literary form would not be truly free if they were not free to deal with all conceivable extremes.[45] The autonomy of literature should be defended precisely by those who credit the author with the function of reality or the shaping of history. Only by presupposing this autonomy can we let something that is factually unrealized, something that is not yet reality, appear as reality.

The autonomy of art is not the problem that threatens a "progressive" theory of literature. Rather, its threat comes from a reception process in which the recipient would be constantly aware of the nonreality of the experienced reality. But since, as the paradoxical relationship of structure and reception shows, the nonreality in the as-if structure of reality remains hidden from the recipient, this criticism is setting up a straw man. For the recipient, who experiences as reality the reality produced at the hands of a "creator," literature becomes a way of appropriating the world, a history-shaping energy, an "organ of universal understanding."[46] Precisely because art is not categorically bound by a law of reproduction, it can be either regressive or progressive, conservative or liberal. It can anticipate reality over the expectation horizon to a historical situation and confer the nature of reality to it in the reception process. The exemplary essence in artistic representation and in the autonomy of art, which is not to be confused with autarchy, are contingent on each other.

Our reflections on the paradoxical relationship of structure and reception, literature and reality, have attempted to bring to light some basic aspects to be considered in future scholarship about reception. The attitude we have consciously taken toward the question of the part of structural reception handicaps in the reception process does not ignore the fact that the structural givens are only a part of the total reception phenomenon and that the linguistic structures never appear independently. Nevertheless, it is necessary to observe them in isolation, even though this leaves us open to the charge that we are ignoring historical dimensions. Structural forms such as we have discussed not only represent "the unchanging basic forms of literature";[47] they also release aesthetic-affective energies during the reception process. Within the limitations of this representation we have been able to show by a few examples how essentially the release of the energies stored in the structures depends on the reception, even as the structural singularity of a text strongly determines its reception.

The question of the active energies of linguistic structures should be discussed beyond the present context. It seems to me that not a few authors of the past and present have falsely evaluated or paid too little attention to the immanent active potential of verbal structures. An author's choice of a particular structure and presentation determines not only the conditions of his production, but also the kind and degree of reception.[48] Authors who start out from actively aesthetic presumptions and intentions cannot be indifferent to the means of representation they choose. More detailed research into reception could help to close the gap between literary production and literary studies. Perhaps then the underestimation of particular forms of representation—such as documentary literature—would pass out of fashion.

(Translated by Ruth Hein)

Notes

1. "Mimesis und Imitatio: Grundlagen einer neuen Gattungspoetik," *Euphorion* 64 (1970): 125–42 and 65 (1971): 105.
2. *Die Logik der Dichtung*, 2d rev. ed. (Stuttgart, 1968). Now also in English translation: *The Logic of Literature*, trans. Marilynn J. Rose (Bloomington and London, 1973). In the discussion that follows quotations are from pp. 308–30 of the English translation.
3. About the linguistic implications also see Hamburger.
4. The form of the ballad was deliberately omitted because it will be treated later.
5. The comments of Wolfgang Lockemann are unsatisfactory: "Aspekte des Verhaeltnisses von Dichtung und Wirklichkeit. Skizze zu einem System," *Orbis Litterarum* 26 (1971): 171–84, esp. p. 178. Imitatio—no matter what form of presentation—is not a contradiction to mimesis. Imitatio is in its structure different from mimesis, but not in direct opposition.
6. *Brecht on Theatre*, trans. John Willett (New York, 1964), p. 121.
7. Ibid.
8. Hamburger, *Logic*, p. 45: "Statement is always reality statement because the statement-subject is real, in other words, because statement is constituted only through a genuine, real statement-subject."
9. *Brecht on Theatre*, pp. 128; 126.
10. Ibid., pp. 126–27.
11. *Logic*, p. 314.
12. Cf. my comments in the article mentioned in n. 1.
13. *Das Wesen der modernen deutschen Lyrik* (Stuttgart, 1910), vol. 9, *Kunst und Kultur*, p. 16.
14. The structural differentiation between real and simulated medium of expression (Aussagesubjekt) presents great difficulties, from the point of view of literary theory, as well as that of literary criticism. Moreover, one should not

15. say "poetry"—as Lockemann does—if one is speaking about poetic language, and not speak in terms of "simulated reality," if the simulated expression of reality is meant.
15. Theodor W. Adorno, "Zur Dialektik des Engagements," *Die neue Rundschau* 72 (1962): 93–110; quote, p. 105. Not every relationship of poetry to reality is hereby negated. We will return to this point of view in connection with the problem of autonomy.
16. Ibid., p. 105—"Kein Sachgehalt, keine Formkategorie einer Dichtung, die nicht, sei's auch unkenntlich abgewandelt und sich selbst verborgen, aus der empirischen Realitaet stammte, der es sich entringt. Dadurch, wie durch die Umgruppierung der Momente kraft ihres Formgesetzes, verhaelt sich die Dichtung zur Realitaet."
17. For considerations of this kind Cf. Klaus Weimar, "Kritische Bemerkungen zur 'Logik der Dichtung,' " *Deutsche Vierteljahrsschrift* 48 (1974): 10–24, esp. pp. 12–13.
18. "Das Kunstwerk: Sprache und Gestalt," *Wort und Wirklichkeit* (Sechste Folge des Jahrbuches Gehalt und Gedanke), ed. Bayerische Akademie der Schoenen Kuenste (Munich, 1960), pp. 129–63; quote, p. 140.
19. *Logic*, p. 292: "They are special with reference to their logical structure, which in the case of the ballad and its related forms is the fictional, and in that of the first-person narrative the statement structure. More precisely, they are special forms because they have 'disavowed' their innate structure and gained the right of residing in the respective otherwise-structured genre: the ballad in the lyrical, the first-person narrative in the fictional genre." Also p. 308.
20. "Die Kunstballade und die Logik der Dichtung," *GRM N.F.* 22 (1972): 75–86; quotes, p. 77, 79. Cf. Texte und Argumentation bei K. Hamburger, *Logic*, pp. 305ff.
21. "Kunstballade," p. 81.
22. Ibid., pp. 81–82.
23. Ibid., p. 85.
24. Quoted in Hamburger, *Logic*, p. 60.
25. Ibid.
26. Due to frequent misunderstandings note that both cases are concerned with the simulated expression of reality. It is important for the structural analysis, whether the narrator *is* the narration, or whether—as Gero von Wilpert defines: "der Erzaehler als Betrachter an der Handlung keinen Anteil hat" (*Sachwoerterbuch der Literatur*, 5th ed. [Stuttgart, 1969], p. 229 under "Er-Form"). The latter narrative form is frequently still termed the third-person narrative, whereby the fundamental difference between it and Hamburger's category of the third-person narrative is overlooked. Because of the presence of a medium of narration (Aussagesubjekt), Hamburger categorizes this form also as a first-person narrative, which is consistent according to the structure of the language.
27. *Logic*, pp. 58–59. Therefore K. Weimar is incorrect when he states: "die Praefixe 'Als'- und 'Nicht'- koennen nun aber unmoeglich austauschbar sein" (*Kritische Bemerkungen*, p. 13). They are interchangeable according to whether one argues from a structural linguistic point of view, or from a psychological, critical one.
28. It is useless, at this point, to discuss how a reception by different critics can be inconsistent. Structural language analysis as an analysis of texts cannot of

29. I am using the term "Rezeptionsvorgabe" in the sense in which it is defined by Manfred Naumann and others. Cf. M. Naumann, D. Schlenstedt, et al., *Gesellschaft, Literatur, Lesen* (Berlin and Weimar, 1973), pp. 35f.
30. The term folk ballad is used as defined by Hans Glinz, *Textanalyse und Verstehenstheorie*, Vol. 1 (Frankfurt, 1973), p. 21: "Ein schriftkonstituierter und lesend zu rezipierender Text liegt vor, wenn ein geschrieben (gedruckt) vorhandener Text von seinem Autor von vornherein als geschriebener und den Rezipienten auch in geschriebener Form zuzuleitender Text hergestellt wurde." In connection with recording texts, we need not go into the precise delimitations and transitional forms, of which Glinz (p. 21) gives a list of examples, i.e., texts of written construction which are preserved in oral form, or those that are preserved in written form but are to be received orally.
31. I avail myself here of an expression of Käte Hamburger's, in order to make it fruitful for the analysis of the relationship between structure and reception. Cf. Hamburger, *Logic*, p. 292.
32. In order to prevent misunderstandings, be it noted: the difference or the ambivalence are the product of the reception and do not have as a prerequisite a structural ambivalence of the text. The stringency of structural analyses is not brought into question by these indications.
33. N. Fortunatow, "Kuenstlerischer Schaffensprozess und Leserrezeption," *Kunst und Literatur* 1 (1971): 26–44, quote by M. Naumann, *Gesellschaft*, n. p. 78n.35.
34. *Logic*, p. 58.
35. Gottfried Keller, "Die Leute von Seldwyla," *Erzaehlungen*, ed. Jonas Fraenkel (Zurich and Munich, 1927), 1: 85. Page numbers following extracts in the test are from this edition.
36. Franz Stanzel, *Die typischen Erzaehlsituationen im Roman* (Vienna-Stuttgart, 1955), p. 38.
37. Cf. also Hamburger, *Logic*, p. 312.
38. The *form* of the expression of reality becomes, for the reader, totally unreflected, a means of proving the factuality of that which is depicted.
39. This definition of the grammatical function of the predicate appears to be upheld also in newer studies of the time problem; cf. Hermann Gelhaus, "Sind Tempora Ansichtssache?," *Beihefte zur Zeitschrift Wirkendes Wort* 20 (1969): 80—"Das Praeterium drueckt aus, dass ein Tun (-Sein oder Geschehen) im Sprechzeitpunkt abgeschlossen ist."
40. Karl August Ott, "Ueber eine 'logische' Interpretation der Dichtung," *GRM* N.F. 11 (1961): 210–18; quote, p. 215. It is not to be excluded that there were historical or are actual levels of expectation of reception that consider a fictional text with historical content as "past made present" (ibid., p. 216). However one imagines the complex procedure of primary and secondary reception, one runs up against a paradoxical relationship between poetry and reality.
41. A good example is the television series "Bonanza." Because the viewers wanted to become familiar with the scene of the series, the Ponderosa Ranch, a real ranch to be used in filming, was built near Lake Tahoe. Millions of viewers who took it as a reality are responsible for its existence.

42. Cf. H. von Hofmannsthal, "Das Dorf im Gebirge," in *Gesammelte Werke*, ed. Herbert Steiner, Prose I (Frankfurt, 1956), pp. 277–81.
43. Erwin Pracht operates with this comparison; see "Probleme der kuenstlerischen Wiederspiegelung. Literatur und Wahrheit," *Deutsche Zeitschrift fuer Philosophie* 8 (1960): 838–62; quote, p. 846. He concedes that this comparison does not correspond to "dem Wesen der Sache," but he believes it correct to emphasize that the literary world is "ein Abbild der realen" (p. 846).
44. Pracht (ibid., p. 845), offers objections to Wolfgang Kayser's conclusions; cf. W. Kayser, *Die Wahrheit der Dichter* (Hamburg, 1959), p. 54: "Dichtung ist zunaechst eine in sich geschlossene Spielsphaere, eine voellig eigene Welt mit ihren eigenen Gesetzen, unterschieden von aller Realitaet."
45. Karin Kaminski, "Formalismus in der Literaturtheorie," *Weimarer Beitraege* 15 (1969): 103–22; quote, p. 112.
46. Ott's question would be answered in this manner ("Ueber eine 'logische' Interpretation," p. 212): "Auch die alte Frage, unter welchen Bedingungen die Darstellung fiktiver Personen ueberhaupt wahrscheinlich sein kann, wird nirgends beruehrt [d.h. in K. Hamburgers *Logik der Dichtung*, R.T.], so wenig wie die weitere Frage, welche Qualitaeten die Dichtung zu einem 'Organ des Weltverstaendnisses' machen, und in voelligem Dunkel bleibt ebenso das Problem der emotionalen Wirkung der Dichtung, das sich gerade dann prinzipiell stellen muesste, wenn man die Fiktionalitaet des literarisch Dargestellten so absolut behauptet." An answer to the question of plausibility would be found only in terms of a discussion of the problematics of realism.
47. Ott, "Ueber eine 'logische' Interpretation," p. 211.
48. Tarot, *Hugo von Hofmannsthal, Daseinsformen und dichterische Struktur* (Tuebingen, 1970).

CONTEMPORARY GENRE CRITICISM

Paul Hernadi

ORDER WITHOUT BORDERS: RECENT GENRE THEORY IN THE ENGLISH-SPEAKING COUNTRIES

Pace Croce, every piece of literary criticism entails some consideration of genre. There are, of course, more and less explicit ways of genre-alizing about individual texts. The lawyer friend who told me the other night that he had liked a best-selling, slightly pornographic novel better than the same author's earlier volume of humorous poems would hardly think of himself as a genre critic. Yet his casual remark did attest to the usefulness for his discourse of such generic concepts as novel, poem, pornographic, humorous, perhaps even best-selling, and their various combinations. Indeed, I seriously doubt whether the staunchest believer in the uniqueness of some or all works of literature could prove his point without simultaneously disproving it. After all, he would have to describe the characteristics of those allegedly unclassifiable texts and thereby indicate what they, as a class, have in common. This being the case, the basic question is not whether one can classify literary works but whether (and if so, for what purpose) one should classify them.

Many twentieth-century critics seem convinced that the study of genres is mainly useful as an aid for understanding how particular works come to be written and tend to be read by particular writers and readers.[1] But in presenting the results of concrete generic observations, every critic is likely to develop new or endorse old concepts of literature at large. The following rapid survey of recent genre criticism in the English-speaking countries focuses on theories which suggest new or considerably modify certain established ways of looking at the entire realm of imaginative literature.[2] Since the main concern of such theories is the order of verbal art rather than the borders between individual genres, many of them point beyond texts—the central area of literary study—to psychological, sociological, anthropological, and other "contexts" of literature.[3]

Two significant creative writers of the twentieth century, James Joyce and T.S. Eliot, gave novel turns to the ancient Greek tripartition of the style of presentation into authorial, figural, and mixed speech. Plato (and later Aristotle) had restricted the validity of that set of distinctions to the "manner"—as distinguished from the "matter"—of poetic discourse.[4] But post-Renaissance men of letters gradually came to mean genres rather than modes of discourse by "lyric," "dramatic," and "epic" literature. Around 1800, the Schlegel brothers, Schelling, Goethe, Jean Paul Richter, Hegel, and other German writers and philosophers finally established something like a doctrine of holy trinity in modern genre criticism.[5] Offering the familiar triad of freshman English courses on Poetry, Drama, and Fiction, the curriculum of many American colleges and universities bears witness to the survival of the old faith under increasingly powerful attacks.

Joyce incorporated his 1903 Paris sketch of a theory of genres as Stephen Dedalus's observations concerning art in general.[6] Young Stephen argues that the image must always be set between the artist and others in one of the following three forms: the lyrical ("wherein the artist presents his image in immediate relation to himself"), the epical ("wherein he presents his image in mediate relation to himself and to others"), or the dramatic ("wherein he presents his image in immediate relation to others"). We are not told how the three modes of presentation might be distinguished in other arts perhaps because, as the purist Stephen deplores, "even in literature, the highest and most spiritual art, the forms are often confused." Whether or not the author of *A Portrait* and of Joyce's later works would fully endorse the following imaginative distinctions, his younger self is permitted to present them at considerable length.

> The lyrical form is in fact the simplest verbal gesture of an instant of emotion.... He who utters it is more conscious of the instant of emotion than of himself as feeling emotion.... The narrative is no longer purely personal. The personality of

> the artist passes into the narration itself, flowing round the persons and the action like a vital sea.... The dramatic form is reached when the vitality which has flowed and eddied round each person fills every person with such vital force that he or she assumes a proper and intangible esthetic life. The personality of the artist ... finally ... impersonalizes himself, so to speak.... The artist, like the God of the creation, remains ... invisible, refined out of existence, indifferent, paring his fingernails. (pp. 250ff.)

Far from shunning generic interplay, T.S. Eliot postulates its necessity in a published lecture on *The Three Voices of Poetry*.[7] Without explicit reference to John Stuart Mill, he revives Mill's concept of lyric poetry[8] as "soliloquy overheard" and argues that part of our enjoyment of great literature results from our "overhearing" words which the poet, in the lyric voice, addresses to himself. Of course, "if the poem were exclusively for the author, it would be in a private and unknown language" and therefore no poem at all. Accordingly, Eliot is convinced that at least one of the two other voices must be heard in every lyric poem. Yet the lyric voice must not be completely silent in works written for the second or the third voice either: "If the author never spoke to himself, the result would not be poetry, though it might be magnificent rhetoric." Conventionally enough, the second voice is described in terms of narration and the third as a vehicle of drama—the former tells a tale, the latter exhibits an action, to an audience. Yet Eliot's concept of "voice" prompts the suggestive query whether Macbeth's speech beginning "to-morrow, and to-morrow, and to-morrow" especially moves us because "Shakespeare and Macbeth are uttering the words in unison" (pp. 33ff.). And the same vocal metaphor is well suited to convey Eliot's preference, shared by Joyce in practice if not in theory, for generically complex literature: "All that matters is, that in the end the voices should be heard in harmony; and I doubt whether in any real poem only one voice is audible" (p. 37).

The early Joyce and to some extent even the late Eliot fuse concerns of poetic "matter" and "manner." In contrast, Albert Guérard distinguishes and interrelates them.[9] With due apologies for the "fearful symmetry" of his tentative ninefold classification, Guérard suggests that "the lyric, the epic, and the dramatic spirits, severally, can be clothed in lyric, epic, and dramatic form." His examples for the respective genres include (pp. 197ff.) Goethe's "Wanderers Nachtlied" (lyrical lyric), "Ballad of Sir Patrick

Spence" (epic or narrative lyric), and Robert Browning's dramatic monologues (dramatic lyric); Byron's *Don Juan* (lyrical epic), *Iliad* (epic narrative), and *A Tale of Two Cities* (dramatic epic); *The Tempest* (lyrical drama), *Prometheus Unbound* (epic drama), and the "effective plays" of Scribe and Dumas fils (dramatic drama). Guérard's generic observations avoid the dogmatism of many critics who fail to distinguish "form" from "spirit"—the mode of literary evocation from the characteristics of the evoked world—and prefer what they consider pure genres (Guérard's "lyrical lyric," for example) to equally respectable kinds of literature. But his unrevoked, albeit skeptical, adherence to a threefold system of classification prevents Guérard from unifying his insights concerning proverbs, maxims, precepts, popular saws (p. 203), descriptive and philosophical poems (p. 228), personal essays, autobiographical narratives, impressionistic criticism (pp. 261ff.), and oratory (pp. 302–3) into the concept of a fourth genre or, in his terminology, a fourth type of generic form and spirit.

Such a genre emerges from the revival of the pre-Romantic category of didactic literature by the neo-Aristotelian critics of Chicago. Ronald S. Crane's protestation[10] to the contrary, the Chicago concept of didactic literature (as distinguished from philosophy and other forms of assertive discourse) is not very Aristotelian: whereas the Greek philosopher's distinctions according to the objects, means, and manner of mimesis concern the *whole* of imaginative literature *as* a mimetic art, the most general classification suggested by the Chicago critics divides literature into a mimetic and a didactic genre. In a didactic work, Elder Olson declares, everything "exists and has its peculiar character in order to enforce the doctrine."[11] Even though the metaphorical action of didactic allegories "bears, to a superficial view, a close resemblance to a plot," in this kind of poetry "the characters very generally represent the subjects, and the incidents the predicates, of the doctrinal proposition." Mimetic works, by contrast, are "ordered to plot"—a system of incidents which is "not, like allegorical action, complete because it completely expresses a given doctrine but because, as action, it resolves those issues out of which it has begun." Olson insists that speech is mainly meaningful (*lexis*) in didactic works while mimetic literature employs speech as action (*praxis*). "What the poetic character says in the mimetic poem is speech and has meaning; his *saying it* is action, an act of persuading, confessing, commanding, informing, torturing, or what not. His diction may be accounted for in grammatical and lexicographical terms; not so his action." As a result, most of what has been regarded as meaning in mimetic works should rather be considered "not meaning at all, but implications of character, passion, and fortune derived from the interpretation of speech and action" (pp. 54, 65ff., 71). I fail to see why such statements should describe the narrator's or a character's speech in the *Iliad* more accurately than in the *Divine Comedy*—Olson's chief examples for mimetic and didactic literature, respectively. Much as the meaning of any communication partly depends on the situational context, poetic meaning and plot—the thematic dimension and the mimetic—are interdependent aspects rather than competing or incompatible ingredients of literary works.

Crane's analysis of *Tom Jones* as a novel with a comic plot[12] is a more "Aristotelian" contribution to modern genre criticism. In the extant text of the *Poetics*, only tragic drama receives detailed attention, yet Aristotle's framework invites the application of some of the same critical principles to comic works of nondramatic literature also. Accepting the invitation, Crane's article implicitly interrelates Aristotle's remarks on the objects of mimesis, plot structure, and the "qualitative parts" of tragedy. If we recall that Aristotle demanded of the "perfect" tragedy that it should have (1) a basically good man (2) pass from happiness to misery (3) as a consequence of some great error on his part, we are likely to agree that the "three variables" according to which Crane classifies plots are very Aristotelian indeed. These variables are: the general estimate we are induced to form of the hero's *moral character,* as a result of which we wish for him either good or bad fortune at the end; the pleasurable or painful *events that befall* or are likely to befall the hero; and the degree and kind of his *responsibility* for what happens to him. Beyond doubt, this conceptual apparatus is far more sophisticated than the particular insight it is intended to substantiate, namely, that "the plot of *Tom Jones* has a pervasively comic form" (pp. 620ff., 632–33). Yet it does not combine as much of a twentieth-century reader's hindsight with Plato's and Aristotle's views of the "matter" of poetic discourse as one might wish and as other critics discussing the tragic-comic dichotomy have succeeded in combining.

The very title of Albert Cook's *The Dark Voyage and the Golden Mean: A Philosophy of Comedy* indicates the bipolar framework in which the actual subject matter of the book, as it is specified by the subtitle, has been placed.[13] In Cook's suggestively argued opinion, tragedy and comedy show the world under the opposed aspects of the Wonderful and the Probable, respectively. Without much need for being overly selective as to appropriate topics, each achieves its goal contrary to expectations: "Where comedy says, 'even in the nonprobable does the predictable take place,' tragedy says, 'even in the probable, the wonderful is manifest'" (p. 44). Cook conceives of the two genres broadly. Like Chaucer's Monk and Fielding (in the Preface to *Joseph Andrews*) long before him, he assumes that tragic and comic works are not necessarily written in the dialogue form of drama: *The Odyssey, Don Quixote, Tom Jones,* and *Finnegans Wake* are among his discussed samples of comedy. Nor does he accept the happy or unhappy outcome of a plot as the basis for generic classification: "*Philoctetes* and *The Tempest* are both profound, and both have a happy ending; one is tragedy, the other comedy" (p. 32). What, then, makes the difference? In accordance with his wonderful-probable dichotomy, Cook contrasts tragedy's reliance on ultimate values (good and evil) to comedy's preoccupation with manners, tragedy's exploration of individual souls to comedy's interest in social contexts (generation, family), tragedy's emphasis on the godlike in man to comedy's stress on qualities men share with beasts and machines. In the area of stage conventions, the tragic soliloquy (character addressing his soul) neatly corresponds to the comic aside (character addressing the audience). But Cook also points out that the asides of stage plays manifest a general tendency inherent in comic works of fiction as well as drama: the deliberate breaking of the reader's or spectator's illusion as to the reality of the imaginative world he is invited to contemplate. Tragic works, by contrast, require that we take them "seriously" so that we shall "identify ourselves as individuals with the protagonist—whence our pity and terror" (pp. 33ff., 45ff.).

Reviving two traditional antinomies of drama criticism (failure-success and aristocrat-bourgeois), Cook insists that unrequited pain and ultimate failure in our probable world are essential to the dignity of the tragic hero. The "active hubris" of an Oedipus, Brutus, Lear, or Othello is to deny man's limitations; each feels that his individuality cannot be conquered and that therefore, like a god, "he can will the perfection of his own action." Yet the wonderful attempt to achieve godhead is "an attempt at which man must always fail," and the active hubris of the aristocratic hero will soon have to be "cured"—expiated—by passive suffering. The "passive hubris" of the comic hero who is a bourgeois in spirit (if not indeed in social status as well) is different: "He wants to make sure that when he puts a nickel in the slot machine of the cosmos he gets a full nickel's worth, even if he has to pound the machine violently." Cook warns against confusing this "pounding of the machine" with active hubris. Whereas the tragic hero "actively creates his fate," the bourgeois hero in passive hubris warps his personality "for equity in material exchanges" (pp. 87ff.). In view of this penetrating observation one is left wondering why Ibsen's and Strindberg's heroes whom Cook declares guilty of passive rather than active hubris should be considered heroes of tragedy at all. Some of them (and many other more recent literary characters) could be better understood as "warped heroes" of works which are only partially tragic because, to a considerable extent, they are also melodramatic, ironic, satirical, or tragicomic.

A similar reduction of varied phenomena within the traditional bipolar system of tragedy and comedy mars Susanne K. Langer's pertinent remarks.[14] *In Philosophy in a New Key,* Langer linked the "emotive content" of art works in general to something "prerational and vital, something of the life rhythms we share with all growing, hungering, moving, and fearing creatures" (p. 211). In *Feeling and Form,* she considers the two "great dramatic forms" not only in the more conventional terms of a "tragic theme" (guilt leading to expiation) and a "comic theme" (vanity leading to exposure). Rather, she argues persuasively that tragic and comic works bear the marks of one of two fundamental "rhythms" of life; they contrast the human awareness of individuation and death to the immortality, as it were, of species as such and the protozoa. While comedy exhibits the vital rhythm of nature's self-preservation, tragedy abstracts the rhythm of self-consummation from the irreversible phases of multicellular life: growth, maturity, and decline. Neither genre is, of course, restricted to treat its prototype in a literal sense; tragedy, for instance, tends to imprint the rhythm of "deathward advance" as a perceptible form on matter involving a time span of days or hours instead of the "decades of biological consumption" (pp. 327, 350f., 360–61). This theory steers clear of the bias often found in philosophically inclined critics who approach the two genres with a preconceived model of the world: Langer does not have to interpret the tragic view of life as an "interim reading" of an ultimately untragic universe; nor need she demand that comedy draw a "magic circle" beyond which its reader must not step lest "the wider and deeper view" of the essentially tragic human existence destroy the pattern of the comic world.[15] Her comprehensive view of death-bound individual existence within the uninterrupted flow of self-perpetuating life welcomes the poetic presentation of either "rhythm." But some of Langer's remarks on individual works—particularly the suggestion that Corneille's and Racine's plays are "heroic comedies" rather than tragedies (p. 337)—reveal some potentially misleading ridgidity in her thought-provoking system.

Eric Bentley's discussion of a greater variety of genres in *The Life of the Drama* exemplifies his concepts of melodrama, farce, tragedy, comedy, and tragicomedy with frequent references to novels, operas, and motion pictures as well as plays.[16] This is not surprising; Bentley's view of drama as the imitation of men's conscious and unconscious conflicts is indebted to such thinkers as Plato, Aristotle, Schopenhauer, Nietzsche, Bergson, and Freud, whose respective pertinent statements rely on a broader empirical foundation than the actor's stage. Bentley describes melodrama and farce as "uninhibited." While melodrama derives its basic formula, innocence surrounded by malevolence, from "more or less paranoid fantasies," farce reveals the fierce pleasure of aggression with which "innocence" retaliates. From an "adult, civilized, healthy" perspective, both genres appear "childish, savage, sick." Yet they employ the unrestrained "naturalism of the dream life": their fairy-tale-like features—indulgence in physical violence, naïve juxtaposition of perfect heroes and contemptible villains—reflect a certain kind of reality, namely, the reality of unconscious drives. According to Bentley, words belonging to these "lower forms" tend to have a wholesome "cathartic" effect on readers and spectators as they help release suppressed fears and desires through the channel of harmless aesthetic responses (pp. 203ff., 216–17, 223, 246, 255ff.).

Tragedy and comedy are "higher forms" precisely because they incorporate rather than simply reject important aspects of melodrama and farce, respectively. Surely, the heroes and villains of tragedy and the fools and knaves of comedy are more complex than the corresponding character types in melodrama and farce. Yet it is not verisimilitude but the subtle distribution of responsibility that makes a play like *Othello* tragic rather than melodramatic. "Iago instigates; Othello is susceptible. Between them, Iago and Othello combine vices of civilization with those of barbarism." Tragedy transcends melodrama as justice transcends revenge: in melodrama, the innocent hero may requite suffering; in tragedy, the guilty hero must endure it (pp. 257, 267–68, 288ff.). Since tragedy thwarts our impulse to identify with innocence and exacts identification with guilt, it promotes self-knowledge instead of melodrama's wishful gratification of the ego. Comedy promotes self-knowledge in a different fashion; unlike farce, it faces the misery of the human condition before it decides "to look the other way." So much can be readily admitted even though Bentley overshoots the mark when he interprets comedy's "Let's not go into that" as "That won't bear going into"—an attitude of "pessimism blacker than tragedy, for tragedy presupposes that everything can be gone into" (pp. 260ff., 298–99).

In Bentley's opinion, tragedy as well as comedy provides "horribly conclusive evidence that life is not worth living," yet both genres ultimately affirm the value of human existence "in defiance of the stated facts." As the concluding chapter of *The Life of the Drama* implies, this paradox is mitigated in one kind of tragicomedy, emphasized in another. Bentley distinguishes works in which tragedy is encountered and transcended from works in which the penetrating eye of comedy refuses "to look the other way." "Tragedy with a comic sequel" elaborates on the final moment of reconciliation—brief if at all present in genuine tragedy. Shakespeare's *Measure for Measure*, Kleist's *Prinz von Homburg*, Goethe's *Iphigenie* and *Faust* are tragicomedies in this sense of the word; they celebrate forgiveness as opposed to "justice," that higher form of revenge (pp. 308–9, 316ff., 319, 331). The other, more somber and more up-to-date kind of tragicomedy could be described as "comedy with a tragic sequel" except that the mood of the unhappy ending tends to cast its shadow on the entire works belonging to this genre. Ibsen's *Wild Duck*, Chekhov's *Cherry Orchard*, Shaw's *Saint Joan*, Pirandello's *Six Characters*, and Brecht's *Mahagonny* are among Bentley's relatively early examples; and those plays have in a sense prepared the way for such more pronounced expressions of tragicomic despair as Beckett's *Godot*, Ionesco's *Chairs*, and other representatives of the Theater of the Absurd. Bentley knows, of course, that comic effects often intensify rather than lighten the gloom permeating this type of modern drama. But he also insists that "even gallows humor is humor," and that a man who truly lost hope "would not be on hand to say so"—especially not in the elaborate form of an artwork (pp. 319–20, 334–35, 345, 350, 352).

In the work of the two most original North American critics, tragedy and comedy merge into the larger pattern of literature in fascinatingly disparate ways. In *Attitudes toward History*, Kenneth Burke deals with literary genres in the light of his private theory of collective and individual behavior—a highly undogmatic blend of (mainly Marxist) sociology and (mainly Freudian) depth psychology.[17] Burke considers "Yes, No, and the intermediate realm of Maybe" as the basic attitudes in forming and reforming human congregations, and the "expressive forms" of literary genres represent for him "various ways in which these attitudes are both subtly and grandly symbolized" (p. 1). The great epic poem, tragedy, comedy, a genre termed humor, and the *carpe diem* type of lyric poetry provide "frames of acceptance." The epic poem makes humility and self-glorification "work together" by magnifying the character of the warlike hero to the size of the situation he confronts; contemplating the hero's deeds, one adopts a realistic sense of one's own limitations but also obtains, through partial identification with the great figure, the "distinction necessary for the needs of self-justification." Humor promotes acceptance the other way round; it is "dwarfing the situation" with an attitude of "happy stupidity," whereby "the gravity of life simply fails to register." Both tragedy and comedy repudiate pride and, as frames of acceptance, advocate the advantage of the average person's limitations. The difference lies in this: while tragedy exalts hubris as the root of awe-inspiring crimes, comedy dismisses it as a laughable mistake. Burke suggests that "the rise of business individualism" in Periclean Athens "sharpened the awareness of personal ambition as a motive in human acts" and ascribes to the three great tragedians a "pious, orthodox, conservative, 'reactionary' attitude" toward this kind of hubris (p. 39).

Burke's remarks on genres offering "frames of rejection" have further, if less direct, bearing on tragedy and comedy. Aware that the acceptance of *A* may involve the rejection of *non-A*, Burke does not contrast acceptance and rejection as mutually exclusive (p. 57). It is therefore in a dialectically qualified sense that elegy, satire, and burlesque reject. Elegy does so by a reversal of the strategy of humor: "It spreads the disproportion between the weakness of the self and the magnitude of the situation." But there is also an element of acceptance in elegy, since a person with a perfected technique of complaint will not shun situations enabling him to use such an equipment. Elegy seeks to develop tolerance to blows of great misfortune by stylistically administering misfortune in small doses; this "homeopathic" strategy is, however, not the best in situations where the blows could have been averted altogether. It seems to me that Burke could have made similar statements about tragedy as well, and his observations concerning satire and burlesque also apply to certain types of comedy. Satire attacks in others the weaknesses and temptations that trouble the satirist himself; it is "an approach *from without* to something *from within.*" In burlesque and its related forms (polemic, caricature), there is no attempt to get inside the victim's psyche, and the biased selection of externals of behavior reaches its "logical conclusion" with the target's "reduction to absurdity" (pp. 44ff.).

Although it is never clearly explained why the grotesque and the didactic belong to the "intermediate realms of Maybe," Burke seems to consider them as manifestations of that third type of "attitude toward history." Since he avowedly views genres as "recordings on the dial," we need not blame him for the tendency of interpreting the indicators in other than literary terms. Yet his various discussions of the grotesque (suggestively described as "the cult of incongruity without the laughter") and the didactic ("today usually called propaganda") are sociologically oriented to the point of making it doubtful whether Burke considers those two "preponderantly transitional" genres as genres of imaginative literature at all (pp. 57ff.).

To be sure, Kenneth Burke's widespread influence on his contemporaries and younger critics hardly relies on his concepts of genre. In contrast, much of Northrop Frye's even greater influence is based on his *Anatomy of Criticism,* offering one of the most ambitious theories of literary classification ever devised.[18] Frye knows, of course, that "the purpose of criticism by genres is not so much to classify as to clarify traditions and affinities, thereby bringing out a large number of literary relationships that would not be noticed as long as there were no context established for them" (pp. 247–48). Accordingly, he employs several principles of generic classification instead of preferring or subordinating, for example, a concept of tragedy to a concept of drama or vice versa. Not unlike Aristotle's coordinated distinctions according to the means, objects, and manners of mimesis, Frye's concepts of *mythoi,* modes, and radicals of presentation help us see literary works in a polycentric framework.

In the third essay of the *Anatomy,* Frye postulates the existence of four "narrative categories of literature broader than, or logically prior to, literary genres" and attempts to place every story that can be told on a gigantic conceptual map with the "romantic," the "tragic," the "comic," and the "ironic" (or "satiric") as points of compass. The four "generic plots" or *mythoi* emerge as movements within a highly desirable world (romance), within a painfully defective world (irony and satire), downward from innocence through hamartia to catastrophe (tragedy), or upward from the fallen world of experience through threatening complications to "a general assumption of post-dated innocence in which everyone lives happily ever after" (comedy) (p. 162). Frye's treatment of tragedy and comedy connects aspects of similarity and difference in an especially stimulating manner. Commenting on God's words about man in *Paradise Lost*—"Sufficient to have stood, though free to fall" (III, 99)—Frye points out that Adam loses freedom by his very use of freedom "just as, for a man who deliberately jumps off a precipice, the law of gravitation acts as fate for the brief remainder of his life." In Frye's view of tragedy, the same act of "narrowing a comparatively free life into a process of causation" is performed by Macbeth when he accepts the logic of usurpation, by Hamlet when he accepts the logic of revenge, and by Lear when he accepts the logic of abdication (pp. 211–12). The plot structure of comedy reverses the process and leads the hero out of bondage into a "stable and harmonious order" which, at the end of most comic works, turns out to have been only temporarily "disrupted by folly, obsession, forgetfulness, 'pride and prejudice'" (p. 171). Without explicit reference to Ludwig Jekels's paper "On the Psychology of Comedy,"[19] Frye suggests a similarly Freudian interpretation: "What normally happens is that a young man wants a young woman, that his desire is resisted by some opposition, usually paternal, and that near the end of the play some twist in the plot enables the hero to have his will." Having said so much, Frye has prepared his reader to consider as characteristic of comedy "a kind of comic Oedipus situation in which the hero replaces his father as lover." In some rare yet revealing instances, even "fear of violating a mother" can occur in otherwise comic works such as *The Marriage of Figaro* or *Tom Jones*. More frequently, however, only "psychological alliance" links the hero's bride to his or her (step)mother (pp. 180–81). Likewise, the hero's way to happiness need not be obstructed by his own father (who may or may not be his rival for the heroine's love). The difficulties often stem from such "father surrogates" as the girl's father, her guardian, or a suitor who is older and wealthier than the hero and thus "partakes of the father's closer relation to established society." With this sociological hint Frye supersedes Jekels, who simply argued that comedy lifts our spirits by displacing Oedipal guilt and the concomitant punishment from son to father. Frye in turn notes how frequently comic works add social criticism to their attack on those who exercise paternal authority over the young lovers; "some sharp observation of the rising power of money and the sort of ruling class it is building up" can be found as early as in Renaissance playwrights, including Ben Jonson (pp. 163ff.).

On the whole, of course, Frye's view of the four *mythoi* is far less indebted to Freud, Marx, and their respective followers than it is to Sir James Frazer's and Carl Gustav Jung's writings on mythology. He regards the four generic plots as four phases in mankind's most comprehensive myths. Corresponding to four phases of the "natural cycle" around the clock (dawn, zenith, sunset, darkness) and the calendar (spring, summer, fall, winter), Comedy, Romance, Tragedy, and Irony (or Satire) emerge from the third essay as four basic patterns of the human imagination. In the first essay Frye argues that all such patterns manifest themselves most clearly in myths: since gods possess the greatest possible power of action, stories about them "operate on the top level of human desire." While the hero of genuine myth is a divine being and thus superior in kind both to men and to their natural environment, the typical hero of romance, legend, and *märchen* is superior to other men not in kind but only in degree even though, in the world evoked by this group of works, the ordinary laws of nature are "slightly suspended." Superior in degree to other men but subject to his natural environment is the hero of most epic and tragedy—the leader. Approximately equal to other members of his society, the "hero" of most comedy and realistic fiction is "one of us." To myth, romance, aristocratic "high mimetic" and realistic "low mimetic" Frye adds irony as a fifth mode. Leaving the point of low mimetic verisimilitude behind, this *mode*—which is not to be confused with the *mythos* of irony already mentioned—shows us characters "inferior in power or intelligence to ourselves, so that we have the sense of looking down on a scene of bondage, frustration, or absurdity." With such "ironic" works as Kafka's *Trial,* modern literature recoils, so to speak, from the realm of plausibility toward the mode of myth, for "the dim outlines of sacrificial rituals and dying gods begin to reappear in it" (pp. 33–34, 42). This reference to the mythic reality of dying gods indicates Frye's implicit awareness of the fact that myths can be projections of human fears as well as human aspirations. Furthermore, Frye attributes much of the subtlety of great literature to "modal counterpoint." The "tonality" of Shakespeare's *Antony and Cleopatra,* for example, is high mimetic, but we may also look at the great leader Marc Antony "ironically, as a man enslaved by passion" (pp. 50–51). Despite the possibility of such interplay between different modes, Frye seems justified in postulating a growing tendency to diminish the hero's power of action both in classical antiquity and in the Western tradition since the early Middle Ages.

Frye's historical account of the "themes" of literature as similarly displaced versions of their archetypes is less convincing. Yet his remarks on theme—Frye's term for Aristotle's *dianoia*, usually translated as "thought"—are highly stimulating. Frye argues that while plot or *mythos* determines the temporal shape of a work as a sequence of hypothetical events, theme or *dianoia* holds the work together in a simultaneous, quasi-spatial pattern of meaning. *Mythos* and *dianoia* thus emerge as complementary aspects of all literature: "the *mythos* is the *dianoia* in movement, the *dianoia* is the *mythos* in *stasis*." Their relative prevalence will make some works primarily "fictional," others primarily "thematic"; predominantly fictional works focus on the "internal fiction of the hero and his society," predominantly thematic works in turn establish a kind of "external fiction" by emphasizing the contemporaneous or posthumous relation between the writer and *his* society—the potential reading public (pp. 52–53, 83).

The relative proximity of works to the fictional or the thematic extreme of literature is one of Frye's concerns in the fourth essay of the *Anatomy*. Here Frye suggests that literary works consist of what ideally are spoken, printed, chanted, and acted verbal structures (pp. 246–47). Works in which the poet addresses his audience belong to the genre of *epos*—we are reminded that by *ta epe* the Greeks meant poems to be recited—while *fiction*, a far less palpably authorial type of literature, appears designed for the printed page. The "singer" of *lyric* poems pretends to be communing with himself or, at any rate, with someone other than his actual listener or reader who, in John Stuart Mill's phrase, "overhears" the lyric utterances. Finally and most conventionally, the unmediated presence of hypothetical figures points to acting as the "radical of presentation" characteristic of *drama*. Although all genres may and, since the invention of the printing press, increasingly do exist in written form, Frye's concept of the "radical of presentation" as the criterion for generic distinctions appears convincing in the light of his witty analogy of the keyboard. "Just as it is possible to distinguish genuine piano music from the piano score of an operetta or symphony, so we may distinguish genuine 'book literature' from books containing the reduced textual scores of recited or acted pieces." Thus, for example, even the least stagelike closet drama can be seen as being "referred back to some kind of theater, however much of a castle in the air," and in Joseph Conrad's novels "the genre of the written word is being assimilated to that of the spoken one" through the introduction of internal narrators (pp. 247–48).

At their purest, the individual radicals of presentation require that either the poet (drama) or the hypothetical figures (epos) or both the poet and the hypothetical figures (fiction) remain "concealed" from the audience, or else that the audience "be concealed from the poet" (lyric). The occasional waiver of a given type of "concealment" will, of course, result in various combinations of two or more generic "rhythms," and Frye's assignment of a special kind of diction to each of the four "radicals" further articulates the possibilities of generic interpenetration (pp. 248ff.). The *Anatomy* connects regularly patterned verse with epos, logically straightforward prose with fiction, the verbalization of a stream of consciousness with lyric, and the permanent suiting of style to the characters and situations of the "internal fiction" with drama. But the respective "rhythms" of recurrence, continuity, association, and decorum are obviously meant to be most congenial with (rather than exclusively constituent of) one of the four genres. From the complex interplay between writer, hero, and their respective "societies" in most works of literature, lyric and epos emerge as predominantly thematic with one significant difference between them. Whereas the lyric poet tends to write "as an individual, emphasizing the separateness of his personality and the distinctness of his vision," the writer working in the epos form (which includes oratorical prose) devotes himself to being a spokesman of his community: "A poetic knowledge and expressive power which is latent or needed in his society comes to articulation in him" (p. 54). Fiction and drama are in turn allied in their relative neglect for the thematic relationship between writer and reader. The chief verbal vehicle of fiction is a kind of prose which tends to be a "transparent medium" presenting its subject matter as "plate glass in a shop window" presents what is behind it, and the generic rhythm of drama can be described as "epos or fiction absorbed by decorum"—a variety of speech rhythms appropriate to individual speakers in different situations (pp. 265, 268–69).

In the foregoing account of Frye's concepts of genre I have

refrained from commenting on terminological contradictions and conceptual discrepancies which, in some of the many pronouncements about Northrop Frye, have been duly censured.[20] All such criticism notwithstanding, his way of looking at literature continues to have a powerful impact on a large variety of critics. There are hundreds, if not thousands, of worthwhile attempts to apply Frye's concepts to such concrete tasks as the interpretation of a particular work or the historical delineation of a more or less self-propelled generic tradition.[21] Furthermore, a great deal of effort in the literary theory of the coming decades is likely to be directed toward correlating some of Frye's genre concepts with those of other major critics, ancient and modern. One important reason for this lies, I believe, in Frye's frequent success in making us see generic traditions and affinities as interdependent forces in what he likes to call the "literary universe" (p. 122).

Notes

1. The following critics stress the importance of genres as flexible, quasi-institutional frames for writers: Harold Elmer Mantz, "Types in Literature," *Modern Language Review* 12 (1917); Norman H. Pearson, "Literary Forms and Types," *English Institute Annual, 1940* (New York, 1941); George Watson, *The Study of Literature* (New York, 1969), Chap. 5; Alistair Fowler, "The Life and Death of Literary Forms," *New Literary History* 2 (1971). Like everything else in this survey, this list is highly selective. Arguments stressing the function of genre concepts as hermeneutic tools for readers include Charles E. Whitmore, "The Validity of Literary Definitions," *PMLA* 39 (1924); E.D. Hirsch, Jr., *Validity in Interpretation* (New Haven, Conn., 1967), Chap. 3; Eliseo Vivas, "Literary Classes: Some Problems," *Genre* 1 (1968); Allan Rodway, "Generic Criticism: The Approach through Type, Mode and Kind," in *Contemporary Criticism,* ed. Malcolm Bradbury and David Palmer, Stratford-upon-Avon Studies, No. 12 (London, 1970). A checklist of currently circulating generic notions can be found in Allan Rodway and Brian Lee, "Coming to Terms," *Essays in Criticism* 14 (1964).
2. In *Beyond Genre: New Directions in Literary Classification* (Ithaca, N.Y., 1972) I tried to place a greater number of British and American theories in an international context. The first and last chapters of that book present my own views on the subject.
3. Guarded concern for the contexts of texts was recently sanctioned by René Wellek, perhaps the most respected spokesman for the intrinsic approach:

"One cannot discuss the nature of tragedy without reference to religion and ritual, or isolate the history of fictional forms from such questions as the status of the teller of the tale or the composition of the audience addressed at a particular historical moment. I have . . . made a possibly oversharp distinction between 'extrinsic' and 'intrinsic' approaches to literature." *Discriminations: Further Concepts of Literature* (New Haven, Conn., 1970), p. 335.

4. Plato, *The Republic*, Book 3 (392c to 394c) and Aristotle, *Poetics,* Chap. 3 (1448a).
5. Cf. Irene Behrens, *Die Lehre von der Einteilung der Dichtkunst* (Halle, 1940).
6. *A Portrait of the Artist As a Young Man* (London, 1916), Chap. 5. Cf. also James Joyce, *Critical Writings,* ed. Ellsworth Mason and Richard Ellmann (New York, 1959), p. 145 for the basic idea of this tripartition and pp. 143ff. on tragedy and comedy.
7. New York, 1954.
8. "What is Poetry?" (1833), *Dissertations and Discussions,* 2d ed. (London, 1867), 1: 71f.
9. *Preface to World Literature* (New York, 1940).
10. *The Languages of Criticism and the Structure of Poetry* (Toronto, 1953), pp. 47, 156ff., 197n. 57.
11. "William Empson, Contemporary Criticism, and Poetic Diction" (1950), in *Critics and Criticism,* ed. R.S. Crane (Chicago, 1952).
12. R.S. Crane, "The Concept of Plot and the Plot of *Tom Jones*" (1950), in *Critics and Criticism* (Chicago, 1952).
13. Cambridge, Mass., 1949.
14. *Philosophy in a New Key* (1942), 6th paperback ed. (New York, 1954); *Feeling and Form* (New York, 1953).
15. The quoted phrases come from two otherwise most penetrating and judicious works: Una Ellis-Fermor, *The Frontiers of Drama,* 2d ed. (London, 1964), p. 147; and David Daiches, *Critical Approaches to Literature* (Englewood Cliffs, N.J., 1956), p. 238.
16. New York, 1964.
17. Paperback ed. (Boston, 1961), reprint of 1937 edition.
18. Princeton, 1957.
19. In *Selected Papers* (New York, 1952). "On the Psychology of Comedy" was first published in German in 1926.
20. Cf. esp. W.K. Wimsatt, "Northrop Frye: Criticism as Myth" and Geoffrey H. Hartman, "Ghostlier Demarcations," in *Northrop Frye in Modern Criticism,* ed. Murrey Krieger (New York, 1966) with a bibliography of publications by and about Frye. For an extensive structuralist critique, cf. Tzvetan Todorov, *Introduction à la littérature fantastique* (Paris, 1970), pp. 15ff.
21. Two examples must suffice: Graham G. Hough, *A Preface to the Faerie Queene* (London, 1962) and Robert Scholes, "Towards a Poetics of Fiction: An Approach through Genre," *Novel* 2 (1969). The attractiveness of Frye's genre concepts beyond the limits of literary criticism is persuasively demonstrated in Hayden White, *Metahistory* (Baltimore, 1973).

Herman P. Salomon

OBSERVATIONS ON THE DEFINITION, EVOLUTION, AND SEPARATION OF GENRES IN THE STUDY OF FRENCH LITERATURE

Among the French literary theoreticians of the sixteenth and seventeenth century—whose purview did not include the novel—we find in regard to genre a rather confused thinking and incoherent exposition, obscured even more by the imprecise nature of their rapidly antiquated terminology. Thus during the seventeenth century, plays went by the name of poems; tragedies and comedies were often indifferently styled comedies, although complex theories on the distinction between the two (or more) kinds of comedy were rampant.[1] During the next century, Voltaire at one point declared that each work of literature must be judged on its own terms and is a genre unto itself, but at other times categorized and legislated using the undefined generic distinctions of the previous centuries.[2] In respect to genres, as in other matters, Voltaire is best remembered for a witticism: *Tous les genres sont bons, hors le genre ennuyeux* (*L'enfant prodigue*, Préface). The death-blow to French interest in concrete definitions of genres was dealt by one of France's greatest literary critics, Ferdinand Brunetière (1849–1906), the introductory volume of whose work *L'évolution des genres dans l'histoire de la littérature* (Paris, 1890) was never followed by the work itself. Some ten reprintings (the last in 1931) testify to the value of Brunetière's history of French literary criticism from the Renaissance through the nineteenth century. The historical part makes up the body of one volume. The idea contained in its first thirty pages, that literary history and biology are related fields and that literary genres are governed by Darwin's laws on the evolution of the species, was roundly ridiculed. Brunetière was henceforth known to many who had not read him as *l'homme de l'évolution des genres* and the study of genres became a ridiculous thing.[3] Brunetière dogmatically maintained his initial stance and published one chapter of the unborn work, the study on the evolution of tragedy.[4] Nowhere, though, did Brunetière attempt to determine the legitimacy of the generic labels he employed to classify the Greek, Latin, and French works whose "evolution" he described, at times with remarkable insight and critical acumen. In one study, unrelated to the evolutionistic doctrine, he tried to establish a dividing line between melodrama and tragedy, which, though his treatment is totally unsystematic and even arbitrary, also provides valuable insights.[5]

There is no thorough assessment of the entire notion of literary genres in French literature, such as that achieved in Italian literary criticism by Benedetto Croce (1866-1952) and his opponents.[6] An appraisal of the problem thus must rely on a few stray and simplistic replies to Croce and on a number of brief historical overviews by more or less noted scholars which have appeared in various obscure publications, never to be reprinted; most of these originated at a convention on literary genres held at Lyons in 1939.[7] The great American expert on French dramatic literature of the seventeenth century, Henry Carrington Lancaster, tried in his doctoral thesis to arrive at a precise distinction between tragedy and tragicomedy in *The French Tragi-Comedy* (Baltimore, 1907), undaunted by the fact that Pierre Corneille first labeled his *Cid* (1636-37) a *tragicomédie* and later changed his mind and decided it was a *tragédie*. It is no doubt significant that Robert Champigny, in three recent volumes, *Le genre romanesque* (Monte Carlo, 1963), *Le Genre poétique* (Monte Carlo, 1963) and *Le Genre dramatique* (Monte Carlo, 1965) makes no attempt to define these promising titles at the outset and does not take into consideration any scholarly doubts on their significance.[8] The criticism which calls itself "New" of the last decades, and its offshoots such as rhetorical criticism and linguistic discourse analysis, were not undertaken on the authority of the idea of genre, and generally do not investigate the actual genres in which writers wrote their texts. Linguistic-structural criticism involves closer attention to form than genres seem to demand, and phenomenological or anthropological structuralist criticism is leading away from the aesthetic subject matter of the literary works rather than to it.[9] The problem that faces students of French literature is that whereas schools and colleges continue to rely heavily and often exclusively for their description of French masterpieces on fossilized generic concepts, literary scholars have failed to test their relevance by actually confronting them with the literary works to which they are perhaps too readily applied.[10]

The provocative title of a staid essay by Jean-Paul Sartre, "Qu'est-ce que la littérature?" (1947), ultimately led to a radical reevaluation, with nihilistic overtones, of the entire concept of literature. If everything that is said or written is literature, including the slogan "I like Ike" and the order of a cup of coffee, the question of generic categories becomes, literally, academic. In a questionable and somewhat rambling lecture Roman Jakobson tried to show where literature begins.[11] The demonstration was carried out much more successfully by the noted Portuguese literary and social historian António José Saraiva in his recent essay "Message et Littérature."[12] Here he convincingly establishes the absolute distinction between the nonliterary and the literary message and between scientific and literary discourse. Within the latter he perceives two activities: music and oratory. He goes on to delimit within oratory the separate genres of dramatic and narrative discourse:

> We do not believe it is possible to reduce the dramatic game (*jeu dramatique*) to the narrative; it is only possible to transform one into the other, just as the simple [i.e., nonliterary] message may be transformed into the literary message by the procedure of translation [i.e., transposition]. When one gives a "summary" of an authentic play, the result is a narrative, not a summarized play. Obviously, this does not mean that one cannot, within the same work, switch from one genre to the other, as is the case in classical epic which is, in reality, an oratorical message that alternately transforms itself into the dramatic game (dialogue, speeches) and narrative; as is also the case with Brechtian theatre, which represents a return to the dramatic game's oratorical origins.... Nor does this mean that one cannot combine both genres, as we find in certain autobiographical narratives which turn to account the identification of the hero with the Locutor. The essential point here is that two distinct structures do exist.[13]

Saraiva, while touching upon the problem of distinguishing "lyrical" poetry from narrative and drama, suggests at the end of his essay that poetry belongs to the subdivision of literature which he calls Music, rather than to the one which he terms Oratory.

> What distinguishes Poetry is its refusal to conform to the conventions of the message. In using the code, the Poet submits it to a system outside of the code. The Poet uses language as a tool without submitting himself to its system. Now, Music is a system outside of Language, wherein there is no room for the Locutor and the Receiver [the terms used by Saraiva: *Locuteur* or *Emetteur*, and *Destinataire* or *Récepteur*, are clearly explained at the outset of his essay], and neither is there [within Music] a relationship between *significant* and *signifié*. (p. 12)

Since Saraiva does not deal in this essay with any national literature in particular (except for stray allusions to the Portuguese poet and critic Fernando Pessoa), his disquisition does not face the problem, peculiar to French literature, of defining "pure poetry." Going beyond the memorable debate between Paul Valéry and Henri Bremond regarding the nature of pure poetry, André Gide was perhaps the first Frenchman to consider the interesting question, put to him by A.E. Housman, as to whether most of the rhymed matter which goes under the label of "French poetry" is, in fact, poetry.[14] A systematic and penetrating attempt to define a separate genre called poetry in French literature appeared in 1971.[15] A. Kibédi Varga, a Hungarian, argues in that study, which is also a bibliographical survey, that within French poetry there may be poetical and nonpoetical uses of verse. He concludes, like Gide, that most rhymed matter in the French language is, in reality, versified rhetorical discourse. His criterion for distinguishing "pure" poetry excludes nearly all French verses written before Baudelaire. Varga's concern is with meaning rather than musicality: real poems do not *possess* a meaning, but they sometimes *offer* one; often they neither possess nor offer meaning, "by their interrogation, they merely postulate a meaning."[16]

The novel, which, as stated above, was excluded from the sixteenth- and seventeenth-century French critical purview, continued, in the eighteenth, to be looked upon as a genre outside of literature.[17] The first systematic attempt to define it as a distinct genre within literature appeared only in 1943, with the publication, under Jean Prévost's direction, of *Problèmes du Roman,* a collection of essays.[18] At stake, as a feature distinguishing novel from drama, was mainly the problem of the presence of the author in the work. This problem has continued to be the preoccupation of even the most recent New Criticism. Curiously, when one considers that the new-critical assumptions referred to above usually seem to exclude genres as a reactionary descriptive straitjacket, some of the foremost New Critics writing in French on French literature have used generic concepts and categories in order to distinguish between novels which attain a greater or smaller degree of verisimilitude.[19] Tzvetan Todorov, one of the rare New Critics to have applied his method to a detailed study of a specific novel, Choderlos de Laclos's *Les Liaisons dangereuses* (1782), seems to have relied exclusively on that novel's epistolary technique (which he calls a *catégorie*) in order to proclaim its perfection as a novel, the "reality" of its personae, and its closeness to the dramatic genre.[20] In so doing, he has overlooked the fact that there is no intrinsic difference between an epistolary novel and one in which the omniscient author narrates the heroine's thoughts (e.g., *La Princesse de Clèves*) and one in which the hero tells his own story (e.g., *Manon Lescaut*) as far as the "impersonality" of the author and the "reality" of the personae are concerned. While Todorov admits the fundamental artificiality or *invraisemblance,* without which this novel could not exist, of two *roués* writing sincere confessions to each other (*Littérature et Signification,* p. 48), he does not notice that a "real" pupil in a Catholic boarding school (even in the twentieth century) would never have received the sexually illuminating letters of a Cécile Volanges (in a "real" convent school letters are opened and read by the "authorities" and, depending on their contents, either confiscated or delivered); a "real" Mme de Volanges, obsessed with the idea of protecting her daughter from the assiduities of a Vicomte de Valmont, would not have sent her daughter to stay with him in an isolated country house. Contrary to Todorov's confident assertion, the letters are often not "perfectly integrated into the novel" and do not "fully justify their presence" (*Littérature et Signification,* p. 43). If *Les liaisons dangereuses* is a masterpiece, and I have no doubt that it is, Todorov's method, entirely founded on a specious subgeneric ("categoric") distinction, does not help the reader to understand its excellence.

A MISLEADING GENERIC DISTINCTION IN FRENCH LITERATURE: TRAGEDY AND COMEDY

In some cases subgeneric categories, if intelligently defined, may be more helpful and less arbitrary than generic distinctions. Students of French dramatic literature are indebted to Gustave Lanson for his distinctions between comedy of manners, comedy of character, and farce, which have led to a better understanding of Molière's highly diversified art.[21] Lanson suggests that the greatness of such works as *Le Misanthrope, Tartuffe, Les Femmes Savantes* and *L'Ecole des Femmes* derives in large part from their fusion of these three categories of comedy, where character, which Molière individualized, is given the greatest weight. French tragedy, on the other hand, after the elimination of the problematic designation "tragicomedy" before the middle of the seventeenth century, has been traditionally viewed as a monolithic block, which is defined principally in its opposition to comedy.[22] Yet, although generations of critics have foisted this ancient concept upon the schools, it is practically impossible to put one's finger on any fundamental difference between, for instance, some tragedies of Racine and some comedies of Molière. Emile Faguet (1847–1916) humorously suggested that tragedy is comedy with a tragic ending and comedy is tragedy with a happy ending.[23] But this distinction does not always hold. Many French tragedies leave their personae alive and well (Corneille's *Polyeucte, Le Cid, Cinna;* Racine's *Bérénice*). Often the tragic ending of a tragedy or the happy ending of a comedy is artificially tacked on (Molière's *Tartuffe*). To some extent this is the case in Racine's *Andromaque*. Hermione might well have married Orestes; Pyrrhus did marry Andromache. They could have lived happily ever after. Such an ending would not have altered the preceding four and a half acts. Perhaps the best way to uncover some of the mechanisms of our enjoyment of Racine's art is to consider *Andromaque* a comedy. If, however, *Andromaque* is indeed a comedy, it is definitely not a farce. Unfortunately, some critics who have been eager to demonstrate comic elements in this play have treated it as a farce. A demonstrably incorrect formula has been substituted for an analysis: Orestes loves Hermione who loves him not; Hermione loves Pyrrhus who loves her not; Pyrrhus loves Andromache who loves him not; Andromache loves the memory of Hector and also her infant son. Harald Weinreich's *Tragische und komische Elemente in Racine's Andromaque* (Münster, 1958) refers to a *Lie-*

beskette ("chain of love") and invokes Bergson's theory of laughter ("du mécanique plaqué sur du vivant": living organisms endowed with machine-like characteristics) which is absolutely inapplicable to the plot of *Andromaque*.

Instead, we should look for the comic strain in the emphasis Racine places on intimacy in lieu of politics. According to sixteenth-century interpretation of an Aristotelian genre distinction, tragedy concerns "noble" people (kings and princes) and "great" (i.e., political) events, whereas comedy is about "base" subjects (household and family problems) and common people. Pyrrhus, Hermione, Andromache, and Orestes are, respectively, head of state, princess royal, queen apparent, and royal ambassador. But their countries are their least worry. Racine's personae concern themselves with family matters to the detriment of affairs of state. Orestes is a lover who sometimes remembers he is an ambassador. Pyrrhus is a suitor who occasionally recalls his kingship. Hermione is a jealous and frustrated woman who incidentally happens to be a princess. The pride, dignity, and power of her rank are not part of her mental makeup. The subject of *Andromaque* is as banal, as "realistic" as the crime stories we read in the newspapers, for instance: "Jilted beauty quarrels violently with lover after learning he is to marry widowed mother of one." The next day's *Evening Standard* may tell us that the unfaithful lover was murdered at the altar during the ceremony.

Britannicus, similarly, *seems,* at first glance, to be about "great interests." The fate of the world might be at stake. Imperial Rome is the backdrop. In reality, Racine has given us *l'envers du décor* (the seamy side) by choosing to concentrate on a family quarrel of the most banal sort, between a reproachful mother and an ungrateful son. Racine states this in his first Preface (1670): "My tragedy is not concerned with Affairs of State: Nero is here depicted in his home life and in his family circle." Were we to omit but the last 150 verses, those recounting the death of Britannicus and its aftermath, we should be left with a *comédie bourgeoise,* resembling in many respects Molière's *Tartuffe,* produced about ten months earlier.[24]

What is the nature of our pleasure when we read *Andromaque, Britannicus,* or *Phèdre* intelligently or see these plays competently performed? Basically, no doubt, one of cruel delight:

> The greater part of our pleasure arises from the fact that . . . we have a clear view of all the circumstances, relations and

> implications of a certain conjuncture of affairs. . . . We are . . . in the position of superior intelligences contemplating with miraculous clairvoyance, the stumblings and fumblings of poor blind mortals straying through the labyrinth of life. Our seat in the theatre is like a throne on the Epicurean Olympus, whence we can view with perfect intelligence, but without participation or responsibility [or risk] the intricate reactions of human destiny.[25]

Do we not take pleasure in seeing others suffer, especially if the suffering is acted out to the hilt?[26] Of course we rationalize our sadism. We know that the actors will be unscathed at the beginning of the next performance; but we are paying for entertainment. Is this any different from what we get out of comedy, in which people are also made unhappy and subjected to merciless confrontations? The better the comedy, the less we feel inclined to boisterous laughter. Molière and Marivaux, intelligently performed, will catch us wiping away a furtive tear. Some scenes of comedy and tragedy may make us smile (for instance, act 2, scene 5 of *Andromaque*).

Dramatic irony is, in a way, a joke the author plays on the characters for the benefit of the spectators and with their connivance. In *Andromaque,* act 3, scene 3, there is an excellent example. Hermione succeeds in convincing herself that Pyrrhus still loves her. The audience knows that her joy is groundless. Racine is playing a game with Hermione's emotions. Though we may squirm a little at the moments of excruciating pain, we enjoy them. Our pleasure, again, is derived from "privileged knowledge," as in Molière's *Tartuffe* when Elmire deceives the impostor into believing that she loves him, or in *Twelfth Night* when Sir Toby deceives Malvolio into thinking that he is loved by Countess Olivia. Malvolio's last words after having been "most notoriously abus'd" are: "I'll be revenged on the whole pack of you."

I would characterize, then, the best of the works of Pierre Corneille (*Nicomède*), the best of Molière (*L'Ecole des Femmes, Tartuffe, Le Misanthrope*), and most of Racine (*Andromaque, Britannicus, Mithridate Iphigénie, Bajazet, Phèdre, Athalie*) as *genera mixta,* an incorporation and juxtaposition of a range of generic categories (perhaps better termed *procédés* or techniques). In this respect their greatness is parallel to that of Shakespeare.[27] Our study of these works should attempt to discover and analyze the *unwritten* poetics which their authors themselves created. In other words, the authors use genres in order to find their way to please their audience ("Le plaisir du spectateur est le seul but de la poésie dramatique"—Pierre Corneille). Students of literature try to determine what genres were used in order to find out how they were entertained.

TOWARD A COMPARATIVE DEFINITION OF FRENCH DRAMA FROM ITS BEGINNINGS (1552) THROUGH *ATHALIE* (1692)

What do we mean by "French" as opposed, for instance, to "English" drama?[28] Verse form, limitations of time, place, and action come readily to mind. Such conventions have been analyzed by Jacques Scherer in a work that encompasses the total French contribution to seventeenth-century drama: *La dramaturgie classique en France* (Paris, 1950).[29] Yet conventions do not fundamentally distinguish one dramatic system from another.

Emile Faguet in his *Drame ancien, drame moderne* (1898) and Daniel Mornet in his *Histoire de la clarté française* (1929) have seen the essence of French drama as a reflection of the French mind. Faguet puts this most succinctly: "Clarity is the very essence of our national genius. What isn't clear, isn't French, and, conversely, we consider to be true everything that is clear" (p. 38). Both critics suggest that the heroes and heroines of French drama may be *too* coherent. They are, says Faguet, afflicted with a single-mindedness which leaves but little room for psychological interpretation.

The English dramatic hero, as far back as Marlowe's Dr. Faustus (1588), and most noticeably in Shakespeare, is far more richly faceted. This is in great measure a matter of language, exceedingly clear in most of French drama, often vague and obscure in Shakespeare. Furness's New Variorum Edition of *Hamlet* (1877) has some 440 lines of commentary summarizing conflicting interpretations of the "To be or not to be" soliloquy, which consists of 34 lines. To summarize all that has been written on Hamlet's soliloquy since 1877 would probably require an entire volume. A recent critic writes that it cannot be paraphrased. There is no logical sequence of thought. Ideas run into one another, carried by currents of half-expressed emotion.[30] Another critic finds passages in Shakespeare where we are given not the poetic apprehension of thought but thought in the process of formation, where "meaning" is composed of an emotional current running full tilt against logical control.[31] What we have in all French seventeenth-century drama and specifically in Racine is well-disciplined oratory obeying the rules of formal rhetoric.

Uncertainty over the meaning of particular words or phrases is at the root of much of the criticism on English tragedy. When Hamlet declares: "For if the sun breed maggots in a dead dog, being a good kissing carrion" (act 2, scene 2, line 181) the New Variorum gives five full pages of elucidation. In French drama up to the present time, although clarity does vary from author to author, the meaning of any given verse or phrase is seldom open to question. The language of Pierre Corneille is sometimes puzzling to the modern French reader, but this is due to forced syntax and archaisms, not, as in Shakespeare, to cryptic expressions and apprehensions.[32]

The greater accumulation of criticism on English tragedy, however, is mostly due to the psychological complexity of so many of its personae. Hundreds of books and articles have attempted to solve the riddle of Hamlet's personality, the most mysterious of Shakespeare's creations. Some critics have seen only the graceful youth, full of delicate sympathies and aspirations. Close scrutiny by other critics has revealed insensitivity, unnecessary cruelty, grossness, embitterment, callousness, brutality, and even a good measure of cowardice. This complexity marks not only the English dramatic hero but also the English dramatic villain.[33] The towering figure of King Claudius, that extraordinary incarnation of royalty, is slowly coming to be recognized as one of the most interesting dramatic creations of all time. Iago's malice has complex motivations (Kittredge), so that his conduct cannot be dismissed as "monstrous" (compare with Narcissus in Racine's *Britannicus*). Kittredge considered the ambiguity, mixed nature, and fundamental inscrutability of Shakespeare's personae as his greatest trait of genius. "By heaven!" cries Othello, "I'll know thy thoughts!" "You cannot," answers Iago, "if my heart were in your hand; nor shall not whils't 'tis in my custody."

In French dramatic heroes scholars have discovered little or no complexity. Pierre Corneille's principal characters are often monomaniacs or fanatics with no baffling incongruities. Racine's heroes are sometimes even simpler than the elder Corneille's, because they analyze themselves so mercilessly. Faguet claims that most of them are not real people, but abstractions. It is only quite recently that *Andromaque* has come to stand out, in this respect, as a (relative) exception.³⁴ I shall deal in the next section with what I call the Shakespearean quality of *Andromaque*, which makes it unique in French seventeenth-century drama.

French drama before *Andromaque* had not freed itself from an aspect which it shared with the epic (see Saraiva's remark, above): a succession of adventures and feats, such as one finds in the long novels characteristic of the first half of the seventeenth century. In the *Cid* (1636–37), for instance, Rodrigue duels with the count, visits *Chimène* in her bower, battles with the Moors, and extends grace to Don Sanche. Corneille's *Horace* seems to culminate at the end of act 4, but starts anew in act 5 with the killing of Camille. Although the elder Corneille paid unending lip service to what he called the "Aristotelian unities" in his prefaces, he was always circumventing them and, in fact, never conformed to them. There was always too much action to compress into twenty-four hours and so much moving about as to make at least one change of place unavoidable. One might well ask why Corneille made so much fuss about these "unities." Corneille as well as most theoreticians on the drama in seventeenth-century France claimed the Ancients as their source and made an authority of a Greek philosopher of the fourth century B.C. whose manuscript fragment on the theater is defective and whose vocabulary we can no longer be sure we understand.³⁵ In fact Aristotle, whom the French knew through Italian analysts of the sixteenth century, never did establish rules for writing drama.³⁶ The few pages he devotes to the subject seem simply to describe the work of the principal dramatists as he knew it. A British scholar, A.W.H. Adkins, pointed out not long ago that Aristotle lived a good while after Greek drama had ceased and that he failed to grasp most of its features.³⁷ A French critic of the early twentieth century, Jules Lemaitre, discussing Corneille's struggles with "Aristotle's rules," deplored that Corneille got bogged down by such petty superficialities: there is really no difference between spreading the action of a play over a period of six hours or two and a half years.³⁸ Time is a vague element in drama; playwrights compress or elongate it at will. Racine's innovation is that most of the action has already taken place before the play begins. He gives us a "situation" produced by events that have been building up for about a year. This "situation" is explosively charged with pent-up emotion; it could remain intact were it not for a spark that sets the mixture aflame. His plots are lucid, clear-cut, rapid-fire. Unities of time, action, and place no longer matter. Does the action take 12 hours? 11 hours? It is irrelevant.

Unconsciously, however, Corneille was caught up in an evolutionary process (Brunetière's theory is surely correct up to and including Racine) that began with France's first drama (Jodelle's *Cléopâtre captive*, 1552) and was to culminate in Racine's nine masterpieces. Faguet used the word "specialization" to describe what happened. The young people of the *Pléiade* in the mid-sixteenth century had begun by translating ancient drama. When they turned to writing original plays in French, they "specialized." They rejected the most spectacular trappings of Greek theater, such as music, dance, song, stage machinery, sculpture, architecture, rhythmic elocution, and stock fables. From its inception French drama concentrated on emotion and tended toward clarity. After a regression into chaos during the transitional period when plays first began to be performed (French drama of the sixteenth century was performed rarely if at all), unnecessary elements, beginning with the chorus, were eliminated. In the course of the seventeenth century the French dramatists concentrated on personal conflict.[39]

Corneille's dramas are far more to the point than Shakespeare's, which, like ancient Greek plays, contain countless oratorical digressions (e.g., Polonius's speeches in *Hamlet*). Yet Corneille did not achieve concision. His personae still strive for eloquence and tend to be repetitive or to deliver speeches not directly related to the plot, especially when they deal with politics. In Racine's dramas there is not a superfluous word.

It was Faguet again who found a term to describe the final stage of French seventeenth-century drama's technical development: a play which conforms to the "unity of curiosity." Greek drama is to a great degree devoid of the surprise element, since audiences were told or were expected to know the story in advance of the play's performance. A French dramatic work of the seventeenth century attempts to stimulate the audience's curiosity from beginning to end. The French dramatist's job is to mask the outcome as much and as long as possible, yet to lead directly and logically to it. Alexandre Dumas fils (1824–95), in one of the long "prefaces" which follow his own plays, compared French drama to a mathematical equation: let there be nothing in it that does not contribute to the denouement; let the denouement be the sum total of the play.[40] Dumas fils was given to exaggerations, but in this case he was close to a definition of what French drama became in Racine's hands.

Racine adopted mythological settings for some of his plays and reintroduced in *Esther* and *Athalie* some of the trappings of Greek drama in modified form. His dramatic system is entirely different from that of Sophocles or Euripides, but it is in a number of respects similar to Shakespeare's. Common features are the atmosphere of violence and brutality which pervades the stage; "sympathetic knowledge of human nature" (Kittredge); adherence to the Judeo-Christian "moral order" (which does not, of course, imply morality in the personae); psychological and structural believability (*vraisemblance*, which is probably the same as "realism"); technical skill (especially the importance both dramatists give the pivotal scene); naturalism. (Racine's dramatic form, in contradiction to what is still generally taught, does not exclude the most brutal manifestations of "sex." *Andromaque* and *Phèdre*, like *King Lear*, show human beings hungering for each other as if they were wild beasts, although unlike some of Shakespeare's personae, they drape their lewdness in a delicate vocabulary. The best example is possibly the scene in *Phèdre*, where the heroine, unswervingly elegant and even majestic in her language, attempts to seduce her stepson. In *Andromaque*, the audience is informed four times in the polite terms of Racinian naturalism that Hermione's inherited volcanic temperament could not be restrained at Pyrrhus's court.) All these similarities between Shakespeare and Racine require further analysis.

A FRENCH SHAKESPEAREAN DRAMA: RACINE'S *ANDROMAQUE*

It is impossible to study structure as a distinct entity from psychological motivation in Racine's dramatic system. As A. Cioranescu put it: "Ce que l'on voit de l'action n'est qu'un reflet du processus psychologique," which is another way of saying that moods rather than events are the raw material of Racine's drama.[41] This makes for simplicity of plot, but not necessarily for psychological simplicity. Faguet and many later critics missed the point of *Andromaque* because they confused simplicity of plot with psychological simplicity. Indeed, in most of Racine's plays, simplicity of plot is matched by simplicity of the characters' psychology. *Andromaque* is exceptional.

Racine's Andromache remains in some measure mysterious after three centuries of critical commentary. A serious analysis of *Andromaque* must involve a psychological approach to the heroine.

Such an enterprise is fraught with danger: one might read into her lines what is not there (a critical failing now often called "psychologism"). How rare such a discussion is in respect to French drama before Montherlant (1896–1969) can be shown by the fact that Andromache's contradictions are sometimes seen as a failing of the playwright. Yet the most lifelike fictional characters are those who embody some unknown quantity or potentiality that might, when it is first encountered, produce surprise.

Horatio shows astonishment at learning that Hamlet has sent Rosencrantz and Guildenstern to their deaths: "So Rosencrantz and Guildenstern go to 't . . . " (in other words: "Did *you* do *that?*"). Horatio's somewhat enigmatic remark and Hamlet's indignant reply are sheer literary genius. The cold-blooded murder and the clumsy justification somehow (though not immediately) fit into the total picture of Hamlet.

Actions and attitudes as widely diversified as Hamlet's are impossible in Racine's dramatic system. Yet at the very beginning of *Andromaque* Racine brings up from the past a striking detail, twice repeated: Andromache had another child killed, *in her arms,* to save her own child. Surely our overall impressions of Andromache include sweetness, purity, virtue; but here is underlying hardness and pitiless maternal egoism that makes us stop and wonder.

Can we solve the riddle of a fictional personality any more than we can know for sure what lies behind a real person's words and actions? Are we not in real life "a haphazard bundle of inconsistent qualities" (Somerset Maugham)? Should we perhaps underline the contradictions and leave it at that? If it is true that a character's value is proportional to his complexity, as Gide's King Saul would have us believe ("Ma valeur est dans ma contradiction"), are we not lessening the appeal of that character by attempting to appraise his contradictions? The great creator of human personality seems to reply affirmatively through the lips of his Hamlet: "Why, look you now, how unworthy a thing you make of me! . . . You would pluck out the heart of my mystery . . . though you can fret me, yet you cannot play upon me" (3. 2).[42]

Here we must make a sharp distinction between Shakespeare and Racine. To each critic his own *Hamlet, Macbeth,* and *Othello.* "The sensibility that informs the plays is so free and open that the critic can all too easily twist them to suit his own predilections."[43] But in *Andromaque* there is too much sustained critical consciousness on the part of the artist to allow for completely subjective interpretation. In other words, Racine's Andromache is probably to a great extent discoverable; Shakespeare's Hamlet is not. Shakespeare and Racine both plant a series of clues; when all are taken into account the result in Shakespeare's case is one of such astonishing richness that our individual reaction to them is a product of choice. Racine's clues, limited in number, correspond to dramatic necessities.

Andromache's secret, then, is known to the author, included as part of her psychological makeup, but also tempered and hidden from full view. Racine is not playing cat-and-mouse with our feelings; he is consciously shaping a character who operates on conscious and subconscious levels.

The word "subconscious" had not been invented in Racine's time, but the concept was developed by Racine's teachers at Port-Royal into something strikingly similar to the one presented by Sigmund Freud more than two centuries later. They called it "la perception de l'imperceptible" or "les pensées de derrière" and described it as "a kind of background and a kind of origin which remains unknown and impenetrable to us during our whole life." Pierre Nicole (1625-95) varied his views on the impenetrability of the subconscious: "We cannot make out with certainty the origin of our actions," and like Pascal (1623-62) and Antoine Arnauld (1612-94) held man responsible for his innermost thoughts.[44]

Racine in *Andromaque* was the first French dramatist to apply the theme of "insufficient knowledge of oneself" consciously. He combined it with three others. One, that of "le charmant ennemi qu'on aime" (*charmant* in the seventeenth century meant "exercising magnetic attraction"), he simply picked up from the popular literature of his time. It runs through nearly all of the contemporary novels and plays. In Pierre Corneille's *Cid*, Chimène "loves" the man who killed her father; in Thomas Corneille's *Timocrate* (1656), the most frequently performed play of the century, a king "loves" and "is loved" by the princess whose country he is destroying. The theme is used time and again by Mairet, Pierre and Thomas Corneille, Quinault, Rotrou, Boyer, Leclerc, and Racine himself, beginning with *Alexandre*.[45]

A theme which Racine introduces in *Andromaque* and which is completely absent only from his last play, *Athalie* (1691), is sex. With all his predecessors "love" is politically, intellectually, rhetorically, or platonically motivated. The passions of many of Racine's heroines, like those of Shakespeare's Ophelia, Juliet, Goneril, Regan, are physically inspired. Finally there is in *Andromaque* the theme of maternal affection. We do not find it again in French literature until Jean-Jacques Rousseau's *Nouvelle Héloïse* (1761).

Insufficient knowledge of the self, irresistible love of an enemy, sex, passionate maternal love: put these together and we have a part of Racine's Andromache. Racine's achievement is to provide some of these themes below the surface of the heroine's composure. Racine's technique is calculated but unobtrusive.

Andromaque, as I have stated before, is a play which transcends the limits of the French dramatic genre of the seventeenth century. But, as Garasa pointed out in a different context, generic individuality is most noticeable in borderline cases.[46] The minds of Racine's characters are entirely revealed through their own words. Mornet indicates that these are nearly always well-wrought, clearly articulated statements, such as might be presented in a court of law. "This widow, this distressed mother," he writes of Andromache, "has vivid recollections of her studies in rhetoric."[47] Mornet shows that even the most emotional monologues, such as Hermione's when she gives vent to her rage and humiliation (5. 1) are in reality only superficially incoherent. Peter France, following a suggestion of Mornet, shows that even Orestes's hallucination is perfectly organized.[48] It seems almost a miracle that, in spite of Andromache's relentless rhetoric, the clarity of her French, the shortness of the play (1648 verses) and of her role (234 verses), she should nevertheless be the least obvious of seventeenth-century French dramatic personae. Within the confining framework of a genre imposed not by rules but by convention and language, Racine is somehow able to convey the mixture of confusion and self-delusion which characterizes Andromache's relationship with Pyrrhus, as it also characterizes the relationship between Shakespearean personae.

I conclude then, with Pierre Kohler, that, although it is impossible to precisely define a literary genre, it is perfectly legitimate to study its evolution (more than the "evolution of the species" in the natural sciences) and that in France (at least until the last decade of the seventeenth century) the dramatic genre is more organic and significant than the narrative or lyric poetry.[49] Our understanding of artistic originality can be deepened, I believe, by comparisons between French dramatic, lyric, and narrative works and those written in other languages.[50] Future generic investigators should examine "certain mixes, migrations, and alternations in generic category, to see what the *literary* gain may be, both in having genres and in refusing to allow generic categories to dictate or predestine the size, scope, content, and manner in any particular literary work."[51] Hirsch suggests that generic concepts, if properly handled, are indispensable to the study of literature in general.[52] Highly publicized contemporary theoreticians of literature use other concepts and methods.[53] In any case, we should never claim orthodoxy for our own preference in these matters. There can be no "scientific" interpretation of literature (*pace* Brunetière and Lucien Goldmann). There are only our own "capriciously sensitive and unaccountable individualities" (Kittredge).[54]

Notes

1. Cf. Delfín Leocadio Garasa, *Los Géneros Literarios* (Buenos Aires, 1969), pp. 102–33. A compact sampling of seventeenth-century terminology may be found in Pierre Nicole, *Traité de la Comédie* (Paris, 1667); critical edition by Georges Couton (Paris, 1961). Cf. Marvin T. Herrick, *Comic Theory in the Sixteenth Century* (Urbana, Ill., 1964) and, *Tragicomedy* (Urban, Ill., 1962). Attention is called to the need for a "history of literary terminology" in A. Kibédi Varga, "Le poème et ses lectures," *Cahiers de l'Association Internationale des Etudes Françaises*, no. 23 (May 1971): 118n.18.
2. Cf. Garasa, *Géneros*, pp. 146–54.
3. Cf. Paul Van Tieghem, *La littérature comparée* (Paris, 1931), pp. 71–72; "La question des genres littéraires," *Hélicon* 1 (1939): 100—"Brunetière gâta dans l'opinion du public compétent une cause qui méritait d'être mieux défendue."
4. "L'évolution d'un genre, La Tragédie," *Etudes Critiques sur l'Histoire de la Littérature Française*, 7th ser. (Paris, 1905), pp. 151–200. Cf. his related preparatory studies "La Doctrine évolutive et l'histoire de la littérature," *Revue des Deux Mondes* 68 (February 1898): 874–96 (rpt. *Etudes Critiques*, 6th ser. [Paris, 1905]: 1–36); "La Réforme de Malherbe et l'évolution des genres," *R.D.M.* 62 (December 1892): 660–83 (rpt. *Etudes Critiques*, 5th ser., 1ff.); the introduction ("Leçon d'ouverture") to *L'Evolution de la Poésie Lyrique en France au dix-neuvième siècle*, 2 vols. (1894), 1: 1–32.
5. "Mélodrame ou tragédie?," in *Variétés littéraires* (Paris, 1904), pp. 215–42. Cf. Garasa, *Géneros*, pp. 184–94.
6. Garasa, *Géneros*, pp. 195–227; Mario Fubini, *Critica e poesia* (Bari, 1966), pp. 127–257.
7. Cf. Ernest Bovet, *Lyrisme, épopée, drame: Une loi de l'histoire littéraire expliquée par l'évolution générale* (Paris, 1911); René Bray, "Des genres

littéraires, de leur hiérarchie et du principe de cette hiérarchie dans la littérature classique," in *Recueil de travaux publiés à l'occasion du quatrième centenaire de la fondation de l'université, Faculté des Lettres* (Lausanne, 1937), pp. 103–11; Jean Pommier, "L'idée de genre," *Questions de critique et d'Histoire littéraire,* in *Publications de l'Ecole Normale Supérieure, Section des Lettres* (Paris, 1945), 2: 47–81; Pierre Kohler, "Contributions à une philosophie des genres," *Hélicon* 1, no. 3 (1938): 233–44; 2, no. 2–3 (1940): 135–42. The bibliographical survey by Klaus W. Hempfer, "Bibliographie zur Gattungspoetik," *Zeitschrift für Französische Sprache und Literatur* 82 (1972): 53–66, lists many items of scant or dubious relevance. It should be supplemented by Garasa's bibliography, *Géneros,* pp. 327–36.

8. Cf. *Le Genre dramatique,* pp. 147–48: "Y a-t-il lieu de faire ... des distinctions fondamentales entre la comédie, le drame et la tragédie? ... la littérature critique ne semble pas avoir établi que ces termes avaient une signification structurelle stable et profonde ... une grande confusion émane des emplois que les divers critiques font de ces termes.... Chaque théoricien construit son concept du tragique."

9. I have borrowed most of the preceding two sentences from the first page of Rosalie L. Colie, *The Resources of Kind: Genre-theory in the Renaissance* (Berkeley, 1973).

10. Cf. Jean Suberville, *Théorie de l'art et des genres littéraires* (Paris, 1946: 11th ed., Paris, 1969).

11. Cf. "Linguistique et poétique," *Essais de linguistique générale* (Paris, 1963), pp. 209–48; originally in English in T.A. Sebeok, *Style in Language* (New York, 1960).

12. *Poétique* 17, no. 19 (1974): 1–13. This fundamentally important essay should be made available to the widest possible audience.

13. Ibid., p. 10. Footnote 6 on the same page claims that the plays of Gil Vicente (1465?–1537), "the greatest dramatic genius of the Iberian Peninsula," cannot be summarized. On the nongeneric distinction between dramatic (*dramatisch*) and theatrical (*Bühnenmässig*) cf. Emil Staiger, *Grundbegriffe der Poetik* (Zurich, 1946), cited by Garasa, *Géneros,* p. 278; cf. Henri Gouhier, *Renan Auteur Dramatique* (Paris, 1972), pp. 137–38.

14. Cf. Henri Bremond (1865–1933), *Prière et poésie* (Paris, 1926) and *De la poésie pure* (Paris, 1926); A. Gide, *Anthologie de la Poésie française* (Paris, 1949), "Préface."

15. "Le poeme," pp. 107–24. For his effective use of comparative criticism, including many examples of Hungarian poetry, cf. Varga, *Les Constantes du poème* (The Hague, 1963).

16. "Le poeme," p. 124. Cf. Marcel A. Ruff, *Baudelaire l'homme et l'oeuvre* (Paris, 1955), Chap. 10: "Sorcellerie évocatoire."

17. Cf. Georges Claude May, *Le dilemme du roman au XVIII e siècle; étude sur les rapports du roman et de la critique, 1715–1761* (Paris, 1963).

18. It appeared as a special issue of *Confluences* 3, nos. 21–24; cf. the exhaustive bibliography in R. Bourneuf and Réal Ouellet, *L'univers du roman* (Paris, 1972).

19. Cf. *Communications* 8 (1966): *Recherches sémiologiques: L'Analyse structurale du récit; Communications* 11 (1968): *Recherches sémiologiques: Le vraisemblable; Littérature* 1 (February 1971): *Littérature, idéologies, société;* T.

Todorov, *Introduction à la littérature fantastique* (Paris, 1970); *Littérature* 8 (December 1972): *Le fantastique*.
20. The bulk of Todorov's publications are derived from his unpublished thesis, directed by Roland Barthes, on *Les liaisons dangereuses*. Cf. "Les catégories du récit littéraire," *Communications* 8: 125–51; *Littérature et signification* (Paris, 1967). The article by Maurice Roelens, "Le texte et ses 'conditions d'existence': l'exemple des 'Liaisons Dangereuses,' " *Littérature* 1 (February 1971): 73–81, is largely a restatement of Todorov's theories concerning this novel.
21. "Molière et la Farce," *Revue de Paris*, 1 May 1901, pp. 129–33, rpt. *Essais de méthode de critique et d'histoire littéraire* (Paris, 1965), pp. 189–210.
22. A timid exception is Henri Bonnet, *De Malherbe à Sartre, Essai sur les progrès de la conscience esthétique* (Paris, 1964), p. 163. Cf. Peter H. Nurse, *Classical Voices* (London, 1971), pp. 104–6.
23. *Dix-septième siècle* (Paris, n.d.), p. 311. A similar statement was made by Dante in his *De vulgari eloquentia* (II,IV), cited by Garasa, *Géneros*, p. 101.
24. Cf. G. Lanson, *Histoire de la littérature française* (Paris, 1922), pp. 544–45. In a way, even *Britannicus* has a happy ending: the hero comes out on top (as in *Andromaque*). The ensuing murder of Agrippina, announced four times in the course of the play, far from having a tragic impact, strikes me as a case of "good riddance." The same could be said of Narcissus's fate at the hands of the mob.
25. William Archer, *Play-making* (New York, 1912), p. 131.
26. Cf. Emile Faguet, *Drame ancien, drame moderne* (Paris, 1898), pp. 7–8.
27. Cf. Colie, *The Resources of Kind* p. 123 (the same idea applied to Shakespeare). On the comic aspects of *Athalie*, cf. my edition of that play (Paris, 1969), p. 107.
28. "Drama" is used here instead of the misleading word "tragedy." I am aware that Victor Hugo in his Preface to *Cromwell* (1827) used "drama" as a term to encompass works "in which the tragic and the comic coexist," but Hugo did not apply the term to the plays of Corneille, Racine, and Molière.
29. Cf. René Bray, *La formation de la doctrine classique en France* (Paris, 1951); Geoffrey Brereton, *French Tragic Drama in the Sixteenth and Seventeenth Centuries* (London, 1973); Will G. Moore, *The Classical Drama of France* (Oxford, 1971); Antoine Adam, *Le théâtre classique* (Paris, 1970); Donald Stone, Jr., *French Humanist Tragedy* (Manchester, 1974).
30. Arieh Sachs, "To be or not to be," *Scripta Hierosolymitana* 19 (1967): 291.
31. L. C. Knights, *Some Shakespearean Themes and an Approach to Hamlet* (London, 1959), p. 207.
32. See Edward Le Comte, *Poet's Riddles: Essays in Seventeenth Century Explication* (Port Washington, N.Y., 1974).
33. George Lyman Kittredge, *Shakspere* (Cambridge, Mass., 1930); A.C. Bradley, *Shakespearean Tragedy* (London, 1904).
34. Cf. Pierre Quéméneur, "Un théâtre de la nuit," in *H. de Montherlant, homme de théâtre* (Paris, 1960), p. 33: "Racine's heroes progressively obtain more self-knowledge, except in *Andromaque*." Quéméneur obviously did not take into consideration the self-revealing scene of *Andromaque* found in the first two published editions (1668 and 1673), but left out in the subsequent ones published during Racine's lifetime. Many modern editions include it in fine print at the bottom of the scene substituted for it (act 5, scene 3).

35. The word "catharsis," on which countless articles have been written, appears to be a misreading for *sústasin* ("a composition of facts"). Cf. António Freire, "A Catarse Trágica em Aristóteles," *Evphrosyne*, n.s., 3 (1969): 31–45.
36. Cf. Garasa, *Géneros*, pp. 70–87; 102–24.
37. "Aristotle and the best kind of tragedy," *The Classical Quarterly* 16 no. 5 (1966): 78–102.
38. "Corneille et les règles," in Petit de Juleville, *Histoire de la Littérature française* (1912), 4: 280–85; *Corneille et la Poétique d'Aristote* (Paris, 1888).
39. Cf. Brunetière, "L'évolution d'un genre: la tragédie," *Etudes critiques*, pp. 7, 179.
40. Quoted by Brunetière, "Mélodrame ou tragédie?," p. 223. According to Brunetière, Dumas's plays did not conform to this conception.
41. "Baroque et action dramatique: le dehors et le dedans," *Actes 1966 de la 2 e session des journées internationales d'études du baroque*.
42. Cf., however, Harold Skulsky, " 'I Know My Cause': Hamlet's Confidence," *PMLA* 89, no. 3 (May 1974): 477–86.
43. A.L. French, "Hamlet and the Moralists," *The Oxford Review* (Michaelmas, 1967): 41.
44. Un certain fond et une certaine racine qui nous demeure inconnue toute notre vie" (Pierre Nicole, Les visionnaires ou second parti des lettres sur l'hérésie imaginaire, Huit lettres, la première est du 31 dec. 1665, la huitième, fin d'avril 1666, *Visionnaires*, II). "nous ne distinguons point avec certitude par quels principes nous agissons" (*Essais de morale*, III). Elsewhere Nicole writes: "La plus grande partie de nos pensées nous sont inconnues et . . . ne laissent pas d'être dans notre esprit, de s'y faire sentir, de nous conduire, de nous faire tirer des conclusions précises et prendre une infinité de résolutions, de nous pousser et de nous déterminer dans nos jugements, sans que nous en ayons une idée nette et distincte, sans que nous les puissions exprimer sur-le-champ, et sans que nous les puissions le plus souvent découvrir que par beaucoup de réflexions, dont la plupart des hommmes sont incapables." Cf. G. Chinard, *En lisant Pascal* (Paris, 1948), p. 123.
45. Cf. Paul Bénichou, *L'écrivain et ses travaux* (Paris, 1967), pp. 186–91; Daniel Mornet, *Histoire générale de la littérature française* (Paris, 1931). On the general theme of the woman who leaves her own camp for the enemy's, as well as the theme, one of the oldest in French fiction, of the "assassin turned husband," cf. Bénichou, *L'écrivain*, pp. 207–36.
46. *Géneros*, p. 255.
47. *Histoire de la clarté française*, p. 162.
48. *Racine's Rhetoric* (Oxford, 1965), pp. 227–28.
49. "Contributions," p. 247.
50. Cf. Willy R. Berger, "Probleme und Möglichkeiten vergleichender Gattungsforschung," in H. Rüdiger, *Die Gattungen in der Vergleichenden Literaturwissenschaft* (Berlin, 1974), pp. 63–92.
51. Colie, *The Resources of Kind*, p. 103.
52. Cf. Eric Donald Hirsch, *Validity in Interpretation* (New Haven, 1967), p. 109.
53. An evaluation of "New Critical" approaches to Racine may be found in Raymond Picard, *Nouvelle Critique ou nouvelle imposture* (Paris, 1965).
54. Many ideas expressed in this essay were first suggested to me by my teacher Maurice Baudin, Professor Emeritus at New York University.

Klaus Weissenberger

A Morphological Genre Theory: An Answer to a Pluralism of Forms

In Germany, perhaps more than in any other country, there has developed a specific tradition of morphological genre theory. The German morphological tradition was sanctioned by Goethe's classification of epic, lyric, and drama as the only genuine "natural forms" of literature and continued into the twentieth century via the writings of Hegel, Dilthey, Walzel, Petersen, and Müller. This relatively vague and romanticizing concept of the three "natural forms" has served as the ontological foundation for the discussions of the literary subforms, discussions which are characterized by meticulous scholarship with regard to specific details, but which cannot conceal the original weakness of their theoretical foundation.[1]

The difficulty presented by this school, which bases its definition of genre on the poetry of Goethe and the Romantics, is that it appears to postulate one particular model for each genre which is determined by the poetics of German classicism and which found concrete realization in the literature of that period. As a result, every discussion of genre theory is limited to examples drawn from the literature of the classical period or can deal with works from following periods only insofar as they are derived from the former. On the other hand, since genre and subform do not seem to be directly accessible to scholarly investigation, such studies attempt to solve the problem of genre classification by the questionable method of creating more and more subcategories which divert attention from the genre or subform itself. And frequently the criteria for these subcategories are based more on considerations of content than of form; an example is Kayser's classification of the ballad. By this method, subcategorization could continue indefinitely; on the other hand, some works could not be classified at all because they fail a priori to meet criteria which have derived from one specific model. These difficulties present us with two alternatives: we can either view the relationship between a literary work and a genre or subform as being a purely accidental one or a matter of terminological convenience; or we can develop a morphology of genres which does not dissipate into a never-ending subclassification of literary subforms but which, quite to the contrary, makes the ontological foundation of the literary genres accessible to scholarly examination. Only by retaining the "totality of its autonomous character and its ontological dignity"[2] can one do justice to the literary work of art.

It is to Emil Staiger's credit that his *Grundbegriffe der Poetik* [Fundamentals of Poetics] (1946)[3] was the first work to establish a morphology of genres able to withstand the criticism influenced primarily by Croce. Since Staiger's contribution to the topic did not remain the only one in the German-speaking countries, the most severe criticism of these propositions was first voiced by non-German scholars. Unfortunately such criticism focuses too narrowly on unimportant details instead of stressing Staiger's lasting contribution to the understanding of literary genres.

What distinguishes all morphological genre definitions from historical-descriptive ones is their foundation in a synthesizing view of man and life. They conceive of man as a self-contained whole which unites rational understanding with the irrational unconscious and recognize in the nature of man as well a predisposition to become integrated in the "universally human," in the totality of humanity. By establishing an ontology which has ultimate reference to the metaphysical basis of human existence, it becomes possible to understand the individual literary work as the synthesis of all its levels of concretization—from those of prosody to those which function as constituents of a particular genre. It is precisely this "synergetic" quality that characterizes the artistic mode of presentation of any literary work of art. It goes without saying that any literary interpretation which makes the transcendence of the individual elements into a whole the premise for literary creation and therefore places literature in proximity to mysticism must appear suspicious to the historical-descriptive school.

This essay is intended to investigate the most prominent morphological genre theories and to emphasize or point out their genuine contribution to the clarification of this problem. Moreover, an attempt will be made to show how these theories complement each other and how a synthesis of their various insights can contribute to our understanding of literary genres.

In the first part of his "fundamental poetics" Staiger discusses what he considers the three principal genres: "the lyric," "the epic," and "the dramatic" and demonstrates how to free the discussion of genres from the restrictions of historical formalism and normative poetics. In his final chapter, "Vom Grund der poetischen Gattungsbegriffe," Staiger discusses the ontological foundation of his three genres. Although Staiger expressly points out that all his definitions are concerned only with the essential problem and not with terminology, his suggestion that his poetics be understood as a literary-theoretical contribution to philosophical anthropology has in part been misunderstood.[4] Yet it is exactly this concept with which Staiger attempts to make the holistic aspect of the literary work of art accessible to scholarly interpretation. Staiger's anthropology is inherent in or determined by the relation of the literary work to man. And therefore the "structure of the essence of man" (p. 253), which has been made accessible to our understanding by philosophical anthropology, finds its analogy in the structure of the literary art work and in the morphology of the literary genres and their subforms.

The broad range of Staiger's thought can be seen in his view of the triad lyric-epic-dramatic as successive stages of increasing objectivity and intentionality, not unlike the relation of syllable, word, and sentence. Since the syllable has no meaningful content and is pure expression, it corresponds to the unity of sign and thing signified which the lyric strives for. Words imply conceptualization of objects, which is characteristic of the epical structure, and the sentence functions as a superior whole which determines the meaning of the individual parts—analogous to dramatic suspense which results from our comprehension of the action in its totality. In this progression "the lyrical" realizes man's primordial and most intimate awakening to consciousness, whereas "the dramatic" represents the most artistic mode of expression since the function of the parts is always determined by the whole.

By relating his morphology of the poetic genres to Cassirer's philosophy of language and Heidegger's interpretation of Time, Staiger gives his poetics a solid philosophical foundation. Both Cassirer and Heidegger appear to confirm Staiger's triadic classification of the genres. This does not, however, exhaust the significance of the relation of Staiger's poetics to the thought of Cassirer and Heidegger. In addition, it seems to oversimplify matters if we classify Staiger's poetic as "existentialistic" because of this connection.[5] Rather, Cassirer and Heidegger furnished Staiger with conceptual models for the phenomenology of language and for man's subjection to Time which corroborate the morphological foundation of the genres all the more because they establish it independently of literary considerations.

Staiger finds the analogy to the progression lyric-epic-dramatic or syllable-word-sentence in Cassirer's three stages of language: "language in the phase of sensuous expression, language in the phase of concrete expression, language in the phase of conceptual thought" (p. 208). According to Cassirer's philosophical model of language, language develops from "emotional to logical expression" (p. 208) in a process which is analogous to the linguistic development of the individual. The early stage of emotional expression is succeeded by the intentional designation of objects, which in turn is followed by the correlation of objects, the linguistic construction of relationships. The early stages are, of course, not lost and may reappear according to the situation.[6]

This correspondence between the basic forms of literature and the developmental stages of language has convinced Staiger that his basic forms are "literary-theoretical names for fundamental modes of human existence in general" and that "lyric poetry, epic poetry and drama [only exist] because the emotional, representative and logical faculties constitute the essence of man, as a unity as well as a sequence which consists of childhood, youth, and maturity" (p. 209).

This sequence of increasing objectification which derives from Cassirer's philosophy of language finds analogy in the modes of consciousness which are formed by the two poles, soul and mind, and which in the activities "feeling-showing-proving" encompass both the basic forms of poetry and the developmental stages of language. Yet the final sanction for Staiger's ontologically based poetics is provided by its correlation with the concept of the three dimensions of time—past, present, and future—for which Staiger is indebted to Heidegger. Thus, borrowing Heidegger's concept of *Er-innern* ("to remember" in the sense of "to bring inward"), Staiger correlates the lyric with the past, the epic with the present, and the dramatic with the future. This classification appears at first to be paradoxical but becomes less contradictory if we view the past not as distance but as the elimination of the distance from man's primordial condition, which is realized in the lyric. Accordingly, the present is the time dimension of epic representation and the future that of dramatic projection.

By relating the poetic genres to Time as the "Sinn des Seienden," Staiger has carried the ontological interpretation of poetics to its logical conclusion. The correlation of the basic forms with grammatical concepts remains problematic, however. Therefore let us attempt a modification which is actually compatible with Staiger's thesis but which is not limited by such analogies. The lyric, as Staiger understands it, rests on the principle of approaching the [primordial] condition in which space and time do not exist. This gives the lyrical statement a supralogical character and makes it both representative and unique. Staiger designates this the aspect of "pretemporality" or "originality," that is, the passage of time is absent in the lyric, which thus contains the primordial stage before man's experience of temporality. One could even go so far as to claim that the lyric realizes the stage of man's innocent and childlike relationship with God since it invests the immanent statement with a transcendental character and thus points to an ontological condition which precedes revealed religion. This fact becomes especially clear whenever a poem deals with historical subject matter (e.g., the ballad). Either the historical theme evokes a transfigured, glorified condition from the past which corresponds to the supratemporal at-one-ness with the divine, or the historical event is depicted because of its representative character and in the process exchanges its historical character for a supratemporal one.

The epic, on the other hand, represents human existence in the totality of space and time. It is the literary stage which interprets man's individuality in the context of his historical limitation and uniqueness. This fact justifies the detailed descriptions found in epic poetry. This "epic" intent is characteristic, for example, of a great part of Brecht's lyrical and dramatic writing which is dominated by the presentation of historical limitation to such a degree that such poems cannot be considered "lyrical" and his plays can justifiably be designated "epic."

The dramatic, then, represents the literary stage which is based on the tension between historical temporality and supratemporality. This tension results from the equation of historical time with absolute time, which necessarily leads to a conflict between the two. It is the inherent concern of the dramatic to elevate historical limitation to timelessness. This factor is also partially characteristic of the ballad and the *Novelle*, and for this reason both literary forms have been associated with the drama. As soon as this feature is suppressed, the drama takes on either a lyrical character (e.g., the plays of Hofmannstal) or an epic one (e.g., Brecht's epic theater).

Wolfgang Kayser's system of literary genres is closely related to Staiger's "fundamental poetics."[7] However, whereas Staiger concentrated on the elucidation of the concepts lyric, epic, dramatic, Kayser devotes more of his attention to the other pole of genre theory, i.e., to the genre subforms. Although his approach yields valuable insight into the nature of the subforms, the concept of the "human" as a totality, clearly recognizable in Staiger's system, becomes lost. Kayser views the tripartite division of the literary genres as an incontrovertible fact sufficiently corroborated by scholars' recurrent efforts "to understand" it "in greater depth than is necessary, which, of course, is justified by its metaliterary character" (p. 334). Kayser supplements Staiger's appropriation of Cassirer's philosophical model of language with H. Junker's concept of the three functions of language: language "as expression, demand or exhortation, communication or representation" (p. 335). According to Kayser, these brief references make it unnecessary to define the "metaliterary character" of the three genres. For this, Kayser also contents himself with postulating *Urphänomene* of the lyric, the epic, and the dramatic which correspond to the three functions of language. Because of the autonomy of literary language, however, these primal phenomena do not always find direct expression in literature.

In Kayser's opinion, this statement obviates further speculation about the ontological background of the literary genres. Thus he can restrict himself to the realm of literary phenomenology and combine genre theory with the practice of stylistic analysis. Kayser postulates a "structural character" (*Gefügecharakter*) of literary language which is based on the interaction of the various levels of literary realization and which is determined by the stylistic principle appropriate to the particular genre. Only insofar as they belong to a genre can those laws be discovered which Kayser considers to be the "eternal laws according to which the verbal work of art is formed" (p. 387). Thus the focus of his phenomenological analysis shifts from the isolated consideration of a stylistic phenomenon to the general view of the literary work. To be sure, in further subdividing the basic forms, Kayser falls victim to the magic which emanates from the number three.

The problems inherent in Kayser's genre theory can be seen at once in his distinction between "forms of presentation" and the "natural" forms, or "basic attitudes." By "forms of presentation" Kayser means the normative, historically established forms of lyric poetry, epic poetry, and drama in general and their subcategories such as the sonnet, rogue novel, and miracle play. In the category of natural forms belong the lyrical, the epic, and the dramatic, as Staiger wants to have these concepts understood. While there is nothing one could object to in this distinction, it may be argued that Kayser avoids the extraordinarily interesting and rewarding problem of the relationship between the forms of presentation and the natural forms. An explanation of how the former have developed historically from the latter would fill the gap between the genres as ontologically based givens and as "institutions" and would justify Kayser's genre morphology in "practical" terms.

The most problematic aspect of Kayser's system, however, is to be seen in his subdivision of the lyrical, epic, and dramatic natural forms into three "attitudes" each. These attitudes develop as "mixed forms" of the basic attitudes according to Kayser, although he discusses this explicitly only in the case of the lyric. The lyric can therefore be divided into an epic-lyrical attitude (the lyrical naming), into a dramatic-lyrical attitude (the lyrical address), and into the "pure lyrical attitude" (the songlike speech) (p. 339). Kayser even goes so far as to call these "the only three basic attitudes which, as lyrical expression, can create structure" (p. 346) and to derive the *Spruch*, *Ruf*, and *Lied* from them as *the* lyrical subforms.

Kayser considers setting, character, and action to be the structural elements of the epic and dramatic. From this can be derived the setting-epic, the character-epic, and the action-epic or the setting-drama, the character-drama, and the action-drama. By correlating lyrical features with the presentation of setting, epic features with the presentation of character, and dramatic features with the presentation of action, Kayser can validly claim justification for the tripartite subdivision of the lyrical to apply also to the epic and the dramatic without specifically committing himself.

Such a predetermined attitude always has a "mysterious elective affinity" (p. 346) with an appropriate "inner form" which must necessarily complete and shape the attitude. This can be understood as the specific poetic attitude of a subform, and we may see in it the link with the established forms of presentation. Kayser, however, makes no effort to close this obvious gap in his system. Equally questionable is his claim that the attitudes cited above encompass all subforms; even Kayser's examples prove that this is not possible without forcing the point. Instead, therefore, of explaining subforms each time according to the degree to which they represent a mixture of the genres, it seems preferable to determine them from two aspects—on the one hand, from the viewpoint of the poetic attitude ontologically founded in the basic attitudes, and on the other from the aspect of their historical forms of presentation.

Although Staiger's and Kayser's poetics have enjoyed a certain degree of authority in Germany, the voices of their critics have become increasingly audible. Objections come not only from the camp of literary sociology and structuralism, but also from literary critics not unconditionally committed to the new movements. Among them is Friedrich Sengle, whose *Literarische Formenlehre* makes suggestions for reform.[8] Sengle reproves Staiger and his tripartite division of literary genres both for having fallen prey to the magic of the number three and for indulging in aesthetic absolutism. Instead he proposes the introduction of "utilitarian literary forms" and a value-free attitude toward the forms as well as the principle of formal purity. However, Sengle overlooks the fact that he too espouses the principle of three poetic genres. He considers his utilitarian forms to be nonliterary writings. Further, he holds that every poetic genre inherently contains the possibility of undergoing a nonliterary concretization. Sengle chooses the epigram to exemplify an unlimited multiplicity of genres. Implicitly using Staiger's criteria for the lyrical, he postulates that the epigram does not belong in this genre. But the structure of the epigram fulfills the lyrical poetic attitude of the *Spruch;* the fact that in some cases it has a nonliterary nature is based on the specific logic of its language and structure.[9] A comparison might be the *chanson* as a possibly nonliterary form of the *Lied,* or *Bänkelsang* as the nonliterary form of the ballad.

Instead of using the terms "utilitarian literary forms" or "nonliterary writings," it would be far more productive to speak of the "essayistic" as an autonomous literary genre. The so-called utilitarian forms would then represent this genre's nonliterary concretizations. For in its paradoxical stress on the contrast between subject and object, which can be resolved only by an act of "internalization," the essayistic is very close to the lyrical. It is only its cognitive nature that confers on it a teleological aspect which is foreign to the lyrical and which mistakenly seems to tie it to the utilitarian forms. For Sengle the latter are often characterized by the lowest level of style. He is therefore intent on claiming the stylistic levels as such to be genre criteria, since they correspond to the forms of human existence and ontologically justify the utilitarian forms. Sengle's "Continuation of the Old Rhetoric of Tones" seems the most interesting. It would serve to explain both the formal elements of a genre and its specific poetic attitude. This would provide the link, missing in Kayser's system, between the historical forms of presentation and the "natural forms" or genres in the general sense.

Käte Hamburger's contribution to genre morphology is fundamentally different from the literary-aesthetic theories outlined above; it deserves all the more attention in that it does not simply declare these systems invalid but appears to incorporate them from another perspective. Hamburger's work—especially her *Logic of Literature*—has attracted a great deal of attention because she develops a theory of literary genres which derives from the theory of language and which is based on a dual classification rather than on the traditional triad of lyric, epic, and dramatic.[10]

Hamburger faults Staiger because in the final analysis his poetic theory represents "merely interpretations of the generic phenomenon in question, interpretations which themselves only become possible in that fixed, formal classifications were resolved into modes of both experience and expression" (p. 4). Hamburger on the other hand believes that "literary genres remain fixed forms, which as such ultimately resist all interpretation in the sense of an explication of meaning" (p. 4), since inherent in them is an autonomy which we experience directly. The autonomy of the literary genres is based "upon the functions of creative language, i.e., the language which produces literature" (p. 54); and the task of poetics or genre theory can only be to go beyond a consideration of the aesthetic problems of literary language as "verbal art" and to investigate the logico-linguistic functions of creative language. Every aspect of literature is rooted in its linguistic functions, for language is not only the formative material of literature in an aesthetic sense, but also the "medium in which human life takes place" (p. 2). It is precisely this function as medium which distinguishes "creative language" from the noncreative one of the general language system. Therefore the special nature of the former can be understood only from comparison with the latter.

The communicative nature of the general language system is based on the nature of language as statement, since the language system is the "linguistic correlative to the system of reality itself"

(p. 51). All such "reality statements" are based on a subject-object correlation—that is, the statement-subject makes a statement about the statement-object. The different degrees and relationships within this correlation depend on the sentence modalities and on the three types of statement—historical, theoretical, and pragmatic. But the fact that the statement-object has the character of reality does not alter the linguistic function of the statement, for "statement is always reality statement because the statement-subject is real, in other words, because statement is constituted only through a genuine, real statement-subject" (p. 45).

Hamburger distinguishes the system of literature which is manifested in the literary genres from the statement system of nonliterary language. This leads her to a dual classification of literature into the so-called fictional or mimetic and the lyrical or existential genres. Into the first category she places epic and dramatic "natural forms" because they lack a genuine statement-subject and all statement-objects refer to a fictive statement-subject. Hamburger derives the primary arguments in support of this classification from her discussion of the third-person narrative or epic fiction. By analyzing deictic temporal and spatial adverbs she is able to show that these serve to annul the grammatical function of the epic preterit, which is to designate what is past. The cause for this phenomenon of tense is found in the law "that which is narrated is referred not to a real I-origo, but rather to fictive I-origines, and is therefore itself fictive" (p. 73). Thus the narrative is not a reality statement but has the function of representing reality. Recalling Aristotle, Hamburger designates this function as *mimetic*—a concept which, as Hamburger intends it to be understood, has nothing to do with imitation. The fictional genre does not derive from the narrator's field of experience but represents the product of the mimetic narrative function.

According to Hamburger, the same thing applies to the drama as well. Because of the poetological form of the drama, the system of dialogue, she is forced, however, to deny the drama a narrative function and to postulate instead a surrogate mimesis which consists in the drama's being performable on stage. The stage takes on the function of the epic preterit, since despite the "present time" of the performance the performers are not identical with the characters they portray, and thus the stage-present underscores the mimetic nature of the drama.

In Hamburger's system the lyrical genre, in contrast to the mimetic, represents a reality statement because we experience it as the statement of a statement-subject, the "lyric I." Nevertheless, there are fundamental differences between the communicative reality statement—which performs a function in an objective context or a context of reality—and the lyrical statement, for the lyrical statement resists such a function. The difference between the lyrical and the communicative statement is based on the fact that in a lyrical statement the object is not the goal but the occasion. Thus the lyrical statement looses its reality nexus. If, however, it does not carry out this process, it remains on the level of communication.

By interpreting the lyric I as a genuine statement-subject, Käte Hamburger seems to defend the thesis that all lyric poetry is *Erlebnislyrik:* "We experience the lyric statement-subject, and nothing but this. We do not go beyond the experience-field in which it confines us. But this means that we experience the lyric statement as a reality statement, the statement of a genuine statement-subject, which can be referred to nothing but this subject itself" (pp. 270–71). Since, however, Hamburger adopts Husserl's use of the concept of experience "as a comprehensive concept for all acts of consciousness" (p. 277), the experience can be "fictive" or invented; the lyric I, however, will always be regarded as a real statement-subject.

The problems involved in Hamburger's logic of literature can be seen clearly in her effort to classify the literary forms which do not automatically fall within her system. Thus, for example, she is compelled to relate the first-person narrative to the lyrical statement and the ballad, because of its fictional nature, as a foreign body within the lyrical genre. In doing so she runs the risk of becoming a victim of methodological dogmatism in spite of the flexibility of her argumentation. Further, the objection has frequently been raised that Hamburger assigns the same degree of lyrical statement to the amateurish love poem of a high school student as she does to an accomplished poem; but Hamburger makes it very clear that literary evaluation is a problem for literary aesthetics. In terms of the logic of literature, even the high school student's poem must be considered a lyrical statement if it observes the laws of lyrical statement structure.

The most constructive critique of Hamburger's contribution to genre morphology so far has been Rolf Tarot's essay *"Mimesis und Imitatio: Grundlagen einer neuen Gattungspoetik"* [Mimesis and Imitatio—Fundamentals of a New Genre Theory].[11] The starting point for Tarot's critique is Hamburger's classification of the entire dramatic genre as mimetic literature. Tarot points out that her definition of the poetic structure of the drama is based on the assumption that Aristotelian drama is the only dramatic form. However, non-Aristotelian drama, as is proven primarily by Brecht's "epic theater," represents the other basic form of drama. To designate its different logico-linguistic structure Tarot introduces the concept of *imitatio* and distinguishes it from the Aristotelian drama in the following way: "If the actor identifies with the character he presents, then the presentation is mimesis; if the real actor is the narrator (demonstrator) of his character, then the presentation (*Vor-stellung*) is *imitatio*" (p. 130). Thus imitatio is a feigned reality statement because the actor, as narrator of his character, "is not a genuine, but a non-genuine, feigned, imitated statement-subject" (p. 131).

This concept of imitatio allows Tarot not only to explain non-Aristotelian drama in terms of the logic of literature, but also to solve the problem of special forms treated unsatisfactorily by Hamburger. The epic first-person narrative no longer needs to be included within the lyrical genre; rather it is an example of epic imitatio. From this Tarot concludes that "in terms of language theory, the categorical boundary which separates the two fundamentally different modes of creative language runs between mimesis and *imitatio*. This is true not only for the epic and the dramatic presentational forms but also for lyric poetry" (p. 133). Accordingly, the fictional element in the ballad justifies Tarot's characterization of it as a "mimetic structure in the lyric presentational form" (p. 133).

Tarot's genre theory, however, must be expanded by one fundamental consideration. For it is not clear what part the old "natural forms" and subforms play in his system. Tarot states that his categories "encompass all modes of presentation within the 'natural forms' of literature" (p. 141), but he does not explain how this comes about. The designation of the subforms as "presentational forms" does not differ substantially from Kayser's "forms of presentation" and allows the subforms only a historical-descriptive meaning. On the level of literary aesthetics, however, they have in addition an autonomous character which, as Staiger has shown, relates them to the modes of human existence.

Walter Muschg's literary-aesthetic approach appears to afford a quite different sort of solution to this problem. To be sure, his *"Einführung in eine Poetik"* [Introduction to a Poetics] lacks the stringent logic of Hamburger's and Tarot's systems and is characterized by romanticizing formulations; but this is because Muschg was unable to work out more than only an outline of his ideas.[12] There is no question, however, that his ideas constitute an important expansion of the contributions discussed above and furnish a valuable supplement to the various theories of genre morphology.

The poetics which Muschg proposes derives directly from his typology of poetic attitudes based on the distinction between the magical, mystical, and mythical imaginations. He finds correlatives to these attitudes in the personal pronouns I, thou, and it, which represent "the ultimate constants which are recurringly actualized in the human soul. They are innate in man, they constitute his life. Proof of this is furnished by literature, where these primary forms of speech recur in an elemental way.... I, thou, it are the grammatical signs for what we have heretofore called the magical, mystical, and mythical vision" (pp. 62–63).

Like Staiger, Muschg bases his genre theory on ontological considerations. He is not, however, concerned with differentiating between the so-called natural forms; for in his opinion, "the classical canon of genres is based on a generalization from once valid formal tendencies which are now refuted by literature" (p. 61). He perhaps somewhat hastily dismisses these genres as "institutions" and accepts the notion of "primal forms of literature" (p. 61) only insofar as these can be derived from the psychological correlation of literary imagination, language, and imagery. Muschg's ultimate concern is to trace these elements of literature back to archetypal modes of human existence. That his ideas—often only intuitively grasped or insufficiently developed—correspond to provable facts has been shown by modern literary sociology with its objective, fact-oriented methodology. Since Muschg concentrates only on the aesthetic aspect of literature, however, it would be necessary to find support for his ideas in the theory of language as well as in literary-sociological studies.

In his poetics, Muschg distinguishes between the intention of the literary principle in question, which is based on the archetypal nature of the grammatical designations (I, thou, it), and its formal counterpart. He takes as the starting point for his discussion the "language of the first person" (of the I), which is the language of the Orphic poet, the shaman, the magus who finds himself "in harmony with nature" and who knows "the ecstatic joy of self-deification in which the I expands and becomes one with the universe" (p. 63). The individual I of the poet is heightened to an absolute I which invests his language with the demonic power of apprehending the world of objects by the act of naming. This poetic principle is closely related to the stylistic one of realism (i.e., "realism" in a typological rather than in a literary-historical sense). According to Arnold Hauser, the beginnings of realism are to be found in the magical art of the Old Stone Age, when the killing of an animal was guaranteed by the magical-realistic identity which the artist established between the animal and its pictorial representation, thus bringing the animal under man's spell.[13] In his sociology of literature Joseph Strelka has shown convincingly that there is a fundamental attitude which connects the Paleolithic monistic world-view and the "utilitarian-rationalized world-view of an empirical-realistic form of life" and which forms the intellectual-historical and sociological background for all "realistic" style periods.[14]

This "magical" poetic principle which is "conditioned by the nature of the I-like word" (*des ichhaften Wortes;* Muschg, p. 72) has forms of concretization within each genre. The magical form "strives to make manifest the wonder of this flowing-toward-each-other (*Zueinanderfliessen*) of soul and word" (p. 73). Muschg equates this kind of lyric poetry, which he also calls "Orphic" poetry, with Staiger's general concept of the "lyrical," although in Muschg's opinion this encompasses only one aspect of lyric poetry. The concept of "the lyrical" which is derived from the poetry of Goethe and the Romantics and which elevates the originality of the poet's experience to the prime criterion of "the lyrical" represents a revival of the "magical" concept of poetry which was reborn in the eighteenth century as a reaction to the isolation of the modern individual.

The magical epic is best exemplified by the fairy tale, and Muschg even considers magical dramas to be "scenically arranged fairy tales of a demonically aroused soul, the dream visions of silent ecstatics" (p. 84). Common to all three magical genres is the primordial story of "the dream journey of the soul through a resistant spirit-world to the source of life in the Beyond" (p. 76). Unfortunately his concepts are based largely on considerations of content and do not lead to clearly defined formal-aesthetic categories.

The "language of the second person" (of the thou) is that of the "mystical" seer or prophet, who strives to escape from the experience of earthly limitation to the limitlessness of the divine. In principle, it is the language of self-contemplative dialogue, but the tension within the I increases to the point of displacing the focus of existence to a point outside the world. From this phenomenological point of view, Muschg includes "all forms of 'pathetic' thinking and allegorical speech" within mystical literature (p. 92) and finds examples of this visionary basic literary attitude in all three genres.

In purely style-typological terms this "mystical" attitude underlies the phenomenon of romanticism, roots of which sociological investigation has discovered in the New Stone Age. The development from the nomadic culture of the Paleolithic hunters and food-gatherers to the culture of the settled farmers and cattle-breeders of the Neolithic Age is accompanied by a change from monism to dualistic animism and, accordingly, "magical realism" to symbolic irrationalism. In this instance, too, Strelka has shown that there is a literary-sociological line of development which runs from Neolithic geometrism to the metaphysical idealism characteristic of "romantic" periods (pp. 256, 258).

Muschg derives his third literary type from the "language of the third person" (of the it) and sees it exemplified in the "singer" who is filled with mythic imagination. He distinguishes it from the two other types in the following way: "The magus strives for the omnipotence of feeling, the singer strives for omniscience. Whereas the magus' willfulness (*Eigensinn*) lies in his dreamy or intoxicated inwardness, and the mystic's in his fixed gaze towards a transcendent Thou, the singer's is grounded in a hunger for the things of this world" (p. 108). The poetic intention of the mythic poet is the transfiguration of the object world. He draws inspiration from a sensuous bond with life itself, and death apparently has no meaning for him. The form of mythical literature is determined by the principle of naturalness, which also includes the social function.

In this case, too, studies in the sociology of literature furnish concrete evidence in support of Muschg's romanticizing psychologism. For mythic poetry can be understood as a synthesis of magical and mystical poetry which originates in the transitional phenomena that mark the change of style from Paleolithic naturalism to Neolithic geometrism. The stylistic traits of such phenomena represent a stylization and schematization of the naturalistic forms. These transitional styles lead to expressive classicism, which is the synthesis of the realistic and romantic modes of literature and "in which the realistic component embodies the aspect of the surge for reality and the idealistic component the aspect of elevation, of the anagogic in the broadest sense" (Strelka, p. 274).

By basing his typology upon the strict progression of "I, thou, it," Muschg follows a principle which is alien to literature and which, moreover, does not correspond to the course of mankind's intellectual and religious history. That is, the striving for the divine Thou presupposes the experience of man's separation from God, an experience which in religious history follows the Revelation. In literary-typological terms, in other words, the mystical language of the thou follows the mythic language of the it. Magical and mystical literature thus form the two poles of archetypal literary typology, while mythic literature represents a transitional mode or synthesis of the two. Since magical, mystical, and mythical types of literature are to be found within each genre, only the subforms, not the genres themselves, can be associated with a particular mode or type. Muschg himself has given a few hints about how such a classification might be made.

What follows is an attempt to synthesize all of the morphological genre criteria discussed above and to show how they may be applied to lyric poetry in a way that will lead to a comprehensive understanding of the lyrical genre and its subforms. The principal ontological characteristic of lyric poetry is the elimination of historical time and space, which also characterizes all the lyrical subforms. On this rests lyric poetry's claim to "absoluteness," which makes itself felt in its association with a particular subform. This illustrates what Kayser refers to as the "structural character" (*Gefügecharakter*) of the literary work of art.

Rhythm transforms the restrictions and limitations imposed by meter into something natural and self-evident. That is, the deviation from metrical patterns creates in the reader or listener the expectation that such patterns will be fulfilled. The meter is realized, however, not according to a set of fixed rules but in consonance with a physiologically determined emotional response within man. Hence the temporal limitation is changed into timelessness. The same principle also underlies the stanza and rhyme, both of which become natural and self-evident through the realization of their limiting principle. Correspondingly, every word in a lyric poem is related to every other word; this is possible only when such relations are self-evident and are realized within the lyrical structure. Moreover, on the level of imagery, the natural autonomy of lyric poetry can even reach a certain degree of "willfullness" (*Eigenwilligkeit*) provided that such willfullness serves the "unforced" shaping of language to arrive at the unity of word and thing or of sign and thing signified. These elements (prosody and imagery) may be realized either as ritual or as the individual self-fulfillment (*Selbstvollzug*) of the poet, that is, within the range of possibilities from magical to mystical poetry.

These elements of lyric poetry may all be subsumed under the principal stylistic trait of "mutuality" (*Ineinander*) and have their structural equivalent in the specific, often intensely antithetical subject-object relation. This subject-object relation must be presupposed so that by overcoming it the *Ineinander* can be realized. Hamburger designates this process the resorption of the object-relation into the subject-relation. The variability of this relation is one of the determining criteria for the various genre subforms. Strictly speaking, the elimination of historical time and space in the lyric does not result in the elimination of every object-pole; rather, the reference point is simply not preestablished and must in each instance be posited and presented anew. The object-pole takes on a supratemporal and supraspatial character; and even if in some cases the object-reference is not metaphysical, it nevertheless always transcends the subject of the lyrical statement which must stand up to it. Therefore the manner in which this reference point emerges from the lyrical subject and then is resorbed by it in each case determines the poetic attitude of the subform. This attitude must be in harmony with the historical form of presentation if the work is to be successfully realized. This circumstance corresponds to the relationship between the "imitative" and "mimetic" presentational modes and to the spectrum of possibilities from "magical" to "mystical" imagination and imagery. An investigation of the various subforms will elucidate the relationship of these presentational modes to each other.

A justifiable criticism which may be made of both Staiger's and Muschg's interpretations of genres is that both presuppose a development of genres or subforms which ignores the actual facts. Staiger's thesis that "the lyrical" is the ultimate ground of all literature and Muschg's comparable concept of Orphic poetry do not take into account the original teleological function of art. For this reason they exclude from consideration those subforms whose roots can be traced back to a preliterary period, rather than accept them as valid nonliterary forms of lyric poetry and use them in the discussion of their literary equivalents. The two lyrical subforms which, because of their original teleological function, attain the level of the lyrical only as peripheral forms are the *Ruf* and the *Spruch*. Their primarily ritualistic-magical nature is beyond question and serves to establish the object-relation which finds its present-day secularized manifestation in party slogans and other propagandistic formulations. As Hamburger has shown, however, this object-relation must be transformed into a subject-relation if the level of poetic concretization is to be reached.

In this respect, the *Ruf* is the literary mode in which the intention of the poetic attitude is to create from within itself the object-relation as immediate reaction. This is possible only if a continuous relationship between subject and object is presupposed. Connected with this is the self-containment of the subject, which leads to a structuring of the object-pole according to the principle of "inverse projection" (*negative Aussparung*)—that is, the object-relation is not presented directly but can be inferred only from the intention and as a reflection of the lyrical subject. The *Ruf* exemplifies the imitative structure and is an expression of the magical attitude which places the thing under the spell of the word by the act of naming. For this reason, the *Ruf* also lacks any factitive quality which would "guarantee" fulfillment of the intention; it remains merely goal-oriented.

This missing quality is to be found in the *Spruch*. For here there is a complete correspondence of the two poles involving even the rhythm and sound, so that the intention can be invested with its magical power of realization. Because of the principle of complete correspondence, the subjective intention merely represents the other side of the object-pole, which is evoked in this manner. The necessity of this correspondence of the two poles leads to the terseness and pithiness of the *Spruch*. In logico-linguistic terms, one could say that there is a correspondence between the imitative and the teleological structure: the feigned subject-relation corresponds to the real object-relation. That may be the reason why the epigram is only reluctantly classified as lyric poetry. Its logico-linguistic structure as well as its epistemological nature make it appear to be a variation of the "essayistic."

A secularized continuation of the *Spruch* exists in the didactic poem, the lyrical nature of which can be questioned. This is because so many didactic poems have a strictly teleological intention and should therefore be assigned to the "essayistic" genre. There are, however, sufficient examples in which the didactic intent is realized in a mimetic "epicizing" depiction of an exemplary model or in an imitative statement or subjective experience. The subject-pole of the didactic poem, which has been expanded in comparison to that of the *Spruch*, finds correspondence in the object-pole which, as in the *Spruch*, has a pithy form and thus functions as a maxim or précis. The necessary expansion of the subject-pole, which is conditioned both by the subject-pole's relativity in comparison with the object-pole and by the reader who is to be instructed, explains the imbalance of the two parts. This imbalance, however, merely stresses the irrevocability of the object-relation.

In comparison to the *Ruf* and the *Spruch* the *Lied* is the lyrical subform in which the teleological intent and the object-relation disappear and which thus allows the emancipation of the subject by interiorizing this relation. The *Lied* represents the lyrical subform which wholly accentuates the subject-pole and thus invests it with objectivity. By eliminating the object-relation, the lyrical subject claims it for itself and brings about the magical identity of sign and thing signified. The nonpolarized subject-relation leads to the stylistic characteristic that all elements are interdeterminate. This is true for the prosodic elements as well as for the imagery. In this respect, the *Lied* fulfills the conditions which Muschg establishes for the magical lyric. But the *Lied* can be cited as the most convincing example of the fact that the subforms can be realized in all three literary types. It can of course be assumed with some certainty that the original conception of a subform grew out of its coordination with a particular literary type; any association with another type should be viewed as a secondary development.

The *Dinggedicht*—where the identity of presentation and the thing presented serves as the basis for its meaning as an "objective correlative"—can be considered a "mythical" *Lied*. The object reveals itself and determines the form. In the *Dinggedicht*, the magical element of the *Lied* has undergone a transposition to the level of meaning; at the same time, the subjective inwardness has been transformed into an objective one. The "mystical" configuration of the *Lied*, on the other hand, could perhaps be seen in the intention of reattaining the condition of inwardness by overcoming the mythic attitude. This process can be seen in Rilke's poetic development from the *Neue Gedichte* to *Sonette an Orpheus*, which corresponds to the change from a mythic to a mystical poetic attitude. This change even affects Rilke's use of the sonnet form, which served in the *Neue Gedichte* to present a self-contained earthly object. In the *Sonette an Orpheus*, on the other hand, this "self-containment" opens up to reveal a cosmic objectivity; and as a result of this "opening up," the "mythical" poetic attitude is overcome. Stronger mimetic features are to be found in the "mythic" rather than in the "magical" or "mystical" *Lied*.

In contrast to the nonpolarized poetic attitude of the *Lied*, the other lyrical subforms are based on a fully developed subject-object polarity. The ballad is the most problematic of the lyrical subforms; thus many attempts have been made to arrive at a new understanding of it. Its origin in the popular ballad (*Bänkelsang*) reveals a strongly teleological nature, which, as in both the *Ruf* and the *Spruch*, is based on the principle of correspondence. However, this is determined by the public's expectation, which influences the particular strophic form, the formal devices, and the nature of the ballad's oral presentation as well as its subject matter. In the so-called art ballad, public expectation is abandoned in favor of literary expectation, though many of the fundamental features of the popular ballad are retained. One could say that the teleological elements take on a new function and speak of their transposition from a genuine reality-nexus into a feigned one with a mimetic structure. The ballad is basically a kind of mythic poetry, for it gives poetic form and expression to an objective connection with reality which dominates over the subjective sphere. With the transposition of the ballad onto a literary plane, the social conflict in the *Bänkelsang* is transformed into a supratemporal, numinous conflict. As a consequence, if the numinous is denied as an objective referent, the ballad tends to return to the teleological plane.

In addition to its mythic configuration, the ballad also has a magical one, above all in the case of certain folk ballads and their adaptations by Goethe, Eichendorff, and Mörike. Because of their strong subject-relation, the *imitative* reality-nexus dominates in such ballads, and its function as the object-relation is transformed into that of the heightened subject-relation. The same thing is true—and not by accident—of those ballads in which nature is depicted as having magical powers. Their brevity alone suggests a different logico-linguistic structure and poetic mode. We can also speak of a mystical variant of the ballad, but only in a very few cases. Paul Celan's *"Gauner und Ganovenweise"* could be considered an example of the mystical ballad, for here the overcoming of the fictive object-relation does not result from the magical unity of subject and object but from the fact that the subject is expanded to the point of objective equivalence while the object-relation is still retained.[15]

In the idyll the subject-object relation is quite different from that of the ballad. The lyrical subject is set off from the objective world which remains only as the negative pole of a realm the lyrical subject invests with the character of being generally binding. An epic or didactic poetic attitude—that is, a *mimetic* or teleological language structure—underlies the poetic realization of this sphere which achieves an apparent objectivity. Although the character of the idyll is basically mythical, because of this apparent objectivity magical and mystical variants are not uncommon. Storm's *"Abseits,"* for example, must be assigned to the former category; the harmony between man and nature, which leads to the neutralization of temporality, is not so much object-related as it is the reflection of a subject-related understanding of being. Some of Mörike's lyrics, on the other hand, represent the mystical variant; there the lyric eye is absorbed by the cosmic harmony which it has itself created or discovered.

Closely related to the "mythic" *Lied* is the ode, which Muschg includes within the category of mythic poetry and which contains strong mimetic traits. The difference between these two lyrical subforms lies in the fact that the ode fully preserves the subject-object polarity. That is, the lyrical subject creates the object-relation, without becoming submerged in it. Therefore, in spite of the apparent autonomy of the object-pole, a tension between the two poles inevitably arises. The classical forms of the ode allow for this tension, for their freedom is exposed by the rigidity of their form as being only an apparent freedom. The sonnet may also be considered to be a form of the ode, though it is not commonly viewed as such; for in many cases it preserves the tension between the two poles. Once again Rilke's *Sonette an Orpheus* can be cited as an example of how the poet has used a form which is based on this subject-object antithesis only to neutralize the polarity and thus to write a *Lied*. In this one can see the proximity of the "mystical" ode to the "mystical" *Lied,* their generic difference being that the ode retains the subject-object polarity. A great many of Celan's poems could accordingly be designated as "mystical" odes. In the case of Celan it is also evident that the language structure of his "mystical" odes is not mimetic-imitative, but purely imitative.

In the elegy the nature of the antithetical subject-object relation is changed, and the two poles are reconciled. Thus there is a reconciliation between the mimetic and imitative components, and between the mythical and magical elements or the mythical and mystical ones. Goethe's *"Euphrosyne"* is an example of the first variant, for the dominance of the *imitative* component is accompanied by an affirmation of the magical relation between the I and the world. Rilke's *Duineser Elegien*, on the other hand, must be classified as "mystical" elegies, since the lyrical subject intends to make objective reality the vehicle of a higher reality. The same is true of Hölderlin, and in this regard it is significant that the elegies of both poets approach the only fundamentally mystical lyrical subform, i.e., the *Hymne*.

The *Hymne* is diametrically opposed to the *Lied* insofar as it resolves the subject-object antithesis in favor of the object-relation. The lyrical subject becomes subservient to the numinous aspect of the object pole. This reduction of the subject-pole encompasses both prosodic and verbal elements and leads on the one hand to a transcendence of the lyrical subject and on the other to an exalted affirmation of the object-pole. Because of its purely mystical intention, magical and mythical variants are actually foreign to the *Hymne*. One could consider the *Ruf*, since in it the object pole is implied as an inverse projection of the subject pole. A mythical variant of the *Hymne* is the religious hymn, in which the transcendental aspect reveals itself and has become part of a common cultural heritage.

The *Hymne* brings us to the end of the range of lyrical subforms, which extends from total subject-relatedness to complete object-relatedness. We have used the lyrical subforms as concrete examples to demonstrate how the various morphological genre criteria complement each other and how they can contribute, individually and together, to a broader understanding of genre. We have included Muschg's archetypal typology of basic literary "attitudes" in our discussion to show that the genres and their subforms stand in a reciprocal relationship to style periods; this means that not only do the specific configurations of the genres and their subforms reflect the stylistic tendencies of a particular literary-historical period but that they also determine the style, which is characteristic of a period, so that certain genres, subforms, and especially archetypal variants of subforms predominate in one given literary period.

The results of all these attempts at genre morphology have been more or less summarily repudiated by structuralism, a school which claims for itself the questionable reputation of exclusivity. Klaus W. Hempfer's recent structuralist contribution to the genre question can be cited as a representative of this attitude. It seems appropriate to discuss Hempfer's book at this point since he presents the most thorough and comprehensive reworking of genre theories so far and derives his arguments from a critique of traditional genre definitions as well as from a revision and refinement of the structuralist approach.[16]

Of the traditional genre theories, Hempfer accepts as valid only the so-called *expressiv-produktionsästhetischen* conceptions of genre, "which attempt to establish the existence of 'genres' via their expressive function—that is, their role in the production of literature or, in a more general sense, of texts" (p. 80). Hempfer includes the contributions of G. Müller and K. Viëtor to genre morphology within this category. But the above quotation alone makes it clear that an understanding of literature and poetry as verbal works of art is foreign to structuralism, and Hempfer therefore criticizes Viëtor's and Müller's views because they lack "the relation to the process of reception" (p. 80); the preceding discussion of traditional genre theory should, however, have shown that a system of genre morphology can account for this process of reception. Hempfer's equation of literature and poetry with texts, a view which he shares with structuralism, allows him to coordinate literary criticism with generative linguistics and to apply the latest linguistic models to literary criticism in general and to genre definition in particular. In his eagerness finally to be able to establish literary criticism as an exact science, he ignores the fact that his method implies the reduction of literature to a descriptive and communicative language function and bypasses the phenomenon of literary language and creative literature which is based on a transcendence of purely communicative function of language.

The concepts of epic, lyric, and drama Hempfer considers valid only as convenient catchwords, and he maintains that only "modes of writing" (*Schreibweisen*) should be genre-determining. Using Piaget's definition of structure, Hempfer argues that these modes are derived from the "laws of structure" as an integration of "absolute or relative generic invariables (the narrative, the satiric, etc.) which are concretized via particular transformations in the historical genres (epic, verse satire, etc.), whereby these may be based, not only on one, but on the overlapping of two or more modes of writing" (p. 224). The relationship between the invariables and the transformations corresponds to the linguistic model of depth and surface structure. Hempfer must, however, admit that there is no way to foresee when scholarship might be in a position to lay down rules which govern the transformation in any given case. That such mathematical formulas contribute nothing to our understanding of the aesthetic aspect of genre is unfortunately not recognized. In a much more complicated manner Hempfer commits the same error which we already have seen in the attempt to subdivide the genres and subforms into ever smaller categories.

In spite of such basic objections, one must admit that Hempfer does arrive at some genuine though partial insights. The genres cannot, of course, be defined as the sum of the elements but only in terms of the abstract relation of these elements; on the other hand, the individual forms which a genre can take on must be understood "as historical modes of concretization of this abstract relation within the framework of particular socio-cultural systems" (p. 224). As a whole, however, Hempfer's systematic genre theory leaves one with the overall impression that it is a mechanistic genre definition which is alien to the nature of literature; and this makes it difficult to accept even his valid insights. This fact should make it clear that structuralism cannot open new realms in the area of genre theory but leads into a blind alley which is disguised by brilliant formulations.

(Translated by Ruth Hein)

Notes

1. Cf. regarding this topic Karl Viëtor, *Geschichte der deutschen Ode* (1923), Günther Müller, *Geschichte des deutschen Liedes* (1925), Wolfgang Kayser, *Geschichte der deutschen Ballade* (1936), Friedrich Beissner, *Geschichte der deutschen Elegie* (1941), Benno von Wiese, *Novelle* (1963).
2. Cf. Joseph Strelka, *Die gelenkten Musen. Dichtung und Gesellschaft* (Vienna: Europa Verlag, 1971), p 181.
3. The third edition is quoted (Zürich: Atlantis Verlag, 1956).
4. Cf. Edgar Lohner, "The Intrinsic Method: Some Reconsiderations," in *The Disciplines of Criticism. Essays in Literary Theory, Interpretation and History*, ed. Peter Demetz, Thomas Greene, and Lowry Nelson, Jr. (New Haven: Yale University Press, 1968), p. 160.
5. Cf. René Wellek, "Genre Theory, the Lyric, and 'Erlebnis,'" in *Discriminations: Further Concepts of Criticism* (New Haven: Yale University Press, 1970), p. 226.
6. For this reason the three primary poetic types always coexist, but the differing degree to which one becomes conscious of them leads to a different

degree of social relationship: lyric strives for a total freedom from any social reference, while the drama is constituted by it. Perhaps for this reason literary periods with a social tendency, like the Sturm und Drang, "das junge Deutschland," or Naturalism are predominantly nonlyrical in quality and are characterized by a large dramatic output.

7. *Das sprachliche Kunstwerk. Eine Einführung in die Literaturwissenschaft,* 5th ed. (1948: rpt. Bern: Francke Verlag, 1959).
8. *Die literarische Formenlehre. Vorschläge zu ihrer Reform* (Stuttgart: Metzlersche Verlagsbuchhandlung, 1967).
9. Cf. the following discussion of the aphorism as a form of lyric.
10. The English quotations of Käte Hamburger's book are from *The Logic of Literature,* 2d rev. ed., trans. Marilynn J. Rose (Bloomington: Indiana University Press, 1973).
11. *Euphorion* 64 (1970): 125–42.
12. *Die dichterische Phantasie. Einführung in eine Poetik* (Bern: Francke Verlag, 1969).
13. Cf. *Sozialgeschichte der Kunst und Literatur* (Munich, 1953), 1:7.
14. Cf. *Die gelenkten Musen,* p. 257.
15. Cf. the end of the poem: "Aber, aber er bäumt sich, der Baum. Er, auch er steht gegen *die Pest"* in *Die Niemandrose* (Frankfurt: S. Fischer Verlag, 1963), p. 28.
16. *Gattungstheorie,* eds. Klaus W. Hempfer and Wolfgang Weiss (Munich: Wilhelm Fink Verlag, 1973).

Thomas G. Winner

STRUCTURAL AND SEMIOTIC GENRE THEORY

Literary genre theory attempts to typologize works of verbal art, that is, it attempts to determine subtypes composing a universal art form for which there is implied a normative definition. The question at issue between traditional genre theory and structuralist departures is that of the criteria which are used in the effort to isolate hierarchies of invariants and variants that together define the essence of literary art and its various subdivisions.

A variety of descriptive features derived from normative rules, often conceived of as fixed and unchanging, were employed in traditional approaches to genre theory, which isolated various formal and thematic traits, as well as necessary effects exercised by given types of works upon perceivers (e.g., Aristotle's catharsis). However, largely ignored by traditional genre theory were such issues as the following: the relation of the work of art to its environment, including both its narrow artistic surroundings and the broader enveloping culture; inner and deep relations of the components of the work of art not apparent upon surface-level inspection; the dynamics and mutability of genres including their relation to the artistic creators; the significance of deviations of individual works from ideal types; and, most fundamentally, the identification of the underlying structural attributes held to be distinctive of, and specific to, artistic texts themselves.

Hence traditional descriptions of genre listed traits and normative "rules" which together composed abstract, idealized, unchanging types, fitting no specific work of art completely. Deviations became "exceptions" leading to arguments and discussions in which essentially unsolvable issues such as the following were debated: Are such works as Tolstoy's *War and Peace*, Pasternak's

Doctor Zhivago, Proust's *A la recherche du temps perdu,* and Cervantes's *Don Quixote* "novels"? And can they be accepted as "good literature" if they do not fit the model completely? In drama, a typical question, admitting no final answer was: Are Chekhov's major plays tragedies, as Stanislavski saw and staged them, or comedies, as Chekhov insisted they were?

It has long been apparent that a new methodology is needed, since the old one has become sterile. The first requirements are clearly for a more dynamic, systematic, and holistic approach. Looking to structuralist semiotics for new guidelines would seem to be worthwhile, although the area of structuralist genre theory has hardly developed. The time is ripe, however, for more serious efforts to apply the insights of this approach to the construction of dynamic typologies. The primary tenets of structuralism, briefly summarized here, must constitute a point of departure:

1. A work of art is seen as a system, or structure, being composed of levels in hierarchical arrangement, the elements of which are united by both conflict and harmony.

2. The idea of closed immanent texts is rejected for the concept of autonomy, opening up the issue of the interrelations of structures and the changes effected by contact of structures with each other. However, the direction and nature of development stimulated by the external effect of one structure upon another is governed by the internal laws of the autonomous structures themselves.

3. The rigid Saussurian dichotomy of diachrony and synchrony, discarded as early as 1928 by Roman Jakobson and Jurij Tynjanov, is replaced by the view that all structures are in constant motion and ever-evolving, thus diachronic in character; yet, since evolution is systematic, structures are also to be viewed synchronically (Jakobson and Tynjanov 1928:37).

4. Structure cannot be separated from function. But one function is hardly adequate since all human activity is polyfunctional, although one function tends to dominate others in a hierarchical arrangement. Since functions are subject to change, however, no permanent dominance can be assumed. The aesthetic, or poetic, function, that which is specific to art, although it is even present in weakened forms in extra-artistic structures as well, is characterized uniquely by its autodirection, causing the work to call attention to itself, which emphasizes its inner construction. But this formal quality does not exclude the existence of the semantic component, which in aesthetic structures is peculiarly complex, dif-

fuse, and polysemic, in contrast to its more direct nature in nonartistic texts.

5. In the early 1930s, the above tenets were greatly strengthened by the heuristic assumption of the Prague Linguistic Circle that art can best be understood as a specific kind of sign. All contemporary poetics have been affected in one way or another by this semiotic approach, which insists upon encompassing such complexities as the relation of works of art to each other, to their authors, to their present and potential receivers, all of which affect our understanding of the nature of the work of art itself.

6. Paralleling the rejection of the synchrony/diachrony dichotomy, a work of art, as a semiotic system, is both *langue* and *parole*, but *langue* (or code) is no longer seen as fixed and separate from the variable *parole*, as the Saussurian view is replaced by the assertion of the interrelatedness of these two levels in language as well as in other semiotic systems in very complex ways.

7. From the concept of *langue* and *parole* are derived the key concepts of norm and antinorm, the dynamic relations of which compose the aesthetic function. As seen in the early works of Jan Mukařovský, the leading aesthetician of the Prague Linguistic Circle in the 1930s, the tensions between the norm of a given code and its violation are necessary bases for aesthetic structures. The aesthetic norm, striving for unchanging validity which it can never achieve, is eternally challenged by the continuing and changing individual applications and alterations and defiances of the aesthetic norm (Mukařovský 1937:77). These changes result only in part from necessary adaptations to varied external circumstances. They are frequently deliberate, composing one of the primary means of achieving the aesthetic effect (Mukařovský 1936:32–33). We can think of art as swinging between two poles: from almost complete normativeness, or banality and redundancy, therefore coming close to zero information, to almost total violation of the norm, or of the code, resulting again in close to zero information, since the message could barely be decoded by the receivers. From a diachronic approach, the polar concept defines periods of artistic creation, which appear to oscillate between those which place high value upon normativeness at the expense of innovation (for instance, the seventeenth and eighteenth centuries), and those which place high value on innovation at the expense of normativeness (for instance, the romantic period, the art of the early twentieth century). Such complex and shifting relations between norm and norm violations must form the kernel of

modern structural genre theory. This is true because modern genre theory must isolate compositional and thematic invariants of a given group of texts, in the context of their relationships to individual variations, and further change in norms themselves must be accounted for within the system.

We may well ask why structuralist approaches to genre theory have been so meagerly developed over the past decades. Is it, as Jauss (1970:79) puts it, that normative genre theory of the nineteenth century has given the entire topic a bad name? Or is it rather the greatness of the difficulties in finding common denominators encompassing not only modern art forms but also the art of the Middle Ages and pseudo-art, or popular art, all of which must be understood synchronically and diachronically within Goethe's three "echte Naturformen der Poesie: die klar erzaehlende, die enthusiastisch aufgeregte und die persoenlich handelnde" [the epic, the dramatic, and the lyric]? Whatever the reason, systematic work toward a structuralist or semiotic genre theory, synchronic and diachronic in character, is limited. As the young Polish scholar M. Głowiński reflects, division into the main three genres is to be seen more as a part of the subconscious than the conscious aspect of literary science, while genre theory is characterized by "petrification as well as chaos" (1969:20–21).

Here we will summarize some specific contributions to genre theory consciously made by those considering themselves structuralists. In an early approach, Mukařovský suggested that genre should no longer be based on such thematic criteria as the heroic, the lyrical, and the dramatic but should rather be based on formal elements and their interrelationships, because genre is "a stabilized system of creative devices" (1929:396) similar to a code which permits an infinite number of individual performances. In considering receptions of works of art, Mukařovský also pointed out that the awareness of genre (ibid.:395) on the part of the perceiver builds up certain expectations which may or may not be fulfilled. As the Russian formalist critic Ejxenbaum has observed, when a work of literature is transferred to another literary culture, such expectations, or lack of expectations, may become highly significant (1968:2). The short stories of O. Henry, for example, were received in the United States against the background of a well-developed short story tradition, while in Russia, where the short story was not a popular phenomenon, the stories of O. Henry appeared to be an exotic form. These pronouncements by Mukařovský, revealing the influence of Russian "formalism," were later abandoned, since form and meaning were seen as inseparable and understandable only within a broader context.

Felix Vodička, one of the most important literary historians associated with the Prague School, devoted more attention to the question of genre theory, placing it in a historical framework and defining the problem as one of the pragmatics of communication, that is, of the contact between an author and his public, both of whom share, to a certain extent, knowledge about the genre used (1952:35). However, the only substantial study concerning genre that emanated from the Prague Linguistic Circle is J. Veltruský's (1942) study of drama, with little general theoretical application. Veltruský posits two methods for the determination of genre. The first consists of a detailed listing of all poetic devices, their functions within a set of works, and the forms that the given devices take in a given literary type. Since this requires a considerable body of material which, Veltruský states, does not yet exist from the structuralist viewpoint, he chooses a second path, analogous to what Prague scholars call the "semantic gesture," which forms the constructive principle of a particular author for the selection and arrangement of his material. The reconstruction of the "semantic gesture" is, in fact, the assemblage of the invariants of the various works of a single author, defined by their functions in each of the particular author's works. Although Veltruský wanted to extend this method to other literary types as well (1942:408–10), the task remains unfinished.

These early and limited forays into traditional genre theory by members of the Prague Linguistic Circle hardly hint at the wide possibilities for applications of structural principles in the construction of a new artistic typology. We are left with a general point of view of the Prague Linguistic Circle: an artistic structure, composed of dynamic, changeable, hierarchically arranged relationships, encompasses both form and meaning and exhibits complex relationships to other structures and meaning external to it. This approach, relevant to an individual work of art or to the works of a single author or of a period, needs to be thoroughly extended to genres, as well as to any typology of literary texts.

In turning to more recent structural concepts and their possible application to genre theory, we note the strong influence of semiotic views.

The question of poetic versus nonpoetic utterances lies of course at the very heart of structural poetics and aesthetics, and here we must consider Jakobson's formulation of the six-factor and six-function model of the linguistic communication act (1960:353–58). The poetic (aesthetic) function is no longer just one of "others," but is clearly defined in relation to five complementary functions. The aesthetic function was defined as "orientation of the utterance" (ibid.: 356), which, when dominant, characterizes a work of art (1935:82–84). Function is thus a teleological aspect of verbal activity. Since the goal is the key, the very same form can serve different functions (referential, metalingual, phatic, emotive, conative), thereby altering our perceptions of the text (1960:299–302).

We must consider the relation of the poetic quality of a text not only to the intention of the encoder but also to that of the receiver of an aesthetic message. In a poetic utterance, a word is felt primarily as a word which obtains its own weight and value; in poetic language, as Jakobson noted much earlier (1921:41), Husserl's *dinglicher Bezug* is absent; hence a poetic text is self-oriented. Individual elements are brought into new relationships, which are characteristic only of the given text, and of no other text systems. Meaning, in aesthetic texts, is no longer directly communicated because the relation between the signifier and the signified, on the one hand, and the sign and the denotatum, on the other, takes on altered dimensions (1965:11). Because of the complex and elusive relationship between sign and denotatum, the attention of the perceiver is drawn to the artistic structure *qua* structure, to its inner relationships, and only then to the denotatum.

Not only are aesthetic qualities affected by the intention of the author and the receivers, but independently the aesthetic text, in contrast to other texts, emphasizes its formal elements such as grammar and sound patterns. In the most extreme example, poetry, there is the greatest exploitation of the formal qualities of the structure of the natural language. Jakobson has expressed this formal drive in his characterization of the poetic function as projecting the principle of equivalence from the axis of selection onto the axis of combination (1960:358). In verbal art, Jakobson posits, recalling Saussure's distinction between the syntagmatic and paradigmatic axes of the speech act (Saussure 1906–11:122–27), equivalence is shifted from the paradigmatic axis and promoted to the constitutive device of the sequence. Hence, in poetic structures, verbal equations or parallelisms become a constructive principle of the text. Syntactical, morphological, phonemic categories are confronted, juxtaposed, brought into relations of contiguity according to the principles of similarity and contrast, thus communicating their own autonomous significations.

Here then is the basis for a formal distinction between poetic and nonpoetic structures, which lays down guideposts at least. But the framework is yet to be filled, and in the process the outline will inevitably be altered. Turning to the question of units which compose aesthetic systems, the most useful approach is likely to be that based on the concept of text, which is being elaborated by structural theoreticians, especially in Eastern Europe and the Soviet Union.

The linguistic notion of "text" was given a semiotic interpretation by the Russian scholar A.M. Pjatigorskij (1962), who saw the text as an aspect of the "pragmatics" of semiotic communication, which is concerned with the relationship between the sign and its agents: the sender and the receiver(s). According to Pjatigorskij, a text is a complex whole, composed of signals which are, in varied ways, delimited and autonomous. Such a communication has the following characteristics:

1. It is spatially (or acoustically or optically) fixed, so that it is intuitively felt as distinct from a nontext.

2. The fixation of a text is not accidental but is a part of the conscious act of communication by its sender. A text thus is not an accidental conglomerate of features but has a definite inner structure.

3. A text must be comprehensible. That is, it must belong to a social code.

In a more specific application of the concept of "text" to literature by the Polish scholar Maria Renata Mayenowa, the semiotic concept of text is held to mean a certain informing whole, a subject of a sign character, organized in a certain manner, having a beginning and an end, and transmitting finished information from the point of view of its sender (1974:252–308). According to Mayenowa, an integrated text must fulfill the following conditions:

1. It must be the creation of one's sender.

2. It must have the same receiver, that means all "you's" of the possible modal frames should refer to the same person or group of persons.

3. The text must have a unifying theme, or subject matter, that is, everything told in a given "text" must have an "integral" meaning, which implies that every element in the text must be in some way or other related integrally to all other elements of the same text.

4. A text is set off from its environment by a "frame," that is, it has a clearly recognizable beginning and end. Particularly in oral art, the beginning, as well as the end, is frequently couched in formulas, distinguishing it both grammatically and thematically from the remaining text. But written literature also is frequently characterized by traditional beginnings. For example, the following characteristic formula for the beginning of a prose work has developed in written literature since Boccacio: In place X in time Y there lived a person Z (defined by name and social position). When such a formula is established, it can in itself become the object of a "game" of norm breaking or of transforming of the formula into something else. Thus Gogol's *Dead Souls* begins in the following way:

> Into the gates of the inn of the district town there entered a rather nice looking spring carriage in which usually single persons drive about: such as retired colonels, staff captains, landowners with about a hundred souls of peasants—in a word all those whom we call gentlemen of the middling kind. In the carriage sat a man, not beautiful, but not ugly either, neither particularly fat, nor particularly skinny; one cannot say that he was old, however, he was not too young either.

The structure of textual wholes may also be characterized by manners of manipulation of cited utterances, as Jakobson has shown in his discussion of shifters (1957).

A more all-encompassing approach to "text" has been developed by a group of Soviet scholars at the University of Tartu in Estonia, and the Soviet Academy of Sciences in Moscow (cf. Uspenskij et al.:1973), who have applied the notion of "text" to the whole spectrum of cultural behavior, which they define as a hierarchy of semiotic systems, composed of texts. Texts may be understood on three levels. At the lowest level, at the origin of texts, culture is seen as a certain text-generating mechanism, or a collective mechanism for the storage and processing of information (ibid.:17). This information is transmitted in the form of texts composing the next level, where culture is seen as the sum of its texts. Moving to the third level, texts are organized into a hierarchy of semiotic systems.

There are all kinds of cultural texts, including rules of etiquette, prayers, law codes, dress codes, and also artistic texts, which are contrasted to nonaesthetic texts, since artistic texts value devices which are statistically the least frequent, thus carrying a maximum of information. A relationship is posited between artistic and linguistic texts, which, although suggestive, calls for clarification: the notion of artistic texts, since artistic texts are viewed as "secondary modeling systems," linguistic ones being primary. Thus Uspenskij et al. state:

> Under secondary modeling systems we understand such semiotic systems, with the aid of which the models of the world, or of its fragments, are constructed. These systems are secondary in relation to the primary system of natural language, over which they are built—directly (the supra-linguistic system of literature) or in the shape parallel to it (music, painting). (1973:19–20)

If aesthetic texts are constructed "along the lines of language," certain analogies must be implied which have not, unfortunately, been specified in the writings of the Lotman group. However, we assume that there are the following implications. In both primary and secondary modeling systems, the opposition *langue/parole* is operative. That is, an abstract set of rules underlies individual texts, an infinite number of which can be generated. Moreover, the fundamental principles of construction in both primary and secondary modeling systems are based on the paradigmatic axis of selection and the syntagmatic axis of combination. However, while the "secondary" systems select and order their material in a fashion analogous to natural language, different criteria are utilized. In this sense, the Lotmanian thesis bears not only upon a theory of aesthetic texts in general but also upon the problem of genre theory in particular. Aesthetic texts are performances which abide by, or challenge and change, the rules of a given code or *langue*, or genre. Further, the rules of the set, or the genre, limit both the selection and the ordering of materials which compose the text.

Fundamental, then, to a structuralist and semiotic genre theory would be the opposition between semiotic systems and the individual texts generated by them. I have already suggested preliminary formal characteristics of texts, including framing, beginning, end, and integral meaning. Further than that, various works, or texts, may be grouped together by a variety of criteria, which are highly variable, depending upon the common relational features being considered, and which could be depicted by an iconic abstract model uncovering such relevant formal and semantic invariants. Thus, whether our set is all verse, a special type of verse, such as the sonnet, a particular type of sonnet, for instance, the Elizabethan sonnet or all Shakespearean sonnets, or a certain group of paintings and poems transcending the formal artistic divisions depends upon the criteria selected. For example, in a recent essay, the Russian scholar Jurij I. Levin (1973) attempts to type lyrical poetry from the standpoint of the grammatical categories utilized in the various types and subtypes of addressors and addressees functioning within the text of a lyrical poem. Here Levin establishes a system of classifications based on different types of communicative relationships depending upon the first, second, and third person, and on various in-between situations. The goal is to make more precise the usual assertions that the lyric is expressed in the first person in all tenses, the drama in the second, utilizing the present tense, and the epic in the third person and the past tense (cf. Mayenowa 1974:43; Stankiewicz 1961:16–17).

From a structuralist approach, criteria for the identification of genres must be generated from the materials themselves, that is, from the individual texts which are united into sets by certain shared or parallel relations. But further than that we cannot go. As Lévi-Strauss incisively said, it is not the question whether "the touch of a woodpecker's beak does in fact cure a toothache. It is rather whether there is a point of view from which a woodpecker's beak and man's tooth can be seen as 'going together.'" And he continues: classifying, as opposed to nonclassifying, has a value of its own, whatever form the classification may take, whatever the criteria by which we classify our sets (1966:12). Thus we can accept the traditional vertical genre classification preceding from the most general to the most specific as in the diagram on page 264.

Other criteria could be selected, of course, which intersect, cutting across traditional taxonomies, creating horizontal typologies. For example, if we choose the theme of the absurd as a criterion, the set would encompass modern examples in all three traditional genres, the epic, the lyric, and the dramatic. Or certain formal criteria might be utilized, such as linguistic rhythms. In this case, members of one set would include the rhythmic prose of some of the symbolists, rhymed drama, and versified forms of verbal art.

Although sets are high variable, being defined by any relevant criteria, assuming they are heuristic and are not capriciously chosen, this does not mean that from the point of view of structural semiotics, sets, or genres, do not have some more formal and invariant characteristics, among which are the following:

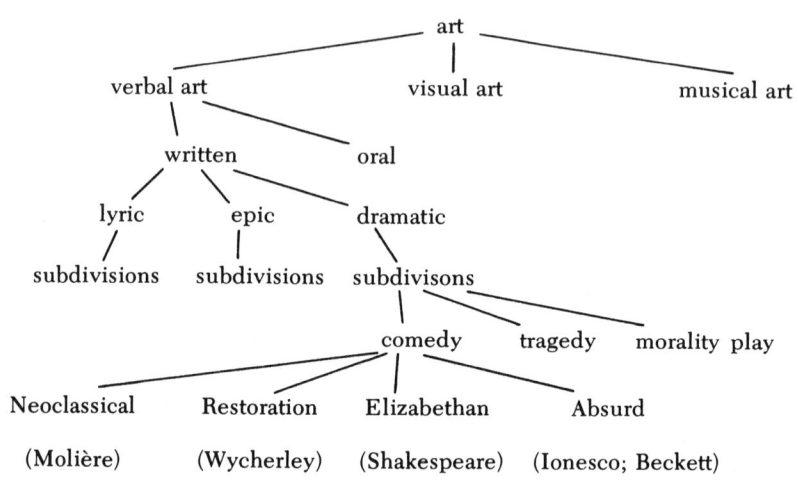

1. Dynamically related diachronic and synchronic characteristics: Since genre represents both the system of artistic norms (rules or devices available to the artist and his receivers at a given time) and the potential artistic deviations and innovations related to these constructs for a given type of artistic utterance, genres are never static and must be studied both synchronically and diachronically. Genre is simultaneously a problem of history and a problem of synchronic structure, an evolving system, which is a dialectical combination of both variants and invariants, that is, of identifications and differentiations. While the invariants serve as identification of a given work or series of works, they are also the basic condition of the historicity of a given genre (cf. Głowiński 1969:31). Yet a synchronic slice cannot isolate invariant features from their associated antinomies, that is, from aspects of change

and differentiation, which act as forces for evolution and differentiation. For each genre, at each given historical period, is a system, and is therefore synchronic in character, but it is simultaneously an ever-evolving series, and hence diachronic in character. Thus normative elements and non-normative elements may coexist in each manifestation of a genre. In fact, since norm violation is raised to one of the constructive principles of the aesthetic function, the non-normative elements are of particular significance in aesthetic structures, whereas their role is less pronounced in non-aesthetic structures.

2. Dynamic relations between the sign, the sender and the receiver, or pragmatics: By his analogy of genre to memory, the Russian critic Mixail Baxtin has pointed to developmental dynamics of genre.

> The literary genre ... represents the most constant ... tendencies of literary evolution. In the genre there are always preserved ... elements of archaic character. But these archaisms are retained in the genre only thanks to their constant renewal, their so to speak contemporanization. A genre is always that and not that, it is always both old and new simultaneously. The genre is reborn and renewed in each new stage of the development of literature and *each individual creation* of a given genre. Thus is expressed the life of a genre. That is why archaic elements retained in the genre are not dead, but remain eternally alive, that is, they remain capable of renewal. A genre lives in the present, but always with the *memory* of its past, of its beginnings. Genre is the representative of creative memory in the process of evolution of literature. It is for this reason that the genre is capable of assuring the unity and uninterruptiveness of this development. (1963:141–42; italics added)

The semiotic area of pragmatics, or the relation of the sign and its agents, the addressor and the receiver, suggests that a genre is a set of conventionalized features, or signals, that are exchanged between the sender and the receiver; they set up certain parameters of expectations. The author, aware of the traditional strictures of a genre, proceeds to "encode" within a certain sphere of possibilities. The converse process of decoding is also effected by the expectation imposed by the genre. The resulting tension between the perception of norm and of its violation is of course strongly influenced by the foreknowledge of the "rules" of the genre. Let me adduce only one example. The code of the nineteenth-century "realistic" short story included certain conventions about the opening and the closing of the story, and of the events that occurred between these two points, which might be roughly formalized in the following manner:

Opening: Introduction of setting and of main protagonist (in location X lived a certain Y).

Action and complication (Y falls in love with Z) and conflict (e.g., a competitor or husband intervenes).

Ending: some resolution of the action.

A Russian reader, expecting Chekhov's mature short stories to exhibit the traditional conventions of the short story genre, would have been "disappointed," since these works lack a traditional opening, often beginning *in medias res,* nor is there the usual "traditional" action and complication, and even the ending is frequently achieved without a resolution. (See Winner 1966: 31–32, 240–41 on "zero endings" in Chekhov.)

3. Multifunctionality: In every aesthetic text other functions participate in addition to the aesthetic one, contributing many levels of meanings. As Jakobson has informed us, the emotive qualities of a lyric focus on the sender, while the conative aspect of the drama is oriented primarily toward the receiver, and the referential element in the epic of a novel returns us strongly to the context (1960:303). Thus emotive, conative, and referential, as well as possibly other functions seem partially to define specific genres and contribute specific meanings.

The foregoing comments suggest some of the directions structuralist theories may take in the construction of new typologies. We see that semiotic and structural poetics views genre as a kind of grammar. Perhaps genre was always seen in this manner. But now such grammars are viewed in dynamic relation to the communicative process, which they regulate and effect but cannot rule. In fact, in the semiotic view, the essence of art is the tension between the creative process of norm breaking and the force of rules. Genres are mutable systems within systems (i.e., within the system of verbal art), they are codes or subcodes, models for the organization of texts, which must be understood both synchronically and diachronically, grammatically and functionally, and which cannot be abstracted from the pragmatic sphere. Clearly, structural semiotics has challenged traditional approaches to artistic classifications based on prior schemes. But a new school of genre theory is hardly born. We have the tools and some first attempts, but most work remains to be done.

References

Baxtin, Mixail. 1963. *Problemy poètiky Dostoevskogo.* Moscow: Sovetskij pisatel.
Ejxenbaum, B.M. 1968. *O. Henry and the Theory of the Short Story.* Translated, with notes and postscript by I.R. Titunik. Michigan Slavic Contributions. Ann Arbor, 1968. Originally published in Russian in *Zvezda* 6 (1925):291–308.
Głowiński, Michał. 1969. *Powieść młodopolska.* Studium z poetyki historycznej. Warsaw: Warsaw PAN.
Jakobson, Roman. 1921. *Novejšaja russkaja poèzija.* Prague: Typografia Politika.
———. 1935. *The Dominant.* From the unpublished text of lectures on the Russian Formalist School delivered at the Masaryk University in Brno, Spring 1935. Translated from the Czech by Herbert Eagle in *Russian Poetics: Formalist and Structuralist Views.* Edited by Ladislav Matejka and Krystyna Pomorska. Cambridge: MIT Press, 1971, pp. 82–87.
———. 1957. *Shifters, Verbal Categories, and the Russian Verb.* Harvard University Department of Slavic Languages.
———. 1960. "Linguistics and Poetics." In *Style in Language.* Edited by Thomas Sebeok. New York: Wiley, pp. 350–77.
———. 1965. "Vers une science de l'art poétique." In *Théorie de la littérature. Textes des Formalistes russes.* Edited and translated by Tzvetan Todorov. Paris: Seuil, pp. 9–13.
Jakobson, Roman and Jurij Tynjanov. 1928. Problemy izučenija literary i jazyka. *Novyj Lef* 12:35–37.
Jauss, Hans-Robert. 1970. Littérature médiévale et théorie des genres. *Poétique* 1:79–101.
Lévi-Strauss, Claude. 1966. *The Savage Mind.* Chicago: University of Chicago Press.
Levin, Jurij I. 1973. Lirika s kommunikativnoj točki zrenija. In Van der Eng and Grygar: 177–95.
Mayenowa, Maria Renata. 1974. *Poetyka teoretyczna. Zagadnienia języka.* Warsaw: Ossolineum.
Mukařovský, Jan. 1929. O současné poetice. *Plán* 1, no. 7: 387–97.
———. 1936. *Aesthetic Function, Norm and Value as Social Facts.* Translated from the Czech by Mark E. Suino. Ann Arbor: Michigan Slavic Contributions, 1970.
———. 1937. *Estetická norma.* Republished in Jan Mukařovský. *Studie z estetiky.* Prague: Odeon, 1966, pp. 223–25. Originally published as *La norme esthétique.* Travaux du IXe congrès international de philosophie. Vol. 12 Paris, 1937.
Pjatigorskij, A.M. 1962. "Nekotorye obščie zamečanija otnositel'no rassmotrenija teksta kak raznovidnosti signala." In *Strukturno-tipologičeskie issledovanija.* Edited by T.N. Mološnoj. Moscow: ANSSSR. Inst. Slavjanovedenija, pp. 144–54.
Saussure, Ferdinand de. 1906–11. *Cours de la linguistique générale.* Edited by Charles Bally and Albert Sèchehaye. Cited from the English version: *Course in General Linguistics.* New York McGraw-Hill Paperback, 1966.

Stankiewicz, Edward. 1961. "Poetic and Non-Poetic Language." In *Poetics, Poetyka, Poètika*. The Hague: Mouton, pp. 11-23.
Uspenskij, B.A., et al. 1973. Theses on the semiotic study of cultures (As applied to Slavic tests). In Van der Eng and Grygar, 1973, pp. 1-28.
Van der Eng, Jan, and Mojmír Grygar. 1973. *Structure of Texts and Semiotics of Culture*. The Hague: Mouton.
Veltruský, J. 1942. "Drama jako básnické dílo." In Čtení o jazyce a poesii. Edited by B. Havránek and Jan Mukařovský. Prague: Družstevní práce, pp. 403-502.
Vodička, F. 1952. "Literární historie, její problémy a úkoly." In *Ctení o jazyce a poesii*. Edited by B. Havránek and Jan Mukařovský. Prague: Družstevní práce, pp. 309-402.
Winner, Thomas G. 1966. *Chekhov and His Prose*. New York: Holt, Rinehart & Winston.

LIST OF CONTRIBUTORS

BONNET, HENRI
Born in 1904 in Roanne, France.
Ph.D., the Sorbonne.
Present position: Redacteur en Chef du Bulletin des Amis de Marcel Proust.

Books: *Le Progres spiritual dans l'oeuvre de Marcel Proust* (volumes 1 and 2), Paris, 1946, 1949; *Roman et Poésie*, Paris, 1951; *Alphonse Darlu, maître de philosophie de Marcel Proust*, Paris, 1961; *De Malherbe à Sartre*, Paris, 1964; *Marcel Proust de 1907 à 1914, Bibliographie générale* (volume 1), Paris, 1971; *Marcel Proust de 1907 à 1914, Bibliographie complimentaire. "Du côté de chez Swann"* (étude), Paris, 1976.

CHAMPIGNY, ROBERT
Born in 1922 in Chatellerault, France.
Studied at Ecole Normale supérieure, Paris; Agrégation, 1947; Doctorat en lettres, Paris.
Present position: Research Professor of French, Indiana University.

Books—Studies: *Portrait of a Symbolist Hero*, Bloomington, 1954; *Stages on Sartre's Way*, Bloomington, 1959; *Sur un héros païen*, Paris, 1959; *Le Genre poétique*, Monte Carlo, 1963; *Le Genre dramatique*, Monte Carlo, 1965; *Pour une esthétique de l'essai*, Paris, 1967; *Humanism and Human Racism*, The Hague, 1972; *Ontology of the Narrative*, Paris, 1972; *Le Jeu philosophique*, Paris, 1976. — Poetry: *Dépôt*, Paris, 1952; *L'Intermonde*, Paris, 1953; *Brûler*, Paris, 1955; *Monde*, Paris, 1960; *Horizon*, Paris, 1969; *La Mission la Demeure la Roue*, Paris, 1969; *Les Passes*, Paris, 1972; *L'Analyse*, Paris, 1974.

DAEMMRICH, HORST S.
Born in 1930 in Pausa, Germany.
Ph.D., University of Chicago.
Present position: Professor of German at Wayne State University.

Books: *The Challenge of German Literature*, Detroit, 1971; *The Shattered Self. E. T. A. Hoffman's Tragic Vision*, Detroit, 1971; *Literaturkritik in Theorie und Praxis*, Munich, 1974; *Widerholte Spiegelungen. Themen und Motive in der Literatur*, Munich, 1977.

HERNADI, PAUL

Born in 1936 in Budapest.

Ph.D., University of Vienna and Ph.D., Yale University.

Present position: Professor of English and Comparative Literature, Chairman of Comparative Literature, University of Iowa.

Book: *Beyond Genre: New Directions in Literary Classification*, Ithaca and London, 1972.

HUISMAN, JOHANNES A.

Born in 1919 in Wijk-bij-Duurstede, Netherlands.

Studied at Nijmegen University; Ph.D., University of Utrecht.

Present position: Chairman, Institute of Old Germanic, Frisian and Scandinavian Studies and Full Professor of Old Germanic Languages and Literature at Utrecht University.

Books: *De Hel-namen in Nederland*, Groningen, 1953; *De namen Betuwe en Veluwe*, Amsterdam, 1958; *Plaatsnamen van sacrale oorsprong*, Groningen, 1959; *Alliteratie in onze tijd*, Groningen, 1959; *Nette en onnette woorden*, Hilversum, 1962; *Het Nederlands tussen dialect en wereldtaal*, Groningen, 1965; *De "vakken achter de streep" in het tijdperk der automatie*, Eindhoven, 1966.

LEVI, ALBERT WILLIAM

Born in 1911 in Indianapolis, Indiana.

Studied at Dartmouth College and the University of Chicago.

Present position: David May Distinguished University Professor of the Humanities at Washington University, St. Louis.

Books: *Rational Belief*, New York, 1941; *General Education in the Social Sciences*, Chicago, 1949; *Varieties of Experience*, Bloomington, 1957; *Philosophy and the Modern World*, Bloomington, 1959 (winner of first Ralph Waldo Emerson Award by Phi Beta Kappa); *Literature, Philosophy and the Imagination*, Bloomington, 1962; *Humanism and Politics*, Bloomington, 1969; *The Humanities Today*, Bloomington, 1970; *Philosophy as Social Expression*, Chicago, 1974.

Editor: *The Six Great Humanistic Essays of John Stuart Mill*, New York, 1963.

MARINO, ADRIAN

Born in 1921 in Iasi, Romania.

Studied at the University of Bucharest and the University of Geneva; Ph.D., University of Bucharest.

Present position: Literary critic and literary aesthetician.

Books: *Life and Works of Aelxandru Macedonski,* Bucharest, 1967, 1969; *Introduction in Literary Criticism,* Bucharest, 1968; *Modern, Modernism, Modernity,* Bucharest, 1969; *Dictionary of Literary Ideas,* I (A–G), Bucharest, 1973; *Ole! España,* Bucharest, 1974; *The Criticism of Literary Ideas,* Bucharest, 1974; *Rumänische Erzähler der Gegenwart,* Bucharest, 1972.

Editor: *Cahiers roumains d'études littéraires,* Bucharest.

Translations: *Kritik der literarischen Begriffe; European Booknotes.*

REICHERT, JOHN

Born in 1935 in Cleveland, Ohio.

Studied at Amherst College; Ph.D., Stanford University.

Present position: Professor of English and Chairman of the English Department at Williams College.

Book: *On Making Sense of Literature,* Chicago, 1978.

ROSENBERG, BRUCE A.

Born in 1934 in New York City.

Studied at Ohio State University.

Present position: Professor of English, Brown University.

Books: *The Folksongs of Virginia,* Charlottesville, 1969; *Medieval Literature and Folklore Studies,* New Brunswick, 1970; *The Art of the American Folk Preacher,* New York, 1970; *Custer and the Epic of Defeat,* University Park, 1974.

SALOMON, HERMAN P.

Born in 1931 in Amsterdam, Netherlands.

Ph.D., University of Amsterdam; Ph.D., New York University.

Present position: Associate Professor of Romance Literatures, State University of New York at Albany.

Book: *Tartuffe Devant L'Opinion Française*, Paris, 1963.
Edited books: Racine, *Phèdre*, Paris, 1964; Racine, *Athalie*, Paris, 1965; Molière, *Tartuffe*, Paris, 1966.
Editor: *The American Sephardi* (Journal of The Sephardic Studies Program of Yeshiva University, New York City).

STAHL, ERNEST L.

Born in 1902 in Senekal, South Africa.

Studied at the University of Capetown, Oxford University; Ph.D., the University of Bern.

Career: Reader in German Literature, Oxford University, 1945; Taylor Professor of German Language and Literature, Oxford University, 1959; Student Emeritus of Christ Church and Taylor Professor Emeritus, 1969.

Books: *Die religiöse und die philosophische Bildungsidee und die Enstehung des Bildungsromans*, Bern, 1934; *Hölderlin's Symbolism*, Oxford, 1944; *Heinrich von Kleist's Dramas*, Oxford, 1948; *Friedrich Schiller's Drama: Theory and Practice*, Oxford, 1954.

Edited books: Goethe, *Die Leiden des jungen Werther*, Oxford, 1942; Lessing, *Emilia Galotti*, Oxford, 1946; Rilke, *Duineser Elegien*, Oxford, 1965; *The Oxford Book of German Verse*, Oxford, 1967.

Editor: *Oxford German Studies; Anglica Germanica*.

Translation: An abridged version of Goethe's *Faust* in collaboration with Louis MacNeice.

TAROT, ROLF

Born in 1931 in Dortmund, Germany.

Studied at Göttingen and Cologne. Ph.D., University of Cologne; Ph.D. habil., University of Zürich.

Present position: Professor of German Literature, University of Zürich.

Books: *Jakob Bidermanns "Cenodoxus,"* Düsseldorf, 1960; *Hugo von Hofmannsthal: Daseinsformen und dichterische Struktur*, Tübingen, 1970.

Edited books: Grimmelshausen, *Gesammelte Werke in Einzelausgaben*, Tübingen, 1967-70; Jakob Bidermann, *Cenodoxus*, Tübingen, 1963 (Latin), 1965 (German); *Ludi theatrales sacri* (2 volumes), Tübingen, 1967; Christian Reuter, *Schlampampe*, Stuttgart, 1966; Andreas Gryphius, *Cardenio und Celine*, Stuttgart, 1968; Daniel Casper von Lohenstein, *Sophonishe*, Stuttgart, 1970.

WEISSENBERGER, KLAUS H. M.

Born in 1939 in Sydney, Australia.

Studied at the University of Hamburg; Ph.D., University of Southern California.

Present position: Professor of German and Chairman of the Department of German and Russian, Rice University.

Books: *Formen der Elegie von Goethe bis Celan,* Munich, 1969; *Die Elegie bei Paul Celan,* Munich, 1969; *Zwischen Stein und Stern. Mystische Formgebung in der Dichtung von Else Lasker-Schüler, Nelly Sachs und Paul Celan,* Munich, 1976.

WINNER, THOMAS G.

Born in 1917 in Prague.

Ph.D., Columbia University.

Present position: Professor of Slavic Languages and Comparative Literature, Brown University.

Books: *Kazakh Literature and Oral Art,* Durham, 1958; *Chekhov and His Prose,* New York, 1966.

Edited books: Iu. M. Lotman, *Lektsii po struktural' oi poetike,* Providence, 1968; Roman Jakobson, *O cheshskom stikhe, preimuschestvenno v sopostavlenii s russikim,* Providence, 1969; Mark Aldanov, *Zagadka Tolstogo,* Providence, 1969; M. O. Gershenzon, *Mechta i mysl' I. S. Turgeneva,* Providence, 1970; Juri Lotman, *Struktura Khudozhetvennogo teksta,* Providence, 1971; *Tvorcheskie raboty uchenikov Tolstogo v Yasnoi Poljane,* Providence, 1971.

INDEX OF NAMES

Aarne, Antti, 159
Abrahams, Roger, 152, 154, 162
Adam, Antoine, 227
Adams, John, 30
Addison, Joseph, 74, 76
Adkins, A.W., 219
Adorno, Theodor W., 188
Aeschylus, 37
Anderson, Walter, 157, 165
Archer, William, 227
Aristotle, viii, 17, 32, 33, 34, 37, 39, 42, 46, 52, 53, 60, 64, 73, 74, 77, 87, 155, 163, 193, 196, 199, 205, 219, 228, 254
Arlt, W., 144
Arnauld, Antoine, 223
Asher, J.A., 146
Auerbach, Erich, 17, 20
Augustine, Saint, 36, 137
Austen, Jane, 58

Bacon, Francis, 42
Baldwin, C.S., 135, 144, 145, 147, 148
Balzac, Honoré de, 5, 6, 7, 68
Barrès, Maurice, 6
Barrett, William, 150
Barthes, Roland, 11, 16, 227
Bascom, William, 153
Bateson, Gregory, 152
Batteux, Abbé, 42, 55
Batts, M.S., 124, 145
Baudelaire, Charles, 6, 7, 114, 212
Baudeloo, Willem van, 138
Baudin, Maurice, 228
Baumgärtner, K., 145, 146
Baxtin, Mixail, 265, 267
Baybak, M.P., 147
Beauvais, Vincent de, 133
Beckett, Samuel, 264
Beethoven, Ludwig van, 12, 30
Behrens, Irene, 208
Beissner, Friedrich, 252
Ben-Amos, Dan, 153, 154, 162, 165
Bénichou, Paul, 228
Bentley, Eric, 199, 200

Bérard, Victor, 40
Berger, Willy R., 228
Bergmann, R., 149
Bergson, Henri, 40, 199, 215
Béroul, 163
Bertau, K., 145
Besch, W., 146, 149
Beyschlag, Siegfried, 126, 147
Bierwisch, Manfred, 146
Billiar, Donald E., x
Blanchot, Maurice, 56
Blankenburg, Christian Friedrich von, 88
Bloomfield, Morton, 123, 146
Boccaccio, Giovanni, 89, 137, 261
Boileau, Nicolas, 50, 52, 53
Boisdeffre, Pierre de, 16
Bolliac, Cezar, 52, 56
Bond, Donald F., 79
Bonnet, Henri, 3, 227
Booth, Wayne, 75
Borelius, H., 146
Bossuet, Jacques Bénigne, 6
Boueke, D., 149
Bourget, Paul, 5, 6, 7
Bourneuf, R., 226
Bovet, Ernest, 225
Bowra, Cecil M., 148
Boyer, Claude, 223
Bradbury, Malcolm, 207
Bradley, A.C., 36, 227
Bray, René, 225, 227
Brecht, Bertolt, 85, 115, 167, 168, 169, 200, 233, 234, 240
Bremond, Henri, 6, 212, 226
Brereton, Geoffrey, 227
Browning, Robert, 195
Brunetière, Ferdinand, 209, 210, 220, 225, 228
Brunner, F., 145
Bruno, Giordano, 51, 52
Buber, Martin, 150
Burke, Kenneth, 159, 161, 162, 200, 201, 202

Bynum, David, 165
Byron, George Gordon Noel, Lord, 7

Caesar, Gaius Julius, 9
Caragiale, I.L., 52
Cassirer, Ernst, 231, 232
Castelvetro, Lodovico, 74, 79
Catullus, 142
Cederschiöld, G., 146
Celan, Paul, 248, 249
Cervantes, Miguel de, 53, 255
Cézanne, Paul, 14
Champigny, Robert, 95, 210
Chardin, Jean Baptiste Simeon, 14
Charlemagne, 141, 164
Chateaubriand, François René Vicomte de, 5
Chaucer, Geoffrey, 89, 137, 197
Chekhov, Anton Pavlovitch, 54, 200, 255, 266, 268
Chinard, G., 228
Ch'ing Ming, 30
Chomsky, Noam, 127
Chrétien de Troyes, 134, 137, 163
Cintico, Giraldi, 51
Cioranescu, A., 221
Coleridge, Samuel Taylor, 34
Colie, Rosalie L., 226, 227, 228
Condillac, Etienne Bonnot de Mably de, 4, 51
Confucius, 29
Conrad, Joseph, 117, 206
Cook, Albert, 196, 197, 198
Corneille, Pierre, 52, 199, 210, 214, 216, 217, 218, 219, 220, 223, 227, 228
Corneille, Thomas, 223
Courbet, Gustave, 14
Couton, Georges, 225
Crane, Ronald S., 55, 57, 60, 61, 62, 63, 64, 76, 195, 196, 208
Croce, Benedetto, vii, ix, 51, 124, 192, 210, 230
Curtius, Ernst Robert, 125
Cuvier, Georges, baron de, 72

Daemmrich, Horst S., 112, 122
Daiches, David, 208
Dante, 28, 31, 53, 135, 137, 227
Darwin, Charles, 210
Daumier, Honoré, 15
Deanesly, M., 149
De Boor, Helmut, 146
Degas, Edgar, 15
De Gaulle, Charles, 15
Delacroix, Henri, 13
Demetz, Peter, 252

Democritus, 39
Descartes, René, 20, 38, 106
De Vries, H., 145
Dewey, John, 39
Dickens, Charles, viii
Dilthey, Wilhelm, 39, 229
Diomedes, 42
Dostoyevsky, Fedor Mihajlovitch, viii, 6, 21, 22, 23, 24, 38, 54
Doležel, Lubomir, 126, 145
Dovada, R., 55
Dragomirescu, M., 51, 56
Du Bartas, Guillaume de Salluste, Seigneur, 53
Dubos, Charles, 52
Dubuffet, Jean, 14
Dumas, Alexandre (Fils), 195, 220, 228
Dundes, Alan, 152
Dunoyer de Segonzac, Barthélemy Charles, 15
Dupont, E.A., 108
Dürer, Albrecht, 14
Düwel, K., 149

Eagle, Herbert, 267
Eggers, H., 145
Eichendorff, Joseph von, 248
Eis, Gerhard, 146, 148
Ejxenbaum, B.M., 267
Elias, Julius A., 91
Eliot, George, 6
Eliot, Thomas Stearns, 26, 30, 31, 32, 38, 193, 194
Ellis-Fermor, Una, 208
Ellmann, Richard, 208
Else, Gerald, 75, 79
Eng, Jan van der, 268
Erzgraeber, W. 144
Euripides, 221
Eyck, Jan van, 14

Faguet, Emile, 214, 217, 220, 221, 227
Farrar, R.S., 148
Fauriel, Claude Charles, 51, 56
Fayolle, Roger, 56
Feydeau, Ernest, 16
Fielding, Henry, 58, 61, 62, 64, 65, 197
Finck, Werner, 170
Fischer, Hanns, 146, 147
Flaubert, Gustave, 6
Fokkema, D.W., 142
Fontane, Theodor, 179
Fortunatow, N., 189
Foscolo, Ugo, 51
Fowler, Alistair, 207
Fowler, David, 157, 165

INDEX OF NAMES

Fra Angelico, 32
Fraenkel, Jonas, 189
Franz Joseph, Emperor of Austria, 30
Frazer, Sir James, 204
French, A.L., 228
Freud, Sigmund, 74, 199, 204, 223
Fromm, Hans, 145, 147
Frye, Northrop, ix, 42, 55, 57, 59, 66, 69, 70, 73, 75, 76, 78, 202, 203, 204, 205, 206, 207, 208
Fubini, Mario, 56

Galfredus de Vinoslavo, 147
Gallais, Pierre, 148
Garasa, Delfin Leocadio, 224, 225, 226, 227, 228
Gautier, Théophile, 79
Geertz, Clifford, 150
Gelhaus, Hermann, 189
Gennrich, F., 145, 148
Gering, H., 146
Gide, André, 16, 212, 222, 226
Glier, Ingeborg, 148
Głowinski, M., 257, 265, 267
Goethe, Johann Wolfgang von, 6, 34, 37, 46, 86, 89, 90, 91, 92, 115, 131, 138, 166, 193, 194, 200, 229, 242, 248, 249, 257
Gogh, Vincent van, 27
Gogol, Nikolaj Vasilevitch, 261
Goldmann, Lucien, 17, 225
Goris, J.A., 147
Gottfried von Strassburg, 136, 163
Gottsched, Johann Christoph, 87
Gouhier, Henri, 226
Grava, Arnolds, 15
Gravina, V., 52
Gray, Thomas, 62
Greene, Thomas, 252
Greimas, A.J., 98
Grimm, Jakob and Wilhelm, 80
Grimminger, R., 144
Grubmueller, Klaus, 149
Grundmann, H., 149
Grygar, Mojmir, 268
Guarini, Giovanni Battista, 43
Guchmann, M.M., 146
Guerard, Albert, 194, 195
Guevara, Che, 164

Hadlaub, 137
Hakon, King of Norway, 132
Hamburger, Käte, 166, 167, 170, 172, 173, 174, 175, 176, 184, 187, 188, 190, 237, 238, 239, 240, 241, 246, 253
Hardy, Thomas, 6

Hartman, Geoffrey, 208
Hatto, A.T., 144
Haubrichs, W., 145
Hauck, K., 145
Hauptmann, Gerhart, 115, 117
Hauser, Arnold, 242
Havranek, B., 268
Hawthorne, Nathaniel, 5
Haydn, Joseph, 18
Hegel, Georg Wilhelm Friedrich, 86, 106, 193, 229
Heidegger, Martin, 85, 231, 232
Hein, Ruth, 144, 187, 252
Heine, Heinrich, 7
Heinrichs, H.M., 146
Hemingway, Ernest, 20
Hempfer, Klaus, viii, x, 226, 250, 251, 252, 253
Henning, Hans, 145
Henry, O., 257
Henston, Edward F., x
Herkommer, H., 148, 149
Hernadi, Paul, vii, viii, ix, 192
Herrick, Marvin, 225
Hieatt, A.K., 147
Hirsch, Eric Donald, 58, 110, 152, 153, 207, 225, 228
Hitler, Adolf, 164
Hobbes, Thomas, 74
Hofmannsthal, Hugo von, 171, 190, 234
Hölderlin, Friedrich, 53, 250
Homer, 40, 42, 53, 155
Hopper, V.G., 145
Horace, viii, 50, 53, 88, 137
Hough, Graham, 208
Housman, A.E., 212
Hugo, Victor, 6, 9, 52, 110, 227
Huisman, Johannes A., 123, 144, 147
Hume, David, 19
Husserl, Edmund, 239, 259

Ibsen, Henrik, 200
Ihwe, Jens, 146
Ionesco, Eugene, 264
Iouwick, J.H., 16
Iser, Wolfgang, 122
Ittenbach, Max, 145

Jakobson, Roman, 4, 44, 45, 55, 110, 211, 255, 258, 259, 266, 267, 268
James, Henry, 5, 6, 58, 67
Jaspers, Karl, 150
Jauss, Hans Robert, 122, 257, 268
Jekel, Ludwig, 203
Jesus, 110, 164
Jodelle, Etienne, 220

Jodogne, O., 131, 147
Johnson, Samuel, 62, 64, 74, 79
Jolles, André, 55
Jones, George Fenwick, 149
Jones, James, 108
Jonson, Ben, 204
Joyce, James, 109, 154, 193, 194, 208
Jung, Carl Gustav, 204
Junker, H., 234

Kafka, Franz, 204
Kaiser, Gerhard, vii, ix, x
Kames, Henry Home, Lord, 49, 55
Kaminski, Karin, 190
Kant, Immanuel, 3, 19, 38, 39, 85, 87, 106
Kayser, Wolfgang, 190, 234, 235, 236, 237, 240, 244
Keller, Gottfried, 179, 180, 181, 183, 189
Kellogg, Robert, 162, 163, 164
Kennedy, John F., 163, 164
Kierkegaard, Søren, 111, 150
Kinebanian, D.W., 147
Kittredge, George Lyman, 221, 227
Klein, K.K., 148
Kleist, Heinrich von, 89, 200
Klopstock, Friedrich Gottlieb, 87
Kluckhohn, Paul, 91
Knights, L.C., 227
Koch, Josef, 126, 145
Kohler, Pierre, 224, 226
Kreuzer, Helmut, 145
Krieger, Murray, 208
Krolow, Karl, 114
Krupp, Gustav, von Bohlen und Halbach, 30
Kuhn, Hugo, 126, 131, 137, 138, 142, 145, 146, 147, 148, 149

Lachmann, Karl, 130
Laclos, Pierre Choderlos de, 213
Laforgue, Jules, 7
Lämmert, Eberhard, 129, 149
La Motte Houdard (Antoine Houdar de La Motte), 52
Lancaster, Henry Carrington, 210
Lange, Victor, 92
Langer, Susanne K., 198, 199
Langosch, Karl, 131
Lanson, Gustave, 214, 227
La Rochefoucauld, François, Prince de Marcillac, 74
Leclerc, Michel Théodore, 223
Le Comte, Edward, 227
Lee, Brian, 207

Leedy, Paul F., 56
Levin, Jurij I., 263
Lévi-Strauss, Claude, 263, 268
Lehmann, W.P., 147, 149
Leitzmann, Albert, 56
Lenin, 15
Leonardo da Vinci, 14
Lessing, Gotthold Ephraim, 82, 83, 84, 88
Levi, Albert William, 17
Levi, J., 146
Lindgren, K.B., 130
Locke, John, 20
Lockemann, Wolfgang, 187
Lohner, Edgar, 252
Lord, Albert, 151, 156, 160, 165
Lotman, Jurij, 262
Lukács, Georg, 88, 113, 122
Lüthi, Max, 155

Maatje, Frank C., 55, 125, 129, 142
Macedonski, Al. A., 50, 55
MacLean, Norman, 55
Maerlant, Jacob van, 143
Maiorescu, Titu, 50, 55
Malherbe, François de, 227
Malkaraume, Jehan, 134
Mallarmé, Stéphane, 6, 7, 14, 16
Malraux, André, 16
Manet, Edouard, 15
Mann, Thomas, 117
Manoliu, Radu, 55
Mantz, Harold Elmer, 207
Marcel, Gabriel, 111, 150
Marino, Adrian, 41
Marivaux, Pierre Carlet de Chamblain de, 216
Marlowe, Christopher, 217
Marx, Karl, 106, 204
Mason, Ellsworth, 208
Matejka, Ladislav, 267
Maugham, W. Somerset, 222
Maupassant, Guy de, 5, 6, 67
May, Georges Claude, 226
May, Karl, 183
May, Rollo, 150
Mayenowa, Maria Renata, 260, 263, 268
Mayer, H., 149
Meissner, R., 131, 147, 149
Mercier, Sébastian, 52
Meredith, George, 6
Mergell, Bruno, 145
Mérimée, Prosper, 67
Meyer, Conrad Ferdinand, 88, 174, 175
Meyer, H., 147
Mill, John Stuart, 194, 205

INDEX OF NAMES

Milton, John, 79, 152
Mogk, E., 146
Mohr, Wolfgang, 133
Molière, viii, 214, 215, 216, 227
Montherlant, Henri de, 222, 227
Moore, Will G., 227
Mörike, Eduard, 88, 115, 248, 249
Moritz, Karl Philipp, 87
Mornet, Daniel, 217, 224, 228
Morris, William, 75
Mozart, Wolfgang Amadeus, 18, 59
Mukařovský, Jan, 256, 257, 268
Müller, Günther, 90, 91, 92, 144, 229, 251, 252
Muschg, Walter, 240, 241, 242, 243, 244, 245, 247, 249, 250

Naumann, Manfred, 189
Neidhart, 139, 143
Nelson, Lowry, 252
Nerval, Gérard de, 67
Newton, Sir Isaac, 39
Nicolas de Senlis, 141
Nicole, Pierre, 223, 225, 228
Nietzsche, Friedrich, 199
Nodier, Charles, 67
Nurse, Peter H., 227

Ohly, Friedrich, 149
Okken, Lambert, 146
Oksaar, Els, 145
Olrik, Axel, 154, 157
Olson, Elder, 57, 60, 62, 63, 64, 78, 195, 196
Opitz, Martin, 87
Ortega y Gasset, José, 92
Oswald vom Wolkenstein, 142
Otfried von Weissenburg, 140
Ott, Karl August, 189
Ouellet, Réal, 226
Ovid, 134

Palmer, David, 207
Parry, Milman, 151, 156, 157, 158, 160, 165
Pascal, Blaise, 223
Pasternak, Boris, 254
Paulhan, Jean, 14
Pearson, Norman H., 207
Peirce, Charles Sanders, 25
Pessoa, Fernando, 212
Petersen, Julius, 229
Petit de Juleville, 228
Petrarch, 152
Piaget, Jean, 251
Picard, Raymond, 228

Picasso, Pablo, 11, 15, 16
Pirandello, Luigi, 200
Pjatigorskij, A.M., 260, 268
Plato, 42, 106, 199, 208
Poe, Edgar Allan, 6, 105
Pommier, Jean, 226
Pomorska, Krystyna, 267
Pope, Alexander, 52, 56
Posner, Roland, 145, 146
Potocki, Jan, 67
Pound, Ezra, 26, 28, 29, 30, 32, 38, 114
Pracht, Erwin, 185, 190
Prévost, Jean, 213
Price, Martin, 65
Propp, Vladimir, 158, 159, 161
Proust, Marcel, 5, 8, 9, 16, 105, 255
Pushkin, Alexander, 54

Quéméneur, Pierre, 227
Quinault, Philippe, 223
Quintilian, 52

Raabe, Wilhelm, 179
Racine, Jean, viii, 17, 199, 214, 215, 216, 218, 219, 220, 221, 222, 223, 224, 227, 228
Ranke, Friedrich, 149
Rathofer, Johannes, 145
Ravel, Maurice, 12
Reich, Charles A., 165
Reiffenstein, Ingo, 126, 145
Reinmar von Hagenau, 148
Rellstab, Ludwig, 12
Renard, Jules, 12
Rey, Robert, 16
Richardson, Samuel, 6
Richter, David H., x
Richter, Jean Paul, 44, 193
Rilke, Rainer Maria, 7, 88, 247, 249, 250
Riou, Yves-Jean, 148
Robbe-Grillet, Alain, 10, 16
Rodway, Allan, 207
Roelens, Maurice, 227
Rollin, Charles, 43
Rose, Marilynn J., 187, 253
Rosenberg, Bruce, 150
Rostagni, Augusto, 55
Rothacker, Erich, 91
Rotrou, Jean de, 223
Rousseau, Jean Jacques, 6, 224
Rousset, P., 148
Rüdiger, Horst, 228
Ruff, Marcel A., 226
Ruh, Kurt, 146
Rupp, Heinz, 145, 149
Russell, Bertrand, 106

Rusu, L., 51
Ruttkowski, Wolfgang, 144

Sachs, Arieh, 227
Sacks, Sheldon, 57, 62, 63, 64, 65, 78
Saint-Saëns, Charles Camille, 12
Salomon, Herman P., 209
Saraiva, Antonio José, 211, 212, 219
Sartre, Jean Paul, 20, 211, 227
Sattler, Gabriel, 146
Saussure, Ferdinand de, 259, 268
Schelling, Friedrich Wilhelm Joseph, 53, 193
Scherer, Jacques, 217
Schiller, Friedrich, 82, 83, 86, 87, 91, 115, 183
Schirmer, K.H., 144
Schlegel, August Wilhelm, 35, 51, 53, 193
Schlegel, Friedrich, 51, 52, 53, 54, 55, 193
Schleiermacher, Friedrich, 51, 53
Schlenstedt, D., 189
Schneider, Hermann, 137
Scholes, Robert, 208
Schopenhauer, Arthur, 199
Schroeder, W.J., 147
Scott, Walter, 75
Scribe, Eugène, 195
Seboek, T.A., 226, 267
Sengle, Friedrich, 236, 237
Shakespeare, William, viii, 35, 37, 38, 62, 77, 110, 152, 194, 200, 204, 216, 217, 218, 221, 222, 223
Shaw, George Bernard, 200
Shelley, Percy Bysshe, 6
Sidney, Sir Philip, 45
Skulsky, Harold, 228
Smeets, J.R., 147
Sophocles, 38, 221
Sparnaay, H., 147
Spengler, Oswald, 35
Spenser, Edmund, 147
Springarn, J.E., 55
Staël, Anne Louise Madame de, 6
Stahl, Ernest L., 80
Staiger, Emil, vii, 44, 85, 226, 230, 231, 232, 233, 234, 237, 241, 242, 245
Stanislawski, Konstantin, 255
Stankiewicz, Edward, 55, 268
Stanzel, Franz, 189
Stendhal, 6
Stevens, Wallace, 26, 27, 28, 30, 31, 32, 38, 40
Stifter, Adalbert, 117, 119, 122, 175
Stone, Donald, 227

Storm, Theodor, 249
Strelka, Joseph, 242, 243, 252
Suberville, Jean, 226
Susman, Margarethe, 171
Swift, Jonathan, 62, 64
Szondi, Peter, 55

Tarot, Rolf, 166, 190, 239, 240, 241
Thibaudet, Albert, 52
Thomas, H., 148
Thomas d'Angleterre, 163
Thomasin von Zirclaere, 139
Thompson, Stith, 157, 158, 159, 161, 165
Tieck, Ludwig, 85
Tillich, Paul, 150
Timmer, B.J., 165
Todorov, Tzvetan, vii, ix, x, 57, 66, 67, 68, 69, 70, 71, 72, 73, 77, 78, 79, 129, 213, 227, 268
Tolstoi, Alexej Nikolajevitch, 6, 22, 23, 24, 38, 254
Tomachevski, Boris, 55, 56
Touber, A.H., 145
Toulouse-Lautrec, Henri de, 15
Trzynadlowski, Jan, x
Tschirch, Fritz, 145
Turoldus (Théroulde), 163
Tynjanov, Jurij, 255

Ugljanin, Salih, 160
Ulrich von Lichtenstein, 148
Unamuno, Miguel de, 150
Urbanek, T., 149
Uspenskij, B.A., 262, 268

Valadon, Suzanne, 15
Valéry, Paul, 6, 7, 9, 212
Van Dijk, T.A., 128, 129, 146, 147, 149
Van Dyck, Anthonis, 14
Van Rysselberghe, Mme, 16
Van Tieghem, Paul, 55, 225
Vance, E., 146, 148
Varga, Kibédi, 212, 225, 226
Veltrouský, J., 258, 268
Vermeer, Jan, 14
Vianu, Tudor, 55
Vicente, Gil, 226
Viëtor, Karl, vii, ix, 80, 81, 84, 86, 90, 92, 251, 252
Vigny, Alfred Comte de, 6
Vinteuil, 8
Virgil, 135
Vivas, Eliseo, 207
Vodička, Felix, 258, 268
Voelker, P.G., 148, 149

INDEX OF NAMES 281

Voltaire, 52, 54, 209
Voretzsch, K., 146
Vossler, Karl, 55

Wachinger, Burghart, 126
Wackenroder, Wilhelm Heinrich, 51
Wagner, Maria, 172, 173, 174, 176
Wagner, Richard, 53
Walther von der Vogelweide, 138, 139, 146, 147, 148
Walzel, Oskar, 229
Warren, Austin, vii, viii, x
Warton, Thomas, 56
Watson, George, 207
Wehrli, Max, 55
Weidlé, Wladimir, vii, viii, ix, 172
Weimar, Klaus, 188
Weinreich, Harald, 214
Weiss, Wolfgang, 253

Weissenberger, Klaus, 229
Wellek, René, viii, x, 56, 86, 129, 144, 146, 207, 252
Wessels, P.B., 149
Whistler, James MacNeill, 15
Whitman, Walt, 7, 121
Whitmore, Charles E., 207
Wiese, Benno von, 252
Wilpert, Gero von, 188
Wimsatt, W.K., 208
Winner, Thomas G., 255, 266, 268
Wisbey, R., 145
Wisniewsky, R., 147, 148
Wolf, A., 139
Wolfram von Eschenbach, 136, 163
Wordsworth, William, 6, 152

Zagrodzki, T., 147
Zola, Emile, 16